Brexit and Beyond

Brexit and Beyond

Rethinking the Futures of Europe

Edited by

Benjamin Martill and Uta Staiger

First published in 2018 by
UCL Press
University College London
Gower Street
London WC1E 6BT

Available to download free: www.ucl.ac.uk/ucl-press

A CIP catalogue record for this book is available from The British Library.

ISBN: 978–1–78735–277–3 (Hbk)
ISBN: 978–1–78735–276–6 (Pbk)
ISBN: 978–1–78735–275–9 (PDF)
ISBN: 978–1–78735–278–0 (epub)
ISBN: 978–1–78735–279–7 (mobi)
ISBN: 978–1–78735–280–3 (html)
DOI: https://doi.org/10.14324/111.9781787352759

For our families – British and European alike

Acknowledgements

This book would never have seen the light of day without the assistance, support and advice offered to us by our colleagues and friends at UCL and UCL Press.

Our colleagues at the UCL European Institute offered help and advice from the moment we started working on the project. In particular we would like to thank Claudia Sternberg, Christine Reh, Piet Eeckhout and Richard Bellamy, who were instrumental in drumming up support for the project within the European Studies community, and whose efforts ensured the final product would be comprehensive in its coverage of the discipline. We are also much indebted to Oliver Patel for his tireless administrative and intellectual support, both on the book itself and on the various other projects the writing of the volume foisted upon him. We would also like to thank the members of the European Institute's Advisory Board, who followed the book's progress with much interest and encouraged us that there was substantial demand for such a volume in the policy world. The Chair of the Board, Sir John Birch, is particularly deserving of our gratitude for his longstanding commitment to the work of the European Institute, his keen interest in the volume and his helpful insights on its content and audience.

The book has benefited immensely from the helpful staff at UCL Press. We are grateful in particular to Tim Mathews, who first floated the idea of a book on Brexit, and to our editor, Chris Penfold, who has advised on and overseen the process from start to finish. We would also like to thank the two anonymous referees appointed by UCL Press, whose constructive and detailed comments helped us to structure the volume and finesse the arguments therein. Above all, however, we are grateful to all of our contributing authors, who have lent their expertise and their intellect to this project and whose timely and insightful contributions are the very essence of this book. Finally, we would like to thank our families – to whom we have dedicated this book – for their support and patience over the many months whilst we brought the project together.

Benjamin Martill and Uta Staiger
London
November 2017

Contents

Figures and table

Abbreviations

AFSJ	Area of Freedom, Security and Justice
CAP	Common Agricultural Policy
CFSP	Common Foreign and Security Policy
CJEU	Court of Justice of the European Union
CSDP	Common Security and Defence Policy
CTA	Common Travel Area
DExEU	Department for Exiting the European Union
DUP	Democratic Unionist Party
EAW	European Arrest Warrant
ECA	European Communities Act
ECB	European Central Bank
ECHR	European Convention on Human Rights
ECRIS	European Criminal Records Information System
ECSC	European Coal and Steel Community
EDA	European Defence Agency
EDC	European Defence Community
EDPS	European Data Protection Supervisor
EEAS	European External Action Service
EEC	European Economic Community
EFTA	European Free Trade Association
EMU	Economic and Monetary Union
EP	European Parliament
EPC	European Political Cooperation
EU	European Union
EU27	The 27 Member States of the European Union
FAC	Foreign Affairs Council
FCO	Foreign and Commonwealth Office
FLN	Front de Libération Nationale
HRA	Human Rights Act
LREM	La République en Marche
M5S	Five Star Movement

NATO	North Atlantic Treaty Organization
NCA	National Crime Agency
NHS	National Health Service
OPEC	Organization of the Petroleum Exporting Countries
PNR	Passenger Name Record
PSC	Political and Security Committee
QMV	Qualified majority voting
SDG	Sustainable development goal
SIS II	Schengen Information System
TFEU	Treaty on the Functioning of the European Union
TTIP	Transatlantic Trade and Investment Partnership
UK	United Kingdom
UKREP	UK Permanent Representation to the EU
UN	United Nations
UNGA	United Nations General Assembly
UNSC	United Nations Security Council
US	United States
USSR	Union of Soviet Socialist Republics
WTO	World Trade Organization

Contributors

Richard Bellamy is Professor of Political Science in the UCL School of Public Policy and Director of the Max Weber Programme at the European University Institute in Florence.

Chris Bickerton is a Reader in Modern European Politics at Cambridge University, and a Fellow of Queens' College, Cambridge.

Gráinne de Búrca is the Florence Ellinwood Allen Professor of Law and Faculty Director at the Hauser Global Law School, and Director of the Jean Monnet Center for International and Regional Economic Law and Justice, at New York University.

Michelle Cini is Professor of European Politics and Head of the School of Sociology, Politics and International Studies at the University of Bristol.

Deirdre Curtin is Professor of EU Law at the European University Institute in Florence.

Helen Drake is Professor of French and European Studies and Director of the Academy of Diplomacy and International Governance, Loughborough University London.

Piet Eeckhout is Professor of EU Law, Dean of the Faculty of Laws, and Academic Director of the European Institute, at UCL.

John R. Gillingham is a University of Missouri Board of Curators Professor of History.

Andrew Glencross is Senior Lecturer in the Department of Politics and International Relations at Aston University.

Amelia Hadfield is Professor of European and International Relations, and Director of the Jean Monnet Centre for European Studies (CEFEUS), at Canterbury Christ Church University (UK).

Christopher Hill is the Wilson E. Schmidt Distinguished Professor of International Relations at SAIS Europe, and Professor Emeritus of International Relations, University of Cambridge.

Simon Hix is the Harold Laski Professor of Political Science at the London School of Economics and Political Science.

Abby Innes is Assistant Professor in the Political Economy of Central and Eastern Europe at the London School of Economics and Political Science.

Turkuler Isiksel is the James P. Shenton Assistant Professor of the Core Curriculum in the Department of Political Science at Columbia University.

Benjamin Martill is Dahrendorf Fellow in Europe after Brexit at the London School of Economics and Political Science.

Luuk van Middelaar is a former advisor to European Council President Herman Van Rompuy. He holds the chair 'Foundations and Practice of the European Union and its institutions' at the Europa Instituut of Leiden University.

Glyn Morgan is Associate Professor of Political Science at the Maxwell School, Syracuse University.

Kalypso Nicolaïdis is Professor of International Relations, and Director of the Centre for International Studies, at the University of Oxford.

Neill Nugent is Emeritus Professor of Politics at Manchester Metropolitan University.

Kiran Klaus Patel is Professor of European and Global History at Maastricht University.

William E. Paterson is Honorary Professor of German and European Politics at Aston University.

Waltraud Schelkle is Associate Professor of Political Economy at the London School of Economics and Political Science.

Michael Shackleton is Special Professor in European Institutions at Maastricht University.

Jo Shaw is a Professor in the School of Law at the University of Edinburgh where she holds the Salvesen Chair of European Institutions.

Uta Staiger is Executive Director of the European Institute and Pro-Vice Provost (Europe), UCL.

Philippe Van Parijs is Professor in the Faculty of Economic, Social and Political Science of the University of Louvain and a Visiting Professor and Senior Research Fellow at Nuffield College, Oxford.

Amy Verdun is Professor of Political Science and Director of the Jean Monnet Centre of Excellence at the University of Victoria.

Albert Weale is Emeritus Professor of Political Theory and Public Policy in the School of Public Policy, UCL.

Nicholas Wright is a Teaching Fellow in EU Politics in the School of Public Policy, UCL.

Introduction
Brexit and beyond

Benjamin Martill and Uta Staiger

On 23 June 2016, the United Kingdom (UK) went to the polls to decide whether Britain should remain in, or leave, the European Union (EU). The success of the 'leave' vote, by a 51.89 per cent majority, stunned not only the British public but also the major political parties, the polling organisations, and the media, not to mention most political scientists. It also flabbergasted their continental counterparts. Despite the multiple crises in which the Union finds itself embroiled, neither publics nor authorities had fully comprehended the probability of 'Brexit'. Unprecedented in nature, the vote shook whatever remained of the once preponderant *telos* of European integration – encapsulated in the symbolic, if legally vacuous, Treaty commitment to 'ever closer' union' – to the core.[1]

The process of Britain withdrawing from the EU, with which it has been deeply intertwined over the past four decades, will occasion a significant impact on virtually all aspects of the country's political, juridical and economic life. From immigration policy to agriculture subsidies, criminal justice measures to environmental standards, financial services regulations to nuclear power technology, university student fees to employment laws and aviation, Brexit requires rethinking and re-legislating a vast number of policy areas. It also promises to keep authorities (and other stakeholders) busier than ever until withdrawal day, and most likely beyond. Negotiating the terms of Brexit, along with new trade deals previously covered by EU agreements, requires immense capacity and will stretch the civil service to its limits. In addition, amending, repealing or improving existing EU legislation, once transposed into UK law via the Withdrawal Bill (formerly the 'Great Repeal Bill'), is 'one of the largest legislative projects ever undertaken in the UK' (Simson Caird 2017, 5).[2] Expect the Courts, too, to continue to arbitrate on questions of executive competences, and for the devolution settlement to be thorny and contested.

1

But the effects of Brexit will not stop at Britain's borders. As the second largest economy, the third most populous Member State, and a significant net contributor to the EU budget, the UK's departure will send ripples across the continent. As UK nationals and political representatives, including the 73 British Members of the European Parliament (MEPs) leave the institutions, the balance of power among the remaining Member States will shift. So, too, will voting patterns and alliances, the ideological make-up of the institutions, and, potentially, future policy directions. Beyond their relative position in the Union, Member States' domestic politics will be affected, too, not least where they face home-grown Eurosceptic forces. Indeed, the rise of populism is a continent-wide phenomenon, and poses a broader challenge to the Union from both the left and the right of the political spectrum. Moreover, Brexit has prompted a fundamental rethink of the EU's global role, given that the UK's intelligence, military, diplomatic and soft power capacities will no longer be part of the Union (even if they were never placed fully in the service of European goals). And, crucially, it is the very idea of Europe, the pace and parameters of European integration, the place of the nation-state betwixt and between globalising and domestic pressures, and the business of doing politics in twenty-first-century Europe, which will come under intense scrutiny in the years ahead.

The core, underlying claim of this volume is that Brexit is not simply a British phenomenon, but rather a specific manifestation of more general, Europe-wide tensions that have characterised European integration since the 1950s. Viewed from a European perspective, the challenges of Brexit may appear unique in their intensity, but they can also be understood, in more familiar terms, as the latest in a long line of existential crises to have beset the Union since its foundation, as the periodic resurgence of national interests and identities have challenged the ideal of 'ever closer Union' and exposed the tensions underlying the European project. Indeed, the forces behind the Brexit campaign and subsequent vote, as well as many of the issues raised by the decision itself, are reminiscent of two distinct conceptual problems that have characterised politics in Europe since the early days of integration. The first is the tension between supranational control and the defence of national sovereignty, and the conceptual conflict this embodies between a *Europe des patries* (Europe of states) committed to pursuing common national interests, versus a fully fledged United States of Europe (see Moravcsik 1993). The second is the tension between, on the one hand, the dictates of market efficiency and the form of technocratic, depoliticised governance developed in service of this – the so-called 'regulatory state' (Majone 1994) – and, on the other hand, the ever-increasing calls for greater popular contestation and democratic control of the policy agenda (Hix & Follesdal 2006).

This edited volume brings together some of the most notable scholars on European, British and global politics to examine the likely effects of Brexit for the future – or, more accurately, possible *futures* – of Europe and the EU. Substantively, its sets out to answer three 'big questions' looming over the continent as the Brexit process plays out. First, how did we get here? What constellation of events, actions, ideas, practices and socioeconomic factors were involved in bringing about the vote, and how are we to understand the role played by each of these causal factors? Second, what exactly is taking place? How are we to understand the nature of contemporary European and British politics – and what, if anything, is Brexit a case or instance of? Third, what does the future hold for the EU, the UK and EU–UK relations? Why, and how, might different scenarios come about, and with what consequences? And, normatively speaking, what *should* be the future direction of Europe and the EU?

At a time when politics is moving particularly fast, and where questions of such complexity and import must be addressed on both sides of the channel, there has never been a greater need for academics, policymakers, and the public to engage with one another. This book aims to further this cause in three simple respects. First, it addresses most of the major policy areas, actors, institutions, relations and questions across the continent, in order to give insight into the comprehensiveness and complexity of the topic at hand. Second, while rooted in long-standing academic research by the foremost experts in their respective fields, the chapters are short and jargon-free, written in a style that is accessible to those not steeped in the individual disciplines themselves. Third, in line with the (laudable) concern at UCL – and UCL Press – to achieve the broadest possible dissemination of academic knowledge, the book is open access: freely available for anyone to read and download.

Setting the scene: Britain's decision to leave the EU

As a point of departure, let us briefly recall the context in which the referendum on British withdrawal came about. The referendum itself, whilst rooted in the immediate, specific context of the internal politics of David Cameron's Conservative Party, was also the product of a more general discontent with the European project that stretches back decades. Indeed, Britain's relationship to what is now the EU was never a straight-forward one. When Winston Churchill championed the cause of European integration after World War II – in a speech delivered in Zurich – he did not envision the UK being a part of this new Europe, but rather its 'friend and sponsor'. Indeed, when 'the six' European states – France, Germany, Italy, Belgium, Netherlands and Luxembourg – agreed to the creation of a European Coal and Steel Community (ECSC) in 1951, and to the sub-sequent European Economic Community (EEC) in 1957, Britain declined to participate in either venture. The UK also placed itself on the sidelines when the other West European states negotiated the abortive European Defence Community (EDC), agreeing only to an associated role in the pro-posed organisation.

Spurred on by changing political and economic circumstances, however, the UK twice applied to join the EEC in the 1960s. Politically, the disastrous Suez Campaign of October 1956 had demonstrated, to the world, that Britain's claim to be a global – rather than European or regional – power lacked credibility. Economically, moreover, it had become clear by this point that, outside the EEC, the UK would remain the 'sick man of Europe'. And yet, Britain's changing perceptions of the value of EEC membership coincided with the rise of Gaullism in France, and the corresponding rise of anti-American sentiment in the upper-echelons of French politics. Fearing British accession to the EEC as an Anglo-Saxon 'trojan horse', de Gaulle vetoed applications from Harold Macmillan's Conservative government in 1963 and Harold Wilson's Labour government in 1967. When de Gaulle lost power in 1969 – replaced by his more moderate successor, Georges Pompidou – Wilson once again made the case for joining the EEC, and the Labour government was on the verge of negotiating accession in 1970 when they lost the general election to the Conservatives. It was thus left to Conservative Prime Minister Edward Heath to take the UK through the accession process and ensure passage of the 1972 European Communities Act through Parliament, paving the way for British mem-bership of the EEC on 1 January 1973.

The Labour Party, however, and to some extent the Conservative Party, remained deeply divided on the question of British membership of the Common Market. When Labour returned to power in 1974, Wilson made good on his pledge to renegotiate the terms of membership secured by Heath, and to put this to the British people in the form of an in–out referendum. While Wilson's renegotiation was not substantial, and served principally to confuse and irritate other European leaders in Brussels, the result proved sufficient to secure the support of the Labour Cabinet and, subsequently, for Wilson to obtain a majority of 67.23 per cent in favour of remaining in the EEC in the referendum, held on 6 June 1975. The campaign itself demonstrated splits within both major parties, Labour and Conservative, although both party leaders – Harold Wilson and Margaret Thatcher – campaigned to remain in the Common Market. Whilst Labour opponents regarded the EEC as a capitalist project designed to weaken the bargaining power of labour and undermine domestic protection, Conservative sceptics emphasised the threat to national sovereignty and the challenge to British identity posed by European integration.

Labour lost power again in 1979, following a period of significant industrial unrest – the 'Winter of Discontent' – leading to a Conservative government under Prime Minister Margaret Thatcher. Thatcher regarded herself as a classical (Gladstonian) liberal, rather than a traditional Conservative as such, and her zealous belief in the free market and the removal of barriers to trade contributed to her general support for the European project (Van Parijs, Chapter 27). Thatcher was a proponent of further liberalisation of the EEC, supporting the Single European Act of 1986 – which introduced qualified majority voting (QMV) in the Council for the first time – in order to further this aim. Over the course of the late-1980s, however, Thatcher became increasingly hostile to developments in the EEC. Having supported further market integration, she vocally opposed the direction the Community was taking under the entrepreneurial leadership of Commission President Jacques Delors, famously arguing that the European Community should be a 'willing and active cooperation between independent sovereign states' (Thatcher 1988), and pitting herself against the dominant trend towards further integration. Thatcher's hardening opposition to further integration – and in particular to the Exchange Rate Mechanism and the proposed single currency – led directly to the resignation of Geoffrey Howe and the leadership challenge from Michael Heseltine that heralded her fall from power in November 1990 and resulted in John Major replacing her as Conservative leader and prime minister.

The passage of the Maastricht Treaty in 1992 occasioned a significant split in Conservative ranks between pro-Europeans and those who feared the (substantial) supranational elements of the Treaty (including proposals for a common currency and a Common Foreign and Security Policy (CFSP)). Major was able to head off opposition by tying the passing of the Treaty in Parliament to a vote of no confidence in the government (Huber 1996, 269), but the split between pro-Europeans and Eurosceptics remained (and festered), re-opening when David Cameron became prime minister in 2010 at the head of a Conservative–Liberal Democrat coalition. Seeking to settle the issue once and for all, and to head off opposition from the United Kingdom Independence Party (UKIP) which was threatening Conservative majorities in marginal constituencies, Cameron announced an in–out referendum on Britain's EU membership in his Bloomberg Speech in January 2013, contingent on a Conservative victory in the 2015 general election. When Cameron received his majority he duly announced the referendum the following February, after negotiating a deal with the EU to reform the UK's relationship to the Union, setting off the starting gun on four months of intense campaigning by both sides.

Events in British politics moved swiftly following the vote of 23 June 2016 and the 51.89 per cent majority for 'Leave' which resulted. David Cameron resigned the next day, triggering a leadership election in the Conservative Party, in which Theresa May beat sole challenger Andrea Leadsom to become party leader and prime minister. Cameron left it to his successor to trigger Article 50 – the paragraph in the Lisbon Treaty setting out the procedure for withdrawing from the Union – and the letter indicating the UK's intention to leave was delivered on 29 March 2017 by the newly appointed Permanent Representative to the EU, Sir Tim Barrow. This followed the passage of the necessary legislation through Parliament on 13 March, the government having lost a legal challenge against its presumed right to trigger Article 50 by Royal Prerogative.[3] May's vision for Brexit, set out in a speech at Lancaster House in January 2017 and published shortly thereafter as a White Paper (HM Government 2017a), promised no 'back door' membership of the EU. Arguing that 'Brexit means Brexit', May defined her key objectives as access to – but not membership of – the Single Market, a bespoke agreement with the EU without membership of the Customs Union, an end to 'free movement', and an end to the jurisdiction of the European Court of Justice (CJEU). Following shortly after snap elections on 8 June 2017 – during which the Conservative Party lost its slim majority but remained in power thanks to an agreement with the Democratic Unionist Party (DUP) – negotiations between the UK and the EU began on 19 June 2017. With the EU represented by Commission chief negotiator Michel Barnier, on the basis of directives received from the Council, the negotiations are expected to comprise two distinct rounds (on settling outstanding issues, and on future arrangements), and to last until the end of March 2019, unless extended by the Council.[4]

Brexit and the future(s) of Europe: five fault lines

Let us return, then, to the key question animating this volume, namely, the effects of Brexit on Europe and the EU, and how we are to conceptualise the future(s) of Europe after this seismic event. An adequate understanding of Brexit, of course, requires attention to a myriad of different questions and debates, not all of which can be addressed in a single volume. Nevertheless, to set the stage for the subsequent discussion, we suggest that five questions in particular loom large in debates over the future of Europe – in the popular imagination, in academic discourse, and in the contributions to this book. In what follows below, we discuss these five claims in greater detail, positioning each of the chapters in relation to these broader debates to which the authors all speak.

1. How representative is Brexit?

Whether Brexit is idiosyncratically British or representative of a broader regional tendency towards populism represents one timely question. Is the vote best understood as the consequence of Britain's historically awkward 'with but not of' stance, its rabidly Eurosceptic press, or the vicissitudes of its majoritarian democratic system? Or is it better conceptualised as the product of a broader, Europe-wide discontent associated with the fallout from the eurozone crisis, the perceived deficiencies of the EU institutions, and the rise of populism across the continent? In other words, did the Brexit vote represent the 'perfect storm' of contingent factors, or were there deeper, more structural factors at play? The question is an important one since it influences our assessment of the likelihood that we will witness further attempts by Member States to leave the EU in the near future, and thus touches at the viability of the EU itself.

For some contributors to this book, Brexit is best understood as the cumulative outcome of dynamics that are particular to the UK. Britain's imperial history, its (laissez-faire) economic preferences, and the distinctiveness of its legal and political systems, have – according to this view – shaped the 'awkward' role the country has played in European integration to date. De Búrca argues, for instance, that the UK's decision to join the EEC in 1973 represented a pragmatic economic choice rather than a political commitment to the European project, and that deep resistance to the 'federalist' ideal has been a near constant in British attitudes to Europe. Correspondingly, she notes, it 'seems plausible to assume that if a popular referendum on UK withdrawal from the EU had been held on any number of occasions over the four decades of EU membership, the outcome of the vote may well have been the same as in June 2016' (De Búrca, Chapter 4). Hill also discusses the pragmatism of this relationship in his chapter, arguing that Britain's European engagement has been always and above all strategic in nature, and weighed against other commitments, notably the Anglo-American 'special relationship' and the Commonwealth (Hill, Chapter 20). Patel similarly notes the role played by Britain's imperial history in animating the discourse around Britain's post-EU future, predicting trouble ahead as this history becomes more politically salient (Patel, Chapter 12).

Other contributors regard Brexit as representative of more general dissatisfaction with politics on the continent. Bickerton sees Brexit as the 'tip of the iceberg', reflective of a much broader popular disenchantment with the EU's policies which is rooted in the negative effects of economic and monetary integration on national growth models, which have exacerbated the differences between these models whilst simultaneously making reform more difficult (Bickerton, Chapter 14). Van Middelaar, too, attacks the tendency to view Brexit as 'insular British doggedness', pointing instead to the Union's failure to achieve an adequate balance between (economic) freedom and protection as the real driver behind the persistent sense of malaise on the continent (van Middelaar, Chapter 8). Moreover, the effects of a broader discontent is also evident in the contribution by Glencross, who regards the vote as symptomatic of a wider gulf in Europe between elite views on integration and the rejection by voters of the status quo, citing the examples of the French and Dutch opposition to the Constitutional Treaty, the Irish rejection of the Lisbon Treaty, the Greek bailout, and the Dutch rejection of the Association Agreement with Ukraine (Glencross, Chapter 1).

2. How should we understand European integration?

The 'what' of European integration is another key area of contemporary debate. Why do states decide to pool sovereignty, and how does integration proceed over time? What, in other words, does the Union represent? These questions are important for an assessment of where Europe will go next: how we define integration tells us much about where we might look for an assessment of the EU's future. Whether we believe the EU is at base a collection of sovereign states, an international organisation, or a *sui generis* political system, our expectations of its future course are bound to differ. Furthermore, it also matters how we conceive of the *politics* of Europe. Are the EU's aims of cross-border market liberalisation and the protection of pan-European social standards compatible? Do the institutions entrench certain ideological principles – or are they designed specifically to de-politicise conflicts? And what *should* the EU become if it wishes to maintain, or gain, legitimacy? On these questions the authors in this volume represent a significant heterogeneity of opinion.

For some, it is national interests and intergovernmental bargaining that shape, or should shape, the EU's priorities. Gillingham, scathing about the direction integration has taken in the past two decades, argues that the only alternative to 'more Europe' is consensus among and leadership of the 27 Member States, to whom authority should be devolved, effectively doing away with the 'EU policy machinery' and preserving only the Single Market (Gillingham, Chapter 21). Emphasis on the Member States as the driving force is especially strong in discussions of foreign policy, which, as Hadfield reminds us, 'overall remains traditionally intergovernmental', even as other policy domains have become increasingly communitised (Hadfield, Chapter 19). Indeed, while different in outlook, and emphasising the importance of geo-strategic factors in drawing the European states together, the chapters by Hill, Paterson and Drake serve to highlight the context-dependent and historically specific importance of Member States in shaping the direction of EU policy – be they British, German or French, respectively.

Other contributors regard the EU as a far 'denser' institution, one in which sovereignty and national interests are significantly curtailed by the competences afforded the community institutions, which have overtaken the Member States in shaping the EU's agenda. In his chapter, Hix – whom, it should be noted, first argued that the EU constituted a 'political system' in its own right (Hix 1997) – contends the EU has become increasingly centralised with the advent of supranational forms of decision-making, offering Member States little discretion over policy once decisions have been made (Hix, Chapter 7). Bickerton also sees the EU as having moved beyond a mere assemblage of Member States, emphasising the growing centralisation of the EU, the significant differences between 'nation statehood' and 'Member Statehood', and the endurance of the latter through the deep Europeanisation of the British state (Bickerton, Chapter 14).

And what of the *politics* of the Union? Some contributors see the EU as an essentially social democratic project, driven by a desire to regionalise the European social model and regulate globalisation, and as such these authors deplore recent moves in the direction of neoliberalism (since the 1980s) and austerity (since the recession of 2007/8). Van Parijs, for example, argues that the push to create the Single Market in the 1980s represented a Hayekian 'trap' since it entailed the loss of the monopolistic position held by cartels, unions and professional associations at the national level without any corresponding transfer of regulatory competences to the transnational level (Van Parijs, Chapter 27). Van Middelaar offers a similar assessment, arguing the EU has historically been based on a balance between economic freedom and social protection that has, in recent years, become skewed towards economic freedom, at the expense of protection (van Middelaar, Chapter 8). Innes agrees, noting that the EU has itself increasingly become associated with a (damaging) supply-side philosophy in recent years, although she also contends that the EU has unfairly become a scapegoat for the social polarisation that resulted from the UK's supply-side reforms in the 1980s (Innes, Chapter 15). By contrast, others regard the Union as a historically liberalising (and therefore liberating) project. Gillingham, for instance, disagrees with both the diagnosis (of a social democratic Europe) and the prescription (of lessening its free-market credentials), blaming the 'sad story of EU decline' on its move away from the removal of economic barriers ('negative integration') towards the attempt to construct a more comprehensive political community ('positive integration') (Gillingham, Chapter 21).

3. What is wrong with the EU?

Something is rotten in Europe – this much almost all the contributors seem to agree on. Where they disagree is on the principal drivers of Europe's predicament. A number of different diagnoses are offered in the volume, each of which leads to a divergent prescription for solving the problem. Together the contributions highlight three areas where the EU's problems are most evidently manifest: (1) Euroscepticism and the legitimacy crisis, (2) structural problems with the eurozone, and (3) the migration and refugee crises. In practice, these different problems blend into one another to contribute to the present 'omni-crisis' in Europe, although some contributors ascribe greater significance to certain factors over others.

Euroscepticism and the legitimacy crisis: In the years since the Maastricht Treaty, Euroscepticism has moved from the political margins to the centre of political attention. In his chapter, Hix attributes the EU's unpopularity to its becoming involved in redistributive debates over national tax and spending in the wake of the financial crisis of 2007/8 and the ensuing eurozone crisis, since these actions served to politicise the activities of the community institutions and undermine the EU's credentials as an apolitical regulatory state (Hix, Chapter 7). In a similar vein, Isiksel regards the EU's legitimacy crisis as the inevitable consequence of the substitution of *principled support* for integration with *economic pay-offs*, since little in the way of long-term public engagement and identification could ever be expected to emerge from the claim that 'you're better off thanks to the EU'. For this reason, she argues, the EU's institutions 'experience every crisis of competence, every economic slump, as an existential crisis' (Isiksel, Chapter 26). Staiger similarly identifies the sources of the EU's legitimacy crisis in the failure of its institutions to establish the trust of the electorate and to purposively channel debate and dissent in constructive ways; this being the only way, she argues, to avoid the 'destructive excess' that has characterised populist movements across Europe and which was a significant contributor to the Brexit vote (Staiger, Chapter 25). Nugent agrees with this assessment, noting the popularity of Eurosceptic parties in Austria, France, Greece, Hungary, the Netherlands, Poland and the UK in 2015–16, and the concomitant decline in the EU's 'output legitimacy'. In an era of public distrust, he suggests, calls for 'more Europe' are no longer feasible (Nugent, Chapter 5). This concern, finally, is also echoed by Shackleton, who argues that the EU struggles to obtain legitimacy either through fostering a common identity or delivering for its citizens, since there is widespread distrust of Brussels at the national level and significant diversity in the policy priorities held by the Member States (Shackleton, Chapter 22).

Structural problems with the eurozone: Deeply entwined with concerns about the EU's legitimacy is its most serious problem to date: the ambitious and flawed project of Economic and Monetary Union (EMU), which, Gillingham argues, has 'plunged the continent into a decade of depression; cheated a generation of young people out of jobs … impoverished southern Europe; driven a thick emotional wedge between creditor and debtor nations … and embittered the public from north to south and east to west' (Gillingham, Chapter 21). For Isiksel, the problem is that EMU has amplified – rather than cushioned – the effects of the global financial crisis, whilst at the same time succeeded in imposing rigid constraints on domestic fiscal policies which have 'deprived national legislatures of key levers of social policy [and] further attenuated democratic control of policymaking at the domestic level' (Isiksel, Chapter 26). In his chapter, Nugent suggests that the problems with the eurozone lie in its incomplete nature, since a currency union must be accompanied by both fiscal and banking union, as well as political union strong enough to make authoritative decisions. The absence of each of these, he argues, meant the euro was 'not built on solid foundations' (Nugent, Chapter 5). Somewhat more optimistically, however, Schelkle notes that the EU has been able to overcome some of the more fundamental problems of the eurozone through post-crisis reforms in banking supervision and fiscal coordination, and thus predicts that the euro will continue to strengthen against the pound after Brexit (Schelkle, Chapter 13).

Migration and refugee crises: Many of the contributors also emphasise the role played by the mismanagement of migration across Europe. For some the problems arise with regard to internal migration – that is, the movement of persons from one Member State to another. Hill regards the downward pressure on wages in the UK resulting from high levels of immigration after the 2004 'big bang' accession, combined with the emergence of the so-called 'gig economy', as a significant contributory factor in the rising tide of populism and Euroscepticism that culminated in the Brexit vote (Hill, Chapter 20). Others consider the EU's mismanagement of the refugee crisis to be the greater problem. Morgan, for instance, regards the risk of 'large-scale domestic terrorism as a consequence of the implosion of Middle Eastern and North African states and the failure to integrate existing Islamic minority populations' as a significant risk, although he contends the problem would be exacerbated, not solved, by Brexit (Morgan, Chapter 3). Nugent locates the problem in the interaction between the internal and external faces of EU migration, since Schengen, which was designed to allow for free movement within the Union, was not able to deal – justly or administratively – with the influx of thousands of external migrants into the zone (Nugent, Chapter 5).

4. Can sovereignty and democracy function in a globalised world?

Another key strand of debate concerns the democratic implications of globalisation and supranational governance. The status of sovereignty and democracy under conditions of transnational interdependence, such as those characterising the relations between the EU Member States, has been brought to the fore by Brexit, not least given the Leave campaign's emphasis on 'taking back control'. Arguments over the meaning of 'control' touch at the very heart of what democracy and sovereignty mean, and – as is always the case with essentially contested concepts – open up a host of important questions about how these terms should be understood and applied. Within Europe – home to the world's most significant experiment in post-sovereign governance – questions relating to the legitimacy of transnational governance and the compatibility between national and supranational models of democracy are of paramount importance. Again, the contributors to this volume represent a number of diverse perspectives on the crucial questions of the EU's democratic credentials and the extent to which British membership of the Union, and its impending withdrawal, will affect democracy in the UK.

The authors hold different views on the question of whether there exists a 'democratic deficit' in the EU. Shackleton regards the issue principally as a conceptual one, outlining three models of legitimacy in his chapter – drawn from van Middelaar (2013) – to help frame the debate. He distinguishes between a German model of democratic legitimacy based on a common identity, a Roman model based on the provision of tangible benefits to citizens, and a Greek model based on citizen participation in decision-making (Shackleton, Chapter 22). Nicolaïdis accepts that the Union is 'democratically challenged, in spite of all its mechanisms for representation, delegation and checks on power', arguing the solution lies in grounding the EU's activities in the demands of its citizens – and the emerging European *demos* – whilst capitalising on the Union's ability to remain partially shielded from the short-termism of electoral democracy (Nicolaïdis, Chapter 23). Bellamy, in contrast, regards the extension of national models of democracy to the supranational level as a non-starter, since the trade-off between democracy, sovereignty and economic globalisation makes this ideal unfeasible. Rather than attempt to replicate domestic democracy on a European level, he argues that the EU should offer space for countries to collectively regulate transnational processes, such that they are able to control the externalities of their democratic decisions (Bellamy, Chapter 24). Van Parijs makes a similar argument, noting that all states stand to lose their democratic legitimacy if they fail to regulate their actions under conditions of interdependence, since 'the democratically made decisions of one state [can] undercut those of other states' (Van Parijs, Chapter 27).

The contributors disagree over the effects of Brexit on *British* democracy and the UK's (uncodified) constitution. Some do not regard Brexit as a particular threat to the UK's democratic credentials. De Búrca, for instance, argues that the vote did not represent an attempt either 'to remove domestic constitutional checks and balances within the UK, or to promote popular rule over constitutional government' (De Búrca, Chapter 4). Others are more sceptical, including Weale, who argues that the referendum has strengthened the British executive at the expense of Parliament and the other representational elements of the British constitution, since the government has come to regard itself as holding a mandate from 'the people' which can override both Parliament and the judiciary if need be (Weale, Chapter 2). Eeckhout agrees that Brexit has not *removed* constitutional checks and balances in the UK, but argues that the process of Brexit – and in particular the *Miller* case – highlights the threadbare nature of the British constitution, since parliamentary sovereignty is the only principle that stands, regardless of how its exercise infringes established rights and legislation (Eeckhout, Chapter 18). From a broader constitutional perspective, Wright identifies Brexit as a potential threat to the asymmetric form of devolution that has come to characterise British politics since the 1990s, with the risk of a 'hard border' between the EU and the UK across the border between Northern Ireland and the Republic challenging an important foundation of the Belfast (Good Friday) Agreement and exposing Westminster's overall control of the Brexit process (Wright, Chapter 11).

Others, including Glencross, Bellamy and Innes, argue that certain aspects of the Brexit vote may prove problematic for British democracy in other respects. Glencross, for instance, notes that the Brexit vote represents a broader (and problematic) trend for politicians to legitimise their policies through referendums, since they can, by doing so, delegate decisions back to the sovereign peoples and therefore avoid taking politically risky decisions (Glencross, Chapter 1). Bellamy argues that British democracy will be harmed as a result of the diminished capacity of the UK to deal with problems outside its borders, since Brexit will result in the 'inability to tackle problems that require cooperation between states', thereby undermining the capacity of democratic decision-making at home, rather than enhancing it (Bellamy, Chapter 24). Innes, similarly emphasising the threat to the state's *capacity*, is concerned about the likely intensification of supply-side thinking after Brexit, which threatens the integrity of the state by instrumentalising its powers for private and party-political gain whilst withdrawing the protections it previously offered the public (Innes, Chapter 15).

5. What does the future of Europe look like?

The future of Europe is of paramount concern in capitals and homes across the continent. Whilst prediction is a dangerous game, not least in the complex and ever-changing post-Brexit political environment, indicative future scenarios based on readings of the current situation abound. Some believe that Brexit will be good for Britain and good for the EU, although this is something of a minority position. More common is the claim that Brexit will be damaging both for Britain and for Europe. Others see the outcome as likely to favour one side, either the UK or the EU, depending on the outcome of the negotiations and the ability of either side to best navigate the internal and external challenges that lie ahead. Positions on this question, of course, cannot be separated from the questions addressed above. Whether integration is regarded as a success that can deliver for its Member States, for instance, will influence whether one regards the EU's future as a viable one, and whether one sees the consequences of Brexit as damaging for Britain.

A number of contributors are, to begin with, somewhat sceptical about the long-term prospects for the EU after Brexit. Cini and Verdun summarise this view – which, in the most extreme case, sees the disintegration of the EU – in their discussion of the 'centripetal trajectory', which envisages gradual disengagement from the EU as the Union's inability to solve the various crises on its doorstep become clear and as the various political divides widen (Cini & Verdun, Chapter 6). Gillingham in particular is unconvinced about the EU's viability, arguing that 'Europhoric values' are not enough, and that the Commission and other institutions are too discredited to take a leadership role, meaning the only way forward is for a (difficult to imagine) consensus between the 27 post-Brexit Member States (Gillingham, this volume). Nicolaïdis is also somewhat sceptical of the idea the EU can continue in its present form, arguing that flexibility, differentiation and opt-outs must become the new norm, since 'a mosaic EU is more appealing than pushing half of its states to the brink of exit' (Nicolaïdis, Chapter 23).

The alternative scenario laid out by Cini and Verdun – the 'centrifugal trajectory' – imagines a more positive future for Europe once the 'stumbling block' of British membership has been removed, since the UK has historically blocked – or taken no part in – important moves towards greater integration, and since the lesson of Brexit may be that leaving the EU is seen to have very significant costs (Cini & Verdun, Chapter 6). While few contributors foresee increased pressure for integration at the present time, some authors, such as Hix, do suggest additional competences could be afforded the EU, in a restricted set of policy areas, in return for the Member States being afforded a greater degree of flexibility when it comes to implementation (Hix, Chapter 7). Drake, in her chapter on Anglo-French relations after Brexit, argues that much depends on Emmanuel Macron's efforts to place the European continent back on its political footing, since European integration has always depended upon the key Franco-German access. If Macron succeeds in reconciling France with the EU, and helps construct a 'Europe that protects', Drake argues, then the future of the EU will be all the more secure (Drake, Chapter 10). Moreover, several authors note the beneficial effects of increased debate around the consequences of Brexit, which have galvanised the EU to a certain extent. In her chapter on citizenship rights, for instance, Shaw notes that Brexit has 'given rise to unprecedented civic mobilisation around demands for the protection of acquired rights', highlighting the extent to which EU citizenship has – in perception, if not necessarily in law – evolved into a 'transnational citizenship practice' (Shaw, Chapter 17).

The authors also disagree over the consequences for the UK. Some, such as Gillingham, are optimistic about Britain's prospects outside the Union, arguing the 'Brexit naysayers have ... been wildly off the mark' and suggesting that British withdrawal may not only be non-disruptive, but also positively beneficial (Gillingham, Chapter 21). Other contributors, whilst attuned to the risks of Brexit for the UK, note specific instances in which the negative consequences have perhaps been overblown in existing debates. Hadfield, for example, notes that little will change in UK–EU foreign and defence relations. Indeed, she even suggests that the UK 'could dispose of its awkward reputation within the EU and become a more consistent partner from without' (Hadfield, Chapter 19). Patel, moreover, notes that the Algerian and Greenlandic experiences suggest withdrawal may not lead to 'a complete unwinding of ties', and that the key to Britain after Brexit will lie in longer-term trajectories (Patel, Chapter 12). Curtin's chapter is also instructive in this respect, since she finds a strong precedent in the EU's negotiation of bespoke arrangements on information-sharing with Denmark to suggest that continuity in some policy areas – especially those underneath the political radar – may well be possible after Brexit. Indeed, she concludes, on something of a positive note, that: 'where there is a will, it seems, there may well be a way' (Curtin, Chapter 16).

In contrast, other contributors are decidedly less optimistic about the UK's prospects outside the Union. Schelkle suggests in her chapter that the UK's economy will likely suffer, as the pound will continue to fall against the euro, and since the loss of 'passporting' rights will convince many City firms to relocate to the continent (Schelkle, Chapter 13). Morgan also argues that Britain faces a number of significant risks outside the EU, not least the break-up of the UK as a political community and its exclusion from favourable trade, security and research arrangements (Morgan, Chapter 3). Hill regards the idea of British success outside Europe as anachronistic, claiming the UK will quickly discover that 'the notion of being able to opt in and out of European endeavours is an embarrassing mirage', since – in spite of the wishes of Brexiters – 'the historical clock cannot be wound back' (Hill, Chapter 20). Paterson is similarly sceptical of how realistic the UK's aim of becoming a 'great, global Britain' is, noting that other countries will prioritise trade agreements with the EU and that Brexit is unlikely to stay Germany's inexorable upwards rise within Europe (Paterson, Chapter 9).

The structure of the book

The book is divided into two parts. Part One discusses effects of Brexit on the actors, institutions and relationships that comprise the complex political environment of Europe, with a particular emphasis on the UK, the community institutions and the EU27. Section I examines Brexit from the British perspective, contextualising the vote and inquiring as to the principal issues it raises for the future of the UK. Section II considers the likely effects of Brexit on the functioning of the EU itself, examining how it will impact the politics of the community institutions – the Commission, Council, Parliament, Court and Central Bank – as well as how their own failings may have contributed to Brexit itself. Section III considers the effects of Brexit from the perspective of key Member States, examining how the vote will affect the UK's key bilateral relationships within Europe – with Germany, France and Ireland – and considering previous cases of 'exit' represented by Greenland and Algeria.

Part Two is divided thematically between key issue areas, each of which is likely to experience different effects and dynamics as a consequence of the decision. Section IV examines the political economy of Europe after Brexit, considering how the different economic models in Europe and the UK will be affected, and what the likely impact of Brexit will be on the eurozone. Section V examines the effects of Brexit from a legal perspective, looking at the likely impact of the decision on key areas of EU law – including information-sharing and citizenship rights – and addressing the likely consequences for the British constitution. Section VI adopts a global perspective, asking about the likely consequences of Brexit for the EU's global role, and looking in detail at how the decision will affect foreign, security and defence policy in Europe. It examines, in particular, how Brexit feeds into Europe's assessment of its geostrategic situation, and how it may affect the foreign policymaking architecture in the EU. Section VII considers the state of democracy in Europe and discusses important concerns about the legitimacy of the European project, with contributors reflecting upon the future of democracy in the EU after Brexit, as well as how the EU may attempt to solve its 'legitimacy crisis'. Finally, Section VIII addresses the 'idea of Europe' itself, considering the role of identity politics in explaining both support for – and opposition to – European integration, and assessing the role of ideas and emotions more generally in European politics.

Part One
Actors and institutions

I: Brexit and the UK

1
Cameron's European legacy

How Brexit demonstrates the flawed politics of simple solutions

Andrew Glencross

'To govern is to make believe', proclaimed Machiavelli. David Cameron presumably encountered this dictum while studying Philosophy, Politics and Economics at Oxford, but he was unable to put it into practice as prime minister. For if the vote for Brexit on 23 June 2016 demonstrated anything, it was that a majority of the British electorate did not believe what political elites were saying in favour of EU membership. Many in the losing camp cried foul, claiming the other lot won by playing fast and loose with the truth. Yet fixating on the bucket-load of mendacity on offer (from both sides) during the campaign is to miss the wood for the trees. Although David Cameron subsequently blamed populism as a sentiment fuelled by 'a movement of unhappiness and concern about the state of the world' (*Guardian* 2016), the responsibility equally lies much closer to home. What made the untruths about Brexit believable was a politics of simple solutions promoted by Cameron, which ultimately undid him. This damaging legacy will cast a long shadow over British politics as the country adapts to life outside the EU and also stands as a stark warning to other EU leaders on how not to approach European integration.

Cameron saw an in–out referendum as a straightforward fix to internal Conservative Party strife over European integration (Copsey & Haughton 2014). When announced in January 2013, it appeared a low-risk option since winning a parliamentary majority was far from a given. At that time the prime minister was more concerned with quashing Eurosceptic backbenchers' mischief-making under the coalition agreement with the Liberal Democrats. By 2016, Cameron was perhaps entitled to feel confident about his favoured political tactic of managing domestic challenges by forcing voters to choose between the status quo and an unknown future. He had already won two referendums on this basic premise, defeating supporters of the alternative vote (2011) as well as partisans of Scottish independence (2014).

In fact, the former prime minister's rise to the top came on the back of an equally simple expedient: he won the party leadership by promising to withdraw Tory MEPs from the centre-right grouping in the European Parliament. It was a neat way to burnish his Eurosceptic credentials at no domestic cost – although Angela Merkel never understood why Cameron chose to lose influence in the European Parliament. Disdain for EU consensus was also the basis of his fateful renegotiation strategy prior to the Brexit vote. Here again he resorted to a simplistic conceit of talking tough in the hope it might win concessions sufficient to mollify soft Eurosceptics (Glencross 2016).

In reality, the UK's renegotiated terms of EU membership, announced in February 2016, failed to convince the sceptics; measures to address labour migration, in particular, were abstruse and legally uncertain. It was this lacklustre outcome that derailed the subsequent referendum campaign. Cameron had wanted a clear message about winning a better deal for the country in a reformed EU. Instead, it was the Leave camp that had the simpler, more persuasive policy slogan: take back control.

The serried ranks of elites, experts and even foreign leaders such as President Obama mobilised by the government should have made short work of the less well-funded Leave camp. What only Brexiters could offer, though, was a peremptory solution to a multitude of political grievances. Brexit was successfully presented as a way to end Brussels' interference, fund the NHS, and reduce immigration. It was not even that EU withdrawal was always presented as a panacea. Rather, it was the one policy option that had never been tried, meaning attempts to discredit its potential risks were necessarily hypothetical. Voters' desire to break the mould is precisely what populists elsewhere in Europe want to tap into by offering, as with Beppe Grillo in Italy or Marine Le Pen in France, a referendum on membership of the euro. That is why the UK campaign, and its outcome, is of such relevance EU-wide.

As the British government sensed the narrowness of the race, it upped the ante with its increasingly gloomy prognoses about the state of the UK economy and public finances in the event of Brexit. Thus it was not just opponents of EU membership who were engaged in political theatrics. Cameron's Grand Guignol performance, with economic horror at its heart, did little to sway a public sceptical about far more than simply the EU. Having bet his political career on the electorate's status quo bias, the politics of simple solutions backfired on him. The reverse suffered was not just a personal one. Estimates of constituency-level results reveal that 63 per cent of UK constituencies returned a majority for the Leave side (Hanretty 2016). This amounts to a wholesale disavowal of the country's elected representatives, since only 158 MPs openly declared support for leaving the EU (BBC News 2016).

Commentators naturally jumped on the chance to explain this gulf between governed and governing. Initial academic analysis focused on social inequality as the font of electors' frustration with the EU and the domestic governing class in general (Goodwin & Heath 2016). Portraying Brexit as a delayed rejection of neoliberalism by the left-behind of globalisation is certainly a seductive explanation. It confirms the comforting premise of social-democracy: the belief that politics trumps economics and that the inequities of capitalism can be corrected eventually once voters have had enough of market-driven solutions.

However, what the failure of the Remain campaign truly highlighted was the insularity of the British political establishment. The pro-EU side either misread or, worse, ignored the warnings from recent referendums on European integration. A litany of rejected deals preceded the UK vote: the EU Constitutional Treaty (in two countries), the Lisbon Treaty (in Ireland), the Greek bailout and the Ukraine Association Agreement (the Netherlands). These examples did more than merely illustrate the difficulty of selling the EU status quo. The common thread linking these votes was in fact citizens' refusal to be steamrollered into accepting elite nostrums about European cooperation.

Dissatisfaction with Europe is not reducible to an accounting exercise in which the cons outweigh the pros; it is as much a rejection of the animating spirit that there is no alternative to the current institutional order. In that sense the EU is – rightly or wrongly – perceived by many in Britain and elsewhere as a constraining dystopia. As the Director of Hatcheries and Conditioning in Huxley's *Brave New World* explains, creating a harmonious society requires 'making people like their inescapable social destiny … liking what you've got to do'. EU citizens on the receiving end of austerity, market liberalisation, and the socio-economic strains of free movement experience the Single Market as a not-so-dissimilar conditioning exercise.

Particularly telling in this regard was the 2015 referendum in which Greeks said *Oxi* (no) to a bailout that a near-unanimity of expert opinion suggested was the only way to remain in the eurozone. The Greek vote demonstrated the same lesson as in the UK vote: electors could not be cowed into voting out of fear to accept the current EU system as their inescapable destiny (Boukala & Dimitrakopoulou 2016). Greeks, Brits and others have sought to express the right to be unhappy with the results that lie behind grandiloquent evocations of European unity and prosperity. Direct democracy offers precisely such an opportunity for voicing discontent, which is why referendums on EU issues since the 2005 Constitutional Treaty debacle have had to be handled with such caution. Indeed, the passage of the Lisbon Treaty was premised on an informal agreement by the European Council to avoid ratification by the people (Phinnemore 2013).

But the referendum temptation is hard to resist in a Europe where politicians increasingly struggle to rely on representative democracy to legitimise their policies. What is convenient about delegating policy-making back to the sovereign people is that it allows politicians to distance themselves from any negative ramifications that might occur further down the line. However, the experience in the EU of using direct democracy as a device of empowerment suggests it is of very limited value. Where voters have refused to endorse planned treaty change, recalcitrant Member States have submitted to re-voting on the same treaty, as Ireland has done twice. In other instances, a successor treaty has been passed without referendum consultation, as in the case of France's and the Netherlands' adoption of the Lisbon Treaty. Even in situations where a negative vote has led to the obtention of concessions, as with the opt-out on asylum and immigration policy Denmark was granted after its vote against Maastricht in 1992, the diplomatic pressure to conform with EU norms has greatly diluted the value of these concessions (Adler-Nissen 2015a).

The sovereign people in these instances are being short-changed when they supposedly exercise their sovereignty. When a popular decision has no discernible impact on the status quo, the referendum device thus has the opposite effect from that of empowering citizens. Such an outcome reveals the flaw in expecting that direct democracy can magically compensate for the shortcomings of representative democracy. That explains why those with most to lose from referendums are mainstream politicians such as Cameron or Matteo Renzi, both of whom made a unilateral resort to direct democracy with the objective of sweeping away long-standing problems.

By contrast, it is populist, anti-system parties led by personalities such as Nigel Farage, Geert Wilders, Marine Le Pen or Beppe Grillo that have the biggest incentive to bypass representative democracy. They ostensibly promote rule by the people directly as an alternative to a cartelised party politics of both the centre-left and the centre-right that allegedly ignores popular concerns. What really matters, however, as Jan-Werner Müller (2016b) has explained, is that a referendum offers populists a chance for 'the people to confirm what they have already identified as the single authentic will of the people'.

Allowing the people to decide for themselves is nevertheless a powerful political message that is hard to ignore, although in the British case it was not just external pressure that led Cameron to resort to the expedient of direct democracy. Rather, it was a political pincer movement. He wanted in part to silence the virulent Eurosceptic wing of the Conservative Party that pushed their anti-EU agenda by causing parliamentary mischief. At the same time, the other source of pressure was the electoral potency of UKIP, whose strategy of spatch-cocking anti-immigration sentiment with hostility to the EU made it the most successful party in the 2014 European elections (Ford & Goodwin 2014).

But the appeal to the sovereign people cannot be a replacement for representative democracy, because a government is still required to exercise sovereignty in the aftermath of any referendum. Nowhere is this more obvious than in the case of the UK following the vote on 23 June 2016. British politicians, like their Greek counterparts in 2015, have had to face the consequences that stem from unilateral attempts to resolve complex problems of European interdependence.

Cameron's habit of ruling via easy fixes will have a lasting national impact because it leaves those in power at Westminster and Holyrood at the mercy of the same forces that cost him his job. In the months after the vote, Theresa May and the Scottish first minister counterpart, Nicola Sturgeon, became engaged in an ongoing Project Trust – convincing voters they could negotiate the best way out of the Brexit predicament. May's government interpreted the people's verdict as a call to roll back migration from the EU while retaining strong economic ties. Yet the free movement of people is a non-negotiable pillar of the Single Market – as was made clear to Cameron during the renegotiation. The illusion of getting a better deal outside the EU than as a Member State could only remain believable until formal exit talks began. That helps explain why the government stalled on triggering Article 50 and fought tooth and nail to prevent Parliament having a say on the matter.

Meanwhile in Scotland, First Minister Sturgeon toyed with the idea of leveraging the 62 per cent majority who supported EU membership into a successful independence referendum second time around. Any unilateral move of this sort could only succeed if Scots cast aside concerns about oil revenues and the outstanding dilemma of which currency an independent Scotland would use (Glencross 2016). Indyref 2.0 would in any case mirror the Brexit referendum, becoming a debate centred around hypothetical in or out economic scenarios drawing on expert forecasting.

Cameron's flawed EU policy has thus left UK politicians struggling to restore the electorate's confidence in their ability to make the right decisions and raised the stakes in case they do not. There is no way of knowing beforehand whether Brexit will help or hinder that objective across the UK. What is clear is that – except for blaming EU hostility if a speedy free trade deal cannot be agreed alongside Article 50 negotiations – there are no simple solutions left.

Ironically, the political mess occasioned by Brexit might have a positive impact on the EU at a time of ever-growing populism. Despite certain predictions to the contrary, there was no immediate domino-effect of other governments pledging to hold referendums on leaving. Seen from Europe, British politics in the months after the referendum appeared mostly in a chaotic and cacophonous state as government ministers made claims and counter-claims about preferred outcomes or strategies. That compares negatively with the measured statements of leaders across the EU that the four fundamental freedoms cannot be cherry-picked. This show of unity in a time of crisis is not so common.

More importantly, as revealed by a Bertelsmann survey in the aftermath of the British vote, the difficulties facing the UK seem to have reinforced voters' belief in the importance of the EU and its Single Market (*Financial Times* 2016a). The complexity and risks associated with unravelling the UK's EU membership offer an object lesson to European voters in the limitations of simplistic policy solutions. Contradictions that before existed merely in theory, such as the UK having to renegotiate free trade deals with countries for which there was already an EU one, become of practical relevance to voters. In this fashion, Brexit may potentially re-affirm European solidarity – at a time of great self-doubt – by highlighting once and for all exactly what would be lost without European integration. It is not that Euroscepticism or Europessimism, especially that occasioned by austerity within the eurozone, will disappear. That said, anti-EU populism prospered by claiming elites were too blinkered to see the benefits of reclaiming sovereignty. The throes of Britain's attempt to 'take back control' from Europe could finally reverse this narrative.

2
Brexit and the improvised constitution

Albert Weale

'The fault, dear Brutus, is not in our stars,
But in ourselves ...'

(Cassius, William Shakespeare, *Julius Caesar*, Act 1, Scene 2)

Article 50 of the Lisbon Treaty famously says that any Member State 'may decide to withdraw from the Union in accordance with its own constitutional requirements'. Brexit will have many effects. However, possibly its most important has already occurred, namely its highlighting of the peculiarly improvised nature of the UK's constitution. What does it mean to say that the UK is acting in accordance with its own constitutional requirements, when those requirements have to be made up as we go along? And what does the improvisation mean for the principles of constitutional democracy and the constraining of government power?

In proposing answers to these questions, I am going to suggest that the Brexit referendum creates a political paradox. Ostensibly the use of referendums gives control to the people. In practice, within the UK, however, a referendum reinforces executive power. To understand the paradox, we need to grasp the basic principle of UK constitutional practice. Despite many changes in recent years, that principle is one of identifiable party government, with the governing party responsible to the people through the electoral process. Since a referendum only determines a broad direction of policy, the party in government, as the executive, needs a parliamentary majority. When that majority is threatened, it will need to enhance its party support by risking a general election, a logic nicely revealed in Theresa May's calling a sudden election, in order to secure support for any likely Article 50 agreement. The large majority she sought, but ultimately failed to obtain, would have overcome the objections from the opposition and the Lords to those elements in the EU (Withdrawal) Bill that explicitly enhance executive discretion. The same logic of executive dominance means the neglect of the contrary voices of the peoples who make up the compound polity that is now the UK. Constitutionally the fault is in ourselves.

The British constitution

Once upon a time, as they say in all the fairytales, the British political system held a special place in the study of comparative constitutions. The tale ran as follows. If the USA represented the liberal, France the republican and the USSR the socialist route to modern politics, Great Britain (the UK, Britain, England – the names were used interchangeably, significant in itself) exemplified an evolutionary path. Its democratic politics represented new wine in old bottles. The continuity of its institutions and practices reflected a deep national identity and a widespread willingness to defer to legitimate political authority. Its political strength drew support from the UK's peaceful transition from a monarchical to a democratic regime. Its parliament had avoided the instability of the Third and Fourth French Republics; the UK had not fallen prey to the revolutionary upheaval undergone by Russia; and it had fought successful wars under the continuing scrutiny of parliamentary government. Even a left-wing critic like George Orwell in *The Lion and the Unicorn* (Orwell 1941) thought that England was like a family, its problem being that the wrong members were in charge. The fault was not in the institutions but in those who controlled those institutions.

As with all fairytales, there was much by way of selective perception in this account. The constitutional struggle over Irish Home Rule and independence at the end of the nineteenth and the beginning of the twentieth centuries had to be written out of the picture, as did the UK's colonial reach. The tale also ignored the price paid for continuity and stability. The institutions and practices of the UK constitution often seemed anomalous. How, for example, could one account for the existence of an unelected parliamentary chamber in the form of the House of Lords? Why, in order to resign, did MPs have to accept a notional royal appointment to the Chiltern Hundreds rather than just hand in their notice? How was it possible for a legislative chamber also to function as a supreme court in defiance of the elementary principles of the separation of powers? However, these anomalies could be excused as representing merely the formal elements of the constitution. Writing about the constitution in the nineteenth century, Walter Bagehot (1867, 59) said that it was like an old man who still wore the fashions of his youth: what you see of him is the same; what you do not see is wholly altered.

If all unseen was altered, what was it altered into? Bagehot suggested that the 'efficient secret' of the constitution was its concentration of power in the executive in the form of cabinet government. The cabinet is formed from the members of that party that can secure a parliamentary majority. Since Bagehot wrote, the electoral system has usually delivered a bonus of parliamentary seats to the party winning a simple plurality of the popular vote. The effect has been to underwrite cabinet government, giving governments a secure parliamentary majority on which they could rely. Parliamentary majorities thus manufactured by the electoral system did not require a popular majority. Since 1935 no political party in the UK has won a majority of the popular vote, and a popular minority could be translated into large legislative majorities: 1945, 1979, 1983, 1987 and 1997 being stand-out examples. With little devolution of power, a judiciary that interpreted the public interest as being coextensive with the public policy of the government of the day and with a relatively weak second chamber, UK governments exercised considerable power, revealed most obviously in the significant and frequently mutually self-cancelling alterations of policy from one government to another. British government is party government, and that means government by the party that controls the Commons. As Arend Lijphart (1999, Chapter 2) has shown, the UK system contrasts with many other examples of European governments where there is a greater sharing of power among political parties and political institutions.

Of course, since the UK's first application to join the European Economic Community in 1961, there have been considerable constitutional changes, well identified by Anthony King in his study *The British Constitution* (King 2007). The winnowing of local government under Thatcher, large-scale privatisation programmes, the devolution of powers to Scotland and Wales, the settlement in Northern Ireland, the creation of a separate supreme court, the ending of automatic inheritance of the House of Lords, even a period of coalition government have been significant. But none of these changes has overturned the core principle that a government of the day has the constitutional right to pursue its manifesto commitments provided that it can secure a majority in the House of Commons, or the fact that it is easier in the UK than in other jurisdictions to maintain a secure majority.

Given that a cabinet can carry out its programme, the principal security against misrule is supposed to be electoral accountability. If the UK's electoral system did not deliver a broadly representative legislative chamber, it was at least supposed to deliver responsible government, with this responsibility upheld through the ballot box. However, the use of the referendum as a tool carries one major and unique implication: it abandons the principle of responsible government at a crucial point in the public policy process. Governments cease to be responsible for their programme. A new principle emerges, namely that the policy of the government, and not just the party forming the government, should be determined by a popular vote. To the doctrine of cabinet government has been added a mandate theory of representation, a theory that coheres badly with the principles of constitutional democracy.

The intoxications of mandate theory

Go back to Article 50 and the rule that any Member State 'may decide to withdraw from the Union in accordance with its own constitutional requirements'. The difficulty for the UK, given its flexible constitution, is that there are no established constitutional principles widely accepted as authoritative for making a serious decision on a major question of national destiny. All that the legislation on the referendum said was that a referendum would be held. It said nothing about its constitutional status or significance. In consequence, the surprise result, unsurprisingly, has led to constitutional improvisation. Suddenly, we are all supposed to believe in a mandate theory of British government.

The basic principles of mandate theory can be expressed in three propositions. Firstly, the people is sovereign. Second, the people expresses its will on matters of public policy through a referendum in which a simple majority is decisive. Third, the function of the government is to implement the will of the people as decided by the referendum. Consult almost any government statement since the referendum to see this theory of political authority at work. I cite, almost at random and as just one example, the White Paper on legislating for the UK's withdrawal from the EU: 'The result – by 52 per cent to 48 per cent – was a clear instruction from the people of the UK to leave the EU' (Department for Exiting the European Union 2017, Paragraph 1.7).

An instruction from the people to the government appears at first sight to embody an obviously democratic principle. Yet, as Max Weber (1968, 1126–7) pointed out, the logic of the plebiscite can be to legitimate executive domination. This may seem paradoxical, but it is not. The mandate from a referendum is necessarily an incomplete basis for public policy. A referendum can at best only state a decision of principle, it cannot determine a course of public action. In so far as there is popular will in the result of a mandate, and this is doubtful in itself, that will must be given effect in the circumstances of the day that prevail.

In this context, executives come to see themselves as embodying the higher interests of the nation over the claims of competing political parties. Anything that frustrates the will of the people is simply anti-democratic. The holding of a referendum enhances executive dominance. This logic was at work in the government's wanting to use the royal prerogative, free of parliamentary accountability, as the legal basis for triggering Article 50. Although the High Court and the Supreme Court in the *Miller* case (see Eeckhout, Chapter 18) upheld the principle of parliamentary sovereignty, the result of the Commons vote was to give the government back the mandate that it sought. Yet, because any mandate is essentially incomplete, it raises deep questions about the role of Parliament, the rule of law, and, of course, the assumption that there is a unitary people whose will is to be given expression.

The demands on Parliament

As is well known, the Brexit negotiations involve at least two elements. The first is the settling of the outstanding house-keeping arrangements relating to such matters as the existing budgetary commitments of the UK and the liability for civil servants' pensions. The second, and by far and away the most important in constitutional terms, is an agreement on the framework for future relations between the UK and the EU. Straddling the two is the question of retained rights of EU citizens living in the UK and of UK citizens living in the EU. The choice to leave the EU was not a choice for a singular option, but a choice to enter into negotiations over which of a range of hypothetical options might be adopted. Although it may be clear what the referendum decision was against, it is not clear what it was for. At some point, hypothetical options will have to be turned into practical choices. How will that process be managed?

The prime minister in her letter to the Council president spoke of the UK seeking 'a deep and special relationship' with the future EU. To some ears that sounds suspiciously like an association arrangement as envisaged by Article 217 of the Treaty on the Functioning of the European Union (TFEU). The advantages of an association agreement from the point of view of the UK government is that it encompasses 'a deep and comprehensive free trade area' in which there is freedom of movement for goods, services and capital. It also gives tariff free access for goods and passports for services, alongside customs cooperation. Since the movement of labour is subject to work permits, the government could claim to be delivering on its manifesto promise to reduce migration. Moreover, an association agreement would allow participation in such common EU programmes as Horizon 2020 and Euratom, common transport, aviation, environment, employment and consumer protection policies, creating a link with policy areas, particularly security cooperation, where a UK government would be able to make a serious contribution to the European interest (see Duff 2016).

The snag, however, is that the UK would have to respect EU disciplines on competition, state aids, anti-dumping and public procurement, and these agreements would have to be policed by an agreed authority in which the jurisprudence of the CJEU would play a decisive role. This would be unacceptable to Conservative Eurosceptic backbenchers. Even if it were to offer sufficient guarantees on migration, an association agreement is also unlikely to meet the demands of those same backbench MPs on any budgetary contributions required to participate in specific programmes. We shall never know the full calculations that went into the prime minister's decision to call an election. But it is at least a plausible hypothesis that she wanted to increase her party majority in order to have sufficient control over an otherwise unstable Parliament, so as to be able to secure an association agreement that would have been unacceptable to a significant portion of the backbenchers inherited from the 2015 election. Calling an election at a high point of popularity for the government and a low point of popularity for the opposition held out the promise of greater freedom of action unavailable with a small parliamentary majority. As we know, however, the decision backfired spectacularly.

The rule of law

The rule of law embodies the requirement that a government acts on principles of legal impartiality and the due authorisation of political authority by the legislature. In the modern state, these principles come under constant pressure from the large volume of administrative regulations that governments need to adopt in order to ensure the good working of a modern economic and social order. Many hold that already the legislative scrutiny of executive regulation is defective by virtue of the volume of work that has to be undertaken. In the UK since 1973, much of this administrative activity has been increasingly embedded in EU policy processes. So, the UK's departure from the EU requires the repatriation of the legal powers associated with administrative regulation (in the general sense, not the specific EU sense of that term), known as the EU's *acquis*. This is the domain of the so-called 'Great Repeal Bill'.

The House of Lords Delegated Powers and Regulatory Reform Select Committee (2017) has drawn attention to the dangers of enhancing executive power and discretion as a result of the Great Repeal Bill. That Committee points out that although the government's announced intention is simply to domesticate the powers currently exercised within the framework of the EU, simple transposition of those powers into UK law cannot be assumed to have an equivalent effect. Thus, an existing legal duty on the UK government to send information to an EU body, for example on oil and gas projects, cannot have the same force if the relevant procedure is domesticated. All that the duty could simply mean is that a UK government had a duty to send information to itself. Repealing existing obligations to EU institutions will not leave the legal powers of a UK government unaltered.

Here again we can see how the seemingly democratic logic of the referendum increases executive power. The only way in practical terms of repatriating EU law is to allow the government of the day wide-ranging discretionary powers to determine the details of administrative procedure. These are the so-called 'Henry VIII' clauses, which the proposed bill duly enshrines. The decision of principle in the referendum is inherently incomplete in the context of inherited commitments that have to be unstitched one by one. Within the two-year timescale allowed for by Article 50, it is easy to see the dilemma for the government. Unless the powers under which administrative action is empowered is legislated for in UK law, the government would have no legal powers with which to undertake vital functions. So an omnibus bill is needed. On the other hand, precisely because the legislation has to be omnibus, the transfer of the large number of powers that it entails inevitably means that the significance of many individual elements in the transfer escapes proper scrutiny.

The plurality of the people

A mandate theory of the referendum presupposes a unitary people. To act as a people's agent assumes that the government is responding to the mandate of a single people whose will is determinative. Formally speaking, the UK is a unitary state. There are no constitutionally protected spheres of action assigned to sub-national government. Although the devolution legislation had constitutional effects, its status is that of ordinary statute law. The corollary is that there is a 'British people' whose will was expressed in the referendum result.

However, while this is the formal legal position, the political reality is quite different, and it would be unwise to construct a theory of the popular will based upon the principle that devolution law is merely ordinary statute law. No one supposes that in the foreseeable future the devolution of powers to the Scottish government can be rolled back, and there are few who want any other arrangement other than a substantial devolution of political authority to Northern Ireland. Whatever may be true in legal principle, the UK has become a compound polity over the last twenty years. The peoples of the constituent nations of the UK have a substantive political existence in their own right. A UK government needs to accept the restriction of its authority that has emerged since devolution.

The principle of public choice in compound polities is not that of a simple majority of 'the people' but rather concurrent majorities of the different peoples, in which the majority decision of the whole is a function of the component majorities of the parts. In the case of the Brexit referendum, this condition was not met. The majorities for 'Leave' in England and Wales were complemented by majorities for Remain in Scotland and Northern Ireland. Setting the simple majority principle applied to the UK as a whole against the principle of concurrent majorities, it is clear that there can be an inconsistency, as was the case with Brexit.

There is an interesting contrast in the scope of the UK government's powers between Scotland and Northern Ireland. Section 30 of the 1998 Scotland Act gives the UK prime minister the power to refuse a request for a referendum in Scotland, whereas the Good Friday Agreement (GFA) commits both the Irish and UK governments to recognising a united Ireland if majorities in both countries favour that option. Although if there were a clear majority for independence in Scotland, it might be as difficult politically to resist the move as to resist Irish reunification. Moreover, there are significant differences in the way that executive action would play out, not least because Irish reunification would enable the current Northern Ireland to remain within the EU, whereas an independent Scotland would have to go through the same application process as other candidate countries. The limit of the mandate of the people is found in the existence of a plurality of peoples in the UK.

Conclusions

The paradox of a referendum is that it is often presented as a device of popular control by which political power is returned to the people. In practice, it increases executive power, as the government seeks the freedom from Parliament and legal constraint in order to implement what it sees at the popular will. A popular decision of principle creates the field of power in which a government can seek to act. With an improvised constitution like that of the UK, the paradox is heightened, since the meaning of the referendum result becomes a contest of political wills rather than an interpretation of a basic constitutional process. That is the legacy of an evolutionary and flexible constitution. There is no one else to blame. The fault is in ourselves.

3
Is the EU 'a crap 1950s idea'?

Dominic Cummings, branching histories and the case for Leave

Glyn Morgan

The Brexit campaigns of 2016 – both Leave and Remain – were fought largely through the medium of simplicities, delusions and lies (Shipman 2016). Neither campaign generated much deep political thinking. The Leave campaign floated to victory on a fantastical promise of ending immigration and returning Britain's EU funds to the National Health Service (NHS). The Remain campaign relied on no less fantastical projections of the ruinous short-term economic costs of Brexit (the so-called 'Project Fear'). Dominic Cummings, Leader of the Vote Leave campaign, did more than anyone to focus the campaign debate on bogus issues like the NHS and the impending enlargement of the EU to include Turkey (Cummings 2017a). Nonetheless, in a series of writings authored after the referendum, Cummings has produced various arguments for Brexit that have drawn considerable attention and praise.

Cummings' position is worth considering for two reasons. First, it is useful to know which actual arguments propelled some of the leading figures in the campaign, especially since they chose not to reveal those arguments at the time. Second, Cummings insists on moving beyond vague ruminations on whether Brexit will succeed or fail. He thinks political judgments must be based on 'precise quantitative predictions about well-formed questions'.[1] While Cummings' own judgements are not, I think, at all defensible, those who advocate Britain's re-entry into Europe – which is now in all likelihood a generational project – would do well to follow the form, if not the actual substance, of his approach.

Brexit and disaster-avoidance

Cummings' position on Brexit flows from four more general preoccupations. First, he possesses a deep-seated disdain for the British political and administrative classes, which he variously damns as incompetent, lacking in relevant knowledge and mired in dysfunctional bureaucracies. Second, he has a fascination with the advances of science and technology, and their application to human understanding and societal improvement. Third, he recognises that societies face key moments, when the decisions taken send the society down one or another branch of history. Brexit was one of those key moments; for better or worse, the Leave decision sent Britain down a very different 'branching history' than would have been the case had Leave lost. Fourth, Cummings is a follower of Tetlock's work on forecasting. He thinks that political judgements – and presumably, key political decisions – should be based upon rational probabilistic assessments of specific, measurable, time-defined outcomes (Tetlock & Gardner 2015).

All four of these preoccupations come together in Cummings' case for Leave, which rests on the probabilistic assessment that leaving the EU would improve the chances of '1) Britain contributing positively to the world and 2) minimising dangers … [including] Britain's exposure to the problems caused by the EU'. Viewed more specifically, Cummings' argument proceeds along three tracks. Track one takes the Eurosceptics' conventional ride through Brussels – that familiar wasteland, as they see it, of failure, false promise and dysfunction. The only distinctive feature of this part of Cummings's journey is the Hayekian-inspired claim that the EU lacks the self-correcting mechanisms of the market and the experimental sciences (see Van Parijs, Chapter 27). For Cummings, the EU – 'a crap 1950s idea', as he calls it – is excessively hierarchical and centralised, and as such lacks the error-correcting mechanisms of a national parliamentary government (Shipman 2016, 38). Quoting the physicist David Deutsch, Cummings insists that 'preserving the institutions of error correction is more important than any policy'.

This part of Cummings' argument need not detain us. The idea that the EU is slow-moving and lacks *rapid* error-correcting mechanisms is a plausible criticism to make. Scholars of the EU often make the same point. No fundamental transformation in the EU can take place without a Treaty change, which requires a unanimous decision of all Member States. It's also fair to say that the EU is hierarchical, at least in the sense that its decisions are top-down and taken without much direct democratic input. But it's ludicrous to attribute this problem to excessive centralisation. Indeed, the principal reason why the EU is so slow-moving is due to its highly decentralised and consensual decision-making practices. The EU is such a feeble force in global affairs because it lacks the centralised political system of the other Great Powers. Similarly, the EU has struggled with the eurozone crisis because it lacks the centralised tax and budgetary powers necessary to manage successfully a Monetary Union. More generally, the concept of 'error correction' in politics is more problematic than Cummings seems to recognise. Where there is a clearly agreed aim, it is relatively straightforward to identify an error – this is the case, for example, in computer coding. But in politics, errors are often only identifiable after the event, and even then, the attribution of 'error' remains controversial. Was Western military intervention in Afghanistan in 2001 an error? Was the absence of Western military intervention in Syria in 2012 an error? Was the creation of the EU an error? None of these questions can be answered independently of a justification of our political projects, a justification that will inevitably require an appeal to contestable moral values as much as any probabilistic assessment of outcomes (Morgan 2005).

The second track of Cummings' argument focuses on the idea that 'leaving would improve the probability of ... making Britain the best place in the world for science and education'. Here it is important to recall that Cummings worked in Whitehall as an advisor to the minister of education and is the author of an ambitious project for educational renewal (Cummings 2013). For Cummings, science and education are key evaluative criteria. He predicts that a post-Brexit UK will achieve more, and make a greater scientific contribution to the world, once free of the EU's legal and regulatory regime.

One merit of this argument is that it is sufficiently precise to generate a testable prediction. Post-Brexit Britain will, if this prediction pans out, score higher on objective criteria of scientific success at some specified date in the future (2026?) than the Britain of 2016. Presumably the criteria will include such factors as educational scores on the PISA surveys, citation-weighted research publication rates, scientific prizes, global university rankings and technological patents.

The third track of Cummings' argument is the most interesting. Brexit, he argues, minimises dangers, especially the biggest danger of all: the danger that the free movement of labour will spark a populist backlash that will threaten free trade. As he puts this point:

> 1) … a return to 1930s protectionism would be disastrous, 2) the fastest route to this is continuing with no democratic control over immigration or human rights policies for terrorists and other serious criminals, therefore 3) the best practical policy is to reduce (for a while) unskilled immigration and *increase* high skills immigration particularly those with very hard skills in maths, physics and computer science, 4) this requires getting out of the EU, 5) hopefully it will prod the rest of Europe to limit immigration and therefore limit the extremist forces that otherwise will try to rip down free trade.

This argument conjectures a chain of events leading from 'no [national] democratic control over immigration', a requirement of the EU's Single Market, to the rise of extremist forces demanding 1930s style protectionism, which Cummings rightly considers a disaster. He wants to avoid this disaster by way of another conjecture: a chain of events leading from 'democratic control of unskilled labour' – high-skilled labour would be unaffected – to a broader public tolerance of free trade. Ideally, Cummings would like to see post-Brexit UK prompt the formation of 'new institutions for international cooperation to minimize the probability of disasters' (Cummings 2017a). He seems to think that the UK post-Brexit is in better position to do this than as a member of the EU.

While it is difficult to argue against probabilistic wagers and counterfactual claims, there are significant problems with both the second and third tracks of Cummings' argument. The claim that post-Brexit UK will be well placed to experience a scientific renaissance runs into a number of obvious difficulties. First, the UK already does relatively well on national comparative measures of scientific progress (*Scientific American* 2012). Second, scholars have never been able to identify with any great confidence the conditions likely to produce scientific progress (Taylor 2016). And third, any post-Brexit UK government will have to ensure that the country remains (and is perceived to remain) an attractive place for foreign science, technology, engineering and mathematics (STEM) workers to come to study, live and work. It is very difficult to see how Brexit helps here, especially since it diminishes the status of all workers coming from EU countries. Where once these workers had a status grounded in the EU constitution, they now will be in the UK merely at the pleasure of Her

Majesty's Government (Morgan 2016). The reluctance of the Tory government to allow the CJEU any role in protecting the rights of EU citizens in the UK can only increase the anxieties of such people.

Cummings' wager that Brexit would diminish the chances of an extreme form of protectionism emerging in Britain has some initial plausibility. Certainly, UKIP has pretty much collapsed; in the June 2017 election, the voters it had gained in earlier elections largely fled back to the two major parties. But viewed more closely, his argument about Brexit as a means to avoiding protectionism and increasing the UK's share of global trade is deeply problematic. Here we have to weigh a probabilistic claim together with a preventative claim. How likely is it that – absent a reduction in unskilled immigration – the UK would face an anti-trade backlash leading to 1930s-style protectionism? On the face of it, the UK is an unlikely site for protectionism. No current political party – not even UKIP – favours trade protection. Indeed, a central argument of leading Tory thinkers is that post-Brexit the UK will enter a '"post-geography trading world" where we are much less restricted in having to find partners who are physically close to us' (Fox 2016). Furthermore, opinion surveys suggest that UK public opinion is among the most pro-free trade in the advanced industrial world (Pew Survey 2014). In short, 1930s-style protectionism seems like a rather low probability threat. But even if we were to accept that protectionism represents even a low-level threat, there is little reason to think that ending low-skill immigration offers an effective and efficient solution, especially since this type of immigration is so essential in the hospitality, retail, health care and agricultural sectors of the UK economy (Consterdine 2017). Cummings' remedy is not only unduly costly; it promises to be even more injurious than the underlying ailment.

As to the hope that post-Brexit UK will spring to life as a trading superstar, Cummings' argument is no more persuasive than that of Liam Fox and others in the Tory government. The major problem here is that EU membership does not prohibit any EU Member States from trading successfully around the globe. The fact that the UK has been relatively unsuccessful in key global markets (China, for example) has nothing to do with the EU. Indeed, if the EU were the principal cause of trade failures, then why has Germany proven so much more successful? No less problematic is the suggestion that post-Brexit UK will make gains in this new 'post-geography trading world' sufficient to outweigh any losses from exiting the Single Market. If the UK were to trade under WTO rules and couldn't negotiate new frictionless customs arrangements, it is difficult to see how the UK could retain its domestic car industry, one of the largest sources of UK manufacturing exports, or even its aircraft manufacturing industry (Islam 2017). The other big trade problem facing the UK post-Brexit is that the UK has very little power to force the EU to offer favourable trading conditions. Cummings like other pro-Leave advocates often neglects to mention that as a Regional Trade Association (RTA), the EU is allowed, even under WTO rules, to discriminate against third-party countries. For these reasons, most macro-economic estimates of the effects of leaving the EU predict that Brexit will have a significant trade-lowering and welfare-diminishing impact on the UK economy. In sum, if the goal is to increase trade, Brexit seems like the wrong way to do it.

What disasters should we worry about?

While there's not much to be said in favour of the actual content of Cummings' argument, the general form of his argument is quite sensible. Cummings is right to warn against the vacuity of general claims that Brexit will succeed or fail. He is right to recommend that political judgements be based upon probabilistic wagers and predictions. Cummings is also right to emphasise the importance of identifying threats and thinking about institutions capable of error-correction and disaster-avoidance. Yet even with these admonitions in mind, I think it is possible to reach a very different assessment about the merits of leaving the EU.

At this point, it would be helpful to introduce a few brief distinctions. A threat might be conceptualised as a harm multiplied by the probability of its occurrence. A disaster is a harm with very high costs, whether material costs or value costs. The notion of value costs is important. Political communities stand for certain values – whether liberty, democracy, justice or whatever – and when those core moral values are lost, it might be counted a disaster. Organised political communities guard against threats by way of various preventative mechanisms (whether policies or institutions). These mechanisms must be both effective (i.e. they must work) and efficient (i.e. they must have low ancillary costs). It is no good putting in place preventative mechanisms that impose higher costs – whether material or moral – than those posed by the underlying threat. A surveillance society with unlimited police powers might be effective against terrorism, but it is inefficient, since it requires a sacrifice of some of our core moral values. One further point: political decisions have uncertain outcomes. When taking a major political decision – a decision that initiates a new 'branching history' – a sensible political actor will weigh not only likely costs and benefits, but also the capacities of those bureaucrats, politicians and administrative agencies that must enact that decision.

With these distinctions in place, it's possible to think about some threats that post-Brexit UK faces. To narrow the focus, it might be helpful to limit our attention to threats that jeopardise values that are relatively uncontroversial and widely shared, such as national security and societal wealth. The following threats all seem sufficiently probable and sufficiently costly to these values that they require preventative measures:

(i) the exclusion of the UK from the favourable trade, security and research opportunities enjoyed by other EU Member States;
(ii) the break-up of the UK as a political community and the return of terrorism in Northern Ireland;
(iii) US isolationism and trade protectionism leading to a collapse of the post-war international order;
(iv) Russian aggression in Eastern Europe;
(v) large-scale migration – tens of millions per year – into Southern Europe;
(vi) a major banking and debt crisis in Italy;
(vii) large-scale domestic terrorism as a consequence of the implosion of Middle Eastern and North African states and the failure to integrate existing Islamic minority populations.

We have already discussed threat (i), which will arise as an immediate and direct consequence of Brexit, especially if Brexit takes the form of exiting the Single Market and Customs Union. The seriousness of threat (i) further increases, if the EU were to pursue its own self-interest and seek to ensure that the UK is materially worse off outside the Single Market than inside. The EU certainly has no interest in seeing the UK flourish outside the Single Market, because it might encourage other states to leave. Nor does the EU have anything to gain by allowing the UK to pursue an à la carte strategy, where it enjoyed the benefits of access to the Single Market while bearing none of the costs. A prudent UK government cannot dismiss the possibility that the EU will follow such a realist strategy towards the UK. It must expect the EU to pursue policies designed to diminish the UK's economic and political power.

The threats the UK faces outside the Single Market are only exacerbated by threat (iii), which acts as force multiplier to threat (i). Indeed, if and when the UK exits the EU and its Single Market, the UK becomes much more dependent on the US. Pro-Brexit ministers like Liam Fox speak of the opportunities the UK will have for new trade deals with the US. But it is far from clear that these trade deals will be offered on favourable terms by a US president who emphasises 'America First' and is allergic to international treaties. The most readily available remedy against threats (i) and (iii) is simply for the UK to remain in the EU.

The same remedy can be said about threat (ii). No one has yet come up with a solution to the Northern Ireland problem once the UK leaves the EU. This problem has both an economic and a political dimension. Economically, Brexit presents Northern Ireland with the problem of trading across a new land-border between the UK and the Republic of Ireland. Not only will this land-border make it difficult to sustain the extensive intra-company trade flows that depend upon just-in-time deliveries. But a land-border will likely have a severe impact on the Northern Irish agricultural sector. The political problems are, if anything, even more daunting. The Good Friday Agreement of 1998 presupposes that the UK and the Republic of Ireland are both members of the EU; and it makes explicit reference to the European Convention of Human Rights and to European Courts in safeguarding the rights specified in the Agreement. If the UK pulls out of both the EU and the European Convention on Human Rights (ECHR), as Prime Minister May has urged, then the GFA could unravel and terrorism return to Northern Ireland.

Threats (i), (ii) and (iii) can hardly be dismissed as either improbable or trivial. They are serious threats – threats to security and societal wealth – that would not have arisen had the UK remained in the EU. The case for Brexit does not, however, require that these threats be ignored. A sophisticated case for Brexit could concede that these are genuine threats, but are outweighed by other even more serious threats that Brexit would allow the UK to avoid. Some obvious candidates here are those listed as threats (iv), (v), (vi) and (vii). All of these threats affect the UK only indirectly. Thus if one judged that Eastern and Southern Europe had a high probability of collapse, whether because of external factors (Russian aggression or migration) or internal factors (a financial crisis or domestic terrorism), then Brexit might present itself as an escape. Why shackle the country to a corpse – especially if the corpse is facing impending disaster?

At this point, the threat-based case for and against Brexit turns on a set of probabilistic judgements about which combination of threats is more likely and more harmful. Cummings is right, I think, to maintain that arguments for and against Brexit that took place on this territory would be more fruitful than one that relied upon vague and emotive appeals to the failure or success of Brexit. It must be noted, however, that arguments in the register of threats and disaster-avoidance become altogether more complex once we include more controversial and contestable values than security and societal wealth. For many people in the pro-Brexit camp, national identity remains their ultimate and most important value; and the threats to national identity posed by large-scale immigration are sufficient to justify Brexit even at some expense to security and societal wealth. Conversely, for many people in the anti-Brexit camp transnational solidarity (or cosmopolitanism) is their central value. For these people, the idea that the UK turn inwards and ignore threats to Eastern and Southern Europe would be an anathema. It is not obvious how to resolve or even meliorate disagreements driven by incommensurable values. Perhaps the promise of Cummings' threat-based approach to politics is to allow us to distinguish disagreements about probable outcomes and disagreements about the efficacy of preventative measures – both of which disagreements seem amenable to some form of rational adjudication – from disagreements about fundamental values. Given that the 2016 referendum debate never approached this level of clarity, Cummings' post-referendum writings might be viewed as his own *mea culpa*.

4
How British was the Brexit vote?

Gráinne de Búrca

Understandably, the Brexit debate moved quickly from an initial quest to identify causes of discontent and errors of policy and strategy to focus on the mechanics and the terms of exit as well as on the likely terms of future UK engagement with the EU. But an understanding of the causes of Brexit continues to be of central importance, both for intrinsic reasons as well as for the practical purpose of considering what kind of response, or reform, on the part of the EU – and just as importantly on the part of the UK – may be appropriate. An appreciation of the distinctive and local features of the vote as a reflection of the UK's relationship with the EU, as well as the features that it seems to share with current developments across other democracies worldwide, is therefore worth seeking. Hence this contribution steps back again from the immediacy of the current issues to reflect on the extent to which the vote should be understood primarily as a British decision, caused by persistent concerns and long-standing sentiment within the UK body politic, as well as interrogating more closely the role played by the 'populist wave' sweeping much of the Western world.

A dominant focus in the aftermath of the referendum has been on analysing and situating the Brexit vote as an integral part of a wider set of political developments across the globe, namely the rise in nationalist sentiment and illiberal authoritarianism, and the backlash against the perceived consequences of economic globalisation and migration, somewhat neglecting the distinctive relationship the UK has had with the EU.

Much of the commentary has also emphasised the similarities between the impetus for the Brexit vote and the forces that propelled

Donald Trump to electoral victory in the US. The two events have been grouped together as populist political events which expressed and reflected (i) a reaction against immigration, (ii) concern about economic insecurity, (iii) a rejection of internationalism and transnationalism, (iv) a return to inward-looking (economic) nationalism and (v) a rise in authoritarian and illiberal sentiment. This approach to understanding and explaining Brexit stresses the similarities between the issues that were salient during the Brexit campaign and which seem to have animated the vote to leave the EU and those that are fuelling political developments within other democracies, not only in the US election but also across much of Europe at present.

The local story: Brexit as a British event

A different interpretation of the vote suggests that it is best understood and analysed by paying close attention to the particular context of Great Britain, and that its root causes are to be found less in some kind of contagious, common international backlash against globalisation, and more in Britain's political and cultural distinctiveness and in the experiences and perceptions of EU membership of the 17.5 million people who voted to leave (Le Galès 2016).

This reading of the UK vote views it as something of a vindication of the position expressed by French President Charles de Gaulle when in 1963, and again in 1967, he vetoed the UK's application for EEC membership on the basis (among other reasons) that the UK saw the EEC primarily as a trade bloc and was insufficiently committed to the broader project of European integration. Indeed, since the trajectory of European integration from 1973 until today has unquestionably been one of 'ever closer union', moving from what was essentially a common market project when the UK initially joined to a much more integrated political community by the time of the UK referendum in 2016, the Brexit vote can readily be understood from this perspective as the unsurprising and predictable outcome of calling a popular vote on a challenging political relationship.

The UK, when it set out to join the European Economic Community, sought different things from its membership than did the six founding Member States which had been more explicitly committed to 'ever closer union' since the time of the European Coal and Steel Treaty (and indeed the abortive European Defence and Political Communities in 1952–3).[1] The UK chose not to join the original six in the 1950s, preferring instead to commit to the multilateral free trade system and to its Atlantic relations, which it prioritised over its relations with Western Europe (Carter 1966, Neely 1991). It has been argued that the UK's change of heart in the 1960s was driven by its desire to avoid continued economic decline, and not because of any sudden conversion to the political project of European integration (Campos & Coricelli 2015). Joining the EEC was a pragmatic economic choice and not an indication of any commitment to greater political unity with 'continental' Europe. Moreover, even after it had joined the EEC in 1973, the UK remained an 'awkward partner' (George 1998). While other Member States expressed sharp reservations at various times about aspects of EU policy, with specialised opt-outs being sought for particular interests and issues such as the Danish 'second homes' protocol[2] and the Irish abortion protocol,[3] and while there was a gradual rise in Eurosceptical political movements across the EU from the time of the Maastricht Treaty onward (Mudde 2012), the UK nonetheless remained somewhat exceptional (if not exceptionalist) in its attitude towards the EU. Britain sought and received special treatment in relation to the so-called EU budget rebate (European Parliament 2016), and it adopted a pragmatic, case-by-case approach to the introduction of new areas of EU policy. It secured opt-outs on a range of issues on which it was unwilling to countenance closer integration, notably from EMU and Justice and Home Affairs at the time of the Maastricht Treaty, with other shorter-lived or less successful attempts seen in the Social Protocol attached to the Maastricht Treaty (Falkner 1996, Towers 1992) and the more recent Protocol on the Charter of Fundamental Rights attached to the Lisbon Treaty (Barnard 2008).

In 2000, Helen Wallace wrote that 'British governments have been repeatedly concerned that other European governments would run ahead with cooperative and integrationist adventures that would leave the UK on the margins. Their fears have repeatedly been well-founded' (Wallace 2000). She noted that, despite the UK's enthusiasm for specific EU policies, in particular for the Single Market but also, interestingly, for the development of EU foreign policy, there remained a deep resistance towards European 'federalism' and everything this was assumed to imply (*Economist* 2003). Wallace also noted – tellingly, in view of the circumstances in which the initial decision to hold a referendum on EU membership was taken – that 'typically governments in office have sought to develop a more engaged European policy, while the alternating lead party of opposition has found "Europe" a persuasive and useful subject on to which to differentiate itself from the governing party. There has been a damaging cycle of acrimony, which, hardly surprisingly, has been reflected in ambivalent public opinion on European issues and an image of Britain as an unpredictable partner'. Her comment that British political culture did not yield easily to the pressures of Europeanisation can be supplemented by the findings of a leading market research organisation that British public opinion never entirely warmed to the UK's participation in the EU, with levels of support for membership constantly fluctuating, and regularly overtaken by a majority opposed to membership (Mortimore 2016). Given these numbers, it seems plausible to assume that if a popular referendum on UK withdrawal from the EU had been held on any number of occasions over the four decades of EU membership, the outcome of the vote may well have been the same as in June 2016, long before the apparent populist revolution sweeping the West.

Britain was one of the few European countries to emerge with a sense of victory and strength from World War II. With its network of Commonwealth relationships and firm Atlanticist outlook, as well as its distinctive history and strong sense of independence, the UK's decision to join the EU was a pragmatic one taken for largely economic reasons and with clear reservations about the deeper political project of European integration. And while the experience of EU membership seems to have been broadly positive, and to have generated a commitment to transnational integration amongst the younger generations for whom Britain's post-war history and prior alliances are less salient, it has failed to win over a substantial part of the (predominantly older) public brought up in post-war Britain, for whom the 'take back control' slogan resonated strongly. The sense of exclusion or of having been 'left behind' which seems to have driven some of the Brexit vote was thus not only a sense of being left behind economically, but of being left behind in a changing Britain and Europe which does not reflect some voters' preferences, expectations or sense of belonging (Goodwin & Heath 2016).

Hence the referendum vote in the end reflected a deep split within the British public, with 52 per cent voting to leave and 48 per cent to stay. The most striking cleavages appeared along age and educational lines, with other divisions evident in the urban/rural vote and in the devolved regions (British Election Study 2016; Goodwin & Heath 2016). And though the decision came as a shock, not least given its immense repercussions both for the EU and the UK, the fact that many Britons had never overcome their initial reluctance about joining the EU, nor settled into a stable pattern of support for EU membership, meant the warning signs about the risk of holding a referendum were evident for many years. Indeed, the referendum result can be quite reasonably understood as the predictable outcome of a difficult 43-year relationship between the UK and the EU that had never managed to transcend its reluctant and contested origins, and that never fully won the 'hearts and minds' of the British public.

What are the implications of this interpretation of the Brexit vote? One reading of the significance of the age and educational divide is that as the younger generation matures, majority support could well develop for a much closer relationship with the EU than that currently contemplated by those leading the Brexit movement, or possibly even for renewed EU membership after a period outside the EU. The salience of education points to the importance both of adequate public investment in education as well as the integration of a European civic education component into the national school curriculum. The above analysis is not intended to suggest that other issues and political cleavages were not also at play in, and relevant to, the Brexit vote, but rather to show that there is a compelling indigenous story which merits close attention when we seek to understand what gave rise to the result of the vote in June 2016.

The contagion story: Brexit as a boat on the global tide of populist anti-internationalism

The weight of analysis in the aftermath of the vote, however, has been rather less on the local and longer-term story, and more on an understanding of Brexit as a part of the wave of populist, illiberal, anti-international and nationalist sentiment apparently sweeping the democratic world.

There is a certain risk, in my view, given the broad set of political challenges and changes taking place within many democracies at present, of lumping together in the broad category of populism a range of distinct, albeit at times related, issues that would each benefit from separate analysis. Of these separate issues often lumped together, the first is attitudes towards immigration, a second is economic insecurity, a third is a move against internationalism towards economic and other forms of nationalism, and a fourth is the rise of illiberalism, including a move towards reducing or removing constitutional checks and balances on popular democracy.

Concerns about immigration were unquestionably highly salient in the Brexit vote (Swales 2016; *Economist* 2016). The relevance of economic factors and economic status, on the other hand, seems to have been less straightforward. It is not in doubt that the twin issues of EU-driven austerity policy on the one hand, and EU-promoted economic liberalisation on the other, generated significant discontent and opposition to EU policies and to the Union itself amongst parts of the population. Nevertheless, while there was a clear correlation between unemployment status and the vote to leave, many groups of wealthy and economically secure voters who benefited from economic liberalisation also opted to leave, and many less economically secure voters seem to have been motivated more by issues of identity than by economic interest (O'Neill 2016; Williams 2017).

Can the Brexit vote be understood as an instance of the wider global trend toward economic nationalism and against international cooperation? This reading of the referendum vote is complicated by the stated goal of many outspoken Brexit supporters in the UK for free trade. The opposition of 52 per cent of the population to EU membership seems to have been motivated by opposition to a certain conception of supranationalism (or 'federalism') which the EU was seen to represent, rather than a retreat from economic globalisation or internationalism *per se*. The desire of 'Leavers' to be free seems to have been aimed against European regulation, and not necessarily other alliances or forms of international engagement.

What, then, of the rise in popular support for illiberal authoritarian governments, and the corrosion of constitutional checks and balances in many states? Does the Brexit vote fit within this set of developments? Is the Brexit vote to be categorised alongside the rise of the extreme right across Europe and beyond, somewhere on the same continuum as the growth in support for illiberal autocracy? Such an interpretation would require us to view EU membership as a set of supranational constitutional checks, including the constraints of the EU treaty rules and of the Charter of Fundamental Rights, and to understand the vote to leave the EU as a vote to be free of these constraints. But even if it is reasonable to assume that many of those who voted for Brexit sought to avoid the future application of the EU Treaty rules or of the Charter of Rights, such a vote did not necessarily amount to an attempt to remove domestic constitutional checks and balances within the UK, or to promote popular rule over constitutional government. On the contrary, even if – following the *Miller* judgment – there were protests from the tabloid media at the prospect of the judiciary and the UK Parliament playing a role in the decision to leave the EU,[4] the vote to leave the EU, and the 'take back control' slogan, must still be understood as referring to the restoration of British parliamentary democracy, with its own distinctive set of domestic checks and balances. Even Theresa May's flirtations with the possibility of British withdrawal from the European Convention on Human Rights were accompanied by the prospect of adopting a domestic bill of rights instead (Asthana & Mason 2016; Bates 2017). As far as the rise of the far right is concerned, the UK Conservative Party is a party of the centre-right, while the UK Independence Party, which attracted some extreme right-wing support, has largely collapsed in the aftermath of the vote. Even if the salience of immigration in the Brexit campaign often had an illiberal and xenophobic dimension, and authoritarian values were prominent in the vote to leave the EU (Swales 2016, 14), it would be an over-statement to present the vote as a move towards illiberalism in the UK.

The foregoing analysis has certainly not set out to argue that the broader international context was not highly relevant to the Brexit vote. There is no question that issues gaining traction in the US presidential election and elsewhere resonated with those prominent in the Brexit debate, especially concerns about immigration and, to some extent, economic insecurity. Indeed, it seems likely that these factors tipped the balance in the referendum, proving decisive on the day and leading to the vote to leave the EU. But what I want to suggest is that, while those issues helped to provide a new set of narratives to frame and reinforce traditional Eurosceptic sentiments in the UK, an important part of the explanation for the referendum outcome is local, and lies in the specificities of the UK's relationship with the EU the contestation which has characterised that relationship from the outset, and the structure of British politics. This leads to two conclusions. The first is that the EU needs to examine, and to reflect carefully on, the appropriate responses to the concerns about migration which resonated so successfully in the Brexit debate, as well as to the issues of economic insecurity. But the second is that it would be a mistake to assume that the factors that gave rise to the 'leave' vote in the UK are the same as those that are fuelling the discontent arising in other EU Member States – whether in France, the Netherlands, Germany, or elsewhere across the democratic world. Thus, in the months and years ahead, careful disaggregation of the various factors at play in different contexts, and of the specific and local dimensions of political discontent and popular unrest, will be essential if we are to understand and respond to the challenges driving the populist revolt.

II: Europe's institutional order

5
Brexit

Yet another crisis for the EU

Neill Nugent

Introduction

This chapter puts the Brexit crisis within the context of the many other crises the EU has experienced in recent years. The first part of the chapter identifies and briefly describes the nature of these other crises. The second part shows how, in varying ways, these crises have impacted on the Brexit process, notably by influencing: the referendum outcome; the ways in which the EU is structuring itself to conduct the Brexit negotiations; and the stances being adopted by the EU27 in the negotiations.

The EU's many crises

Brexit is clearly a major crisis for the EU. It is so not only because it is the first time a Member State has sought to withdraw from the Union, but also because the state concerned is a large and powerful Member State whose withdrawal will have damaging political and economic implications for the EU's standing and influence. But Brexit is not the only major crisis the EU has experienced in recent years. Rather, it has experienced, and to some extent is still experiencing, a series of crises. These crises have been so deep as to bring the very viability and continuance of the European integration 'project' seriously into question. Whilst it is not possible here to examine all of the other crises the EU has been experiencing, the 'headline' crises can be outlined. Short descriptions of them will help to bring out how severe, varied and multidimensional the crises have been in their natures and impacts. (More detailed accounts and examinations of the EU's crises can be found in Dinan et al. 2017.)

There have been four main headline crises: the eurozone, migration, governance crises, and the crisis of rising Euroscepticism.

The eurozone crisis

The EU's Economic and Monetary Union (EMU) was not built on solid foundations. A strong currency union needs to be accompanied by an economic union which includes both a fiscal union and a banking union, plus a political union since currency unions need institutional structures that can provide authoritative union-wide decisions on key macroeconomic matters. But, as many academic economists and policy practitioners have noted, both at the time of EMU's creation in the years following the Maastricht Treaty and since, whilst the 'M' in EMU has always been strong, the 'E' has been weak. As for politics, this has been almost totally absent. These design faults remained uncorrected in the years leading up to the eurozone crisis, mainly because eurozone Member States had little appetite for creating strong EU fiscal powers that included the capacity to make significant budgetary transfers between members when necessary.

In consequence, EMU was always likely to succeed only as long as the EU economy remained reasonably buoyant. However, the ripple effects of the collapse of Lehman Brothers in the US in September 2008 quickly led to some eurozone countries – notably Greece, but also including Ireland, Spain, Portugal and Cyprus – becoming financially vulnerable and experiencing severe sovereign debt crises, which in turn exposed the eurozone's structural weaknesses. For there were no semi-automatic mechanisms, as there would be in fully developed economic and monetary unions, to assist EMU Member States experiencing difficulties. States with debt problems were thus forced to seek help – most notably in the form of bailouts – from whatever sources that could be persuaded to be providers. Eventually, a so-called troika of lending sources was created – consisting of the European Commission, the European Central Bank (ECB) and the International Monetary Fund (IMF) – but its approach was strongly influenced by German preferences for recipient states of financial aid to be subject to stiff austerity measures, which resulted in lengthy and unseemly public disputes between donor states on the one hand and beneficiary states and their sympathisers on the other.

Indeed, so severe did tensions between creditor states and the main indebted state – Greece – become during the eurozone crisis that at one point – in 2015, when Greece's debts were, yet again, the focus of crises meetings – the German finance minister, Wolfgang Schäuble, even suggested that Greece and the eurozone could both benefit if the former left, albeit perhaps only temporarily, the system.

The migration crisis

Like the eurozone crisis, the migration crisis also stemmed from a core EU system with design faults being placed under severe strain. In this case, the Schengen System, which contained key arrangements for providing for one of the EU's main policy provisions – free movement of people – was the system under pressure. As with the eurozone crisis, the migration crisis resulted in the EU trying to fix a system only after it had entered crisis conditions.

At the heart of Schengen's inadequacy was insufficient attention to the interplay between internal and external EU migration. While Schengen provided for largely unchecked internal movement of people between signatory states, there was no systemic anticipation of what would be done if hundreds of thousands of migrants suddenly appeared at Schengen's external borders. This is what happened from 2014 onwards, with over one million migrants attempting to gain access to the EU in 2015. They did so for a mixture of push and pull reasons, with the main push reason being the desire of migrants to flee Iraq, Syria and other war-torn and/or impoverished countries, whilst the main pull reason was the lure of living in a peaceful and secure country (with northern EU states, especially Germany, being the main destinations of choice of most migrants) where there was the prospect of employment or welfare assistance. Chancellor Merkel's apparent willingness in the summer of 2015 to allow unlimited numbers of refugees to enter Germany opened the metaphorical floodgates, with Schengen's largely unprotected external borders coupled with its (initially at least) relatively open internal borders making it possible for migrants to have realistic hopes of reaching the northern states.

When the numbers of attempted migrants to the EU exploded in 2015, the EU simply did not have a system in place that could cope. There was no fully functioning common asylum system, whilst the porousness of the EU's external borders undermined the integrity of the intra-EU free travel area. The fact was that, like EMU, Schengen had been designed on the basis of hoping for the best rather than anticipating the worst. The migration crisis resulted in the EU being portrayed very unsympathetically in much of the European media. It was seen as being under siege at its external borders, insufficiently resourced and unable to assist the plights of 'legitimate' migrants. The EU's perceived inadequacies were further enhanced when tragedies occurred with drownings of migrants in the Mediterranean and Aegean seas and when conditions in reception areas and camps were revealed as being appalling.

The EU governance crisis

The EU's governance crisis has contained a number of elements, including a leadership crisis, a legitimacy crisis and a crisis in the relations between Member States.

The leadership crisis has had various dimensions, including concerns that in the economic and migration policy areas it has been unclear who should be, and who is, taking the policy lead. In some respects, Germany has sought to exercise a virtual hegemonic leadership in these spheres, but it has by no means been unchallenged – with the Commission, the European Council, the ECB and other Member States also vying for leadership roles. Of course, EU leadership has always been widely distributed, but the crises have exacerbated the extent and uncertainty of the nature of this distribution. They have done so both by increasing the number of potential leaders (notably by making the ECB a potentially important policy player on economic and financial policy matters) and by complicating who is looked to as, and who feels they should be, the lead player(s) on specific matters.

Regarding the legitimacy dimension of the governance crisis, questions have long been asked about the legitimacy of the EU system, with the 'democratic deficit' of the EU's institutions featuring particularly prominently in such debates. But, as the EU's problems in solving the crises have made its 'output legitimacy' look increasingly weak, and as the powers of the ECB – the least accountable of the EU's institutions – have grown considerably as a result of the banking crisis, so has the EU's legitimacy been further undermined.

As for the crisis in the relations between Member States, the EU has, of course, always been the location for inter-state disagreements as states have sought to defend and advance their own interests and policy preferences. But, the eurozone and migration crises have been the occasions for considerably sharpened disagreements, being focused as they have been on core national policy interests and preferences, and on issues (fiscal and border-related) that touch directly on national sovereignty. For example, the migration crisis saw some states, especially Germany, supporting attempts by the Commission to persuade Schengen members to share the burden of refugee settlement, but others, including most Central and Eastern European states, being strongly opposed to being told what they should do.

The rifts between Germany and Greece demonstrate how less clubbable the EU became during the crises. Greece, which had been on the front line of the eurozone crisis was similarly on the front line of the migration crisis, with the Greek border being the principal external border through which most migrants entered the EU *en route* to Germany and other northern states. Given Germany's treatment of Greece during the eurozone crisis, Greece was not inclined to accommodate Germany during the migration crisis by preventing migrants from travelling north, at least not without the prospect of significant financial assistance and debt relief.

The crisis of rising Euroscepticism

Largely in consequence of the crises outline above, another crisis has loomed large in the life of the EU in recent years: there has been a significant decline in popular support for European integration which has, in turn, been accompanied by increased support for anti-European and deeply Eurosceptic parties. As Webber (2017) notes, in the winter of 2015–16 opinion polls indicated that such parties were the largest in terms of popular support in Austria, France, Greece, Hungary, the Netherlands, Poland and the UK, whilst they were growing fast in Germany, Spain and Italy. Such was the advance of popular disillusionment with integration that anti-European or Eurosceptic parties were the main governing parties in Greece, Poland, Hungary and the UK, whilst they featured as minority governing parties in Finland and Portugal.

The impact of the crises on the Brexit process

The EU's crises have had, and will continue to have, many and varied impacts on the Brexit process. In this section of the chapter, three particular impacts are examined.

The referendum outcome

As measured by public opinion polls, not least the long-standing Commission-organised Eurobarometer polls, the UK has, with only occasional interruptions, been the most consistently Eurosceptic Member State over the years. However, there is no doubt that in the years leading up to the referendum, at least three of the EU's crises – the eurozone crisis, the migration crisis and the legitimacy crisis – played significant parts in furthering UK Euroscepticism by contributing to the picture of a distant and undemocratic EU that could neither cope with, nor solve, the various crises afflicting the Union. Although the UK itself never adopted the euro or joined Schengen, widespread perceptions of these core policies as foundering served to undermine confidence in the EU system. The migration crisis in particular featured frequently in the popular media, often accompanied not by sympathetic headlines addressing the plight of the migrants but rather by ill-defined suggestions of the UK itself being under threat. As for the legitimacy crisis, perhaps the most powerful and effective messages at the fore of the Brexit campaign were the various versions of 'let's take our country/sovereignty/independence back'.

The ways in which the EU is structuring itself to conduct the Brexit negotiations

The crises have witnessed intensified EU-level inter-institutional competition and have further complicated the EU's institutional complexity and surplus of leadership. These developments are, in various ways, feeding into the EU's structural arrangements for conducting the Brexit negotiations, including the following:

- All of the EU's leading political institutions have established a Brexit negotiating team or coordinating unit. 'Under' the European Council team, which is being led by Donald Tusk, the European Council president, are teams from the Commission (led by Michel Barnier), the Council (led by Didier Seeuws), and the European Parliament (led by Guy Verhofstadt).
- 'Major' EU directional decisions have long been made by, or at least channelled through, the European Council. But, as a result of the crises, the European Council has become much more actively involved in such decision-making – with many special summits having been convened to deal with subjects such as the

size and conditions of bailouts during the eurozone crisis, the distribution of migrants during the migration crisis, and sanctions against Russia during the Crimea/Ukraine crisis. Deliberations regarding, and the taking of decisions on, 'macro' issues by the European Council have become, more than ever before, the 'new normal'. In line with this evolving practice, the EU27 heads of state and government made it clear at an informal meeting in December 2016 that they would have their hands firmly on the Brexit negotiations tiller. This would involve adopting 'guidelines that will define the framework for negotiations under Article 50 and [setting] out the overall position and principles that the EU will pursue throughout the negotiation' (Informal meeting of the EU27 2016, 2).

- The detailed application of decisions taken at the EU political level has always been primarily the responsibility of the Commission. The crises reaffirmed this. In the context of the eurozone crisis for example, a host of politically approved directional decisions – such as on tighter fiscal rules and the creation of a banking union – were referred to the Commission for detailed drafting. The Brexit negotiations will follow this practice with the Commission, operating within political guidelines set out by the European Council and, on specific matters, the General Affairs Council, undertaking the detailed and technical negotiations.

- The EP has been greatly irritated by being largely excluded from decision-making in respect of most aspects of the EU's crises, except where legislative measures have been required. Decisions on such major issues as the sizes and conditions of financial bailouts and the imposition of sanctions on Russia have been taken on intergovernmental bases that have excluded the Parliament. But, the EP has a history of making maximum use of the powers it does have, and on Brexit it cannot be bypassed because it has the power of consent over the UK withdrawal agreement. In a resolution it adopted in early April 2017, the Parliament served notice that it will seek to use this power to exert significant influence over the final Brexit agreement (European Parliament 2017a). The EP will not itself be directly involved in the negotiations, but it will – working within plenary-approved guidelines on the EU's aims in the negotiations and via a specially appointed steering committee plus various sub-committees – exercise important roles in helping to shape and guide the negotiations.

The stances of the EU27 in the Brexit negotiations

In the run-up to the April 2017 special meeting of the European Council, when the EU's guidelines for defining the framework for Brexit negotiations were set out (European Council 2017a), the 27 Member State governments and the EU institutions were broadly united in their approaches. This enabled the guidelines to be agreed without too much difficulty. So, amongst the key guidelines were stipulations that: until 'sufficient progress has been achieved' on the size of the UK's 'exit bill' and on the residency and related rights of EU and UK citizens post-Brexit, trade talks will not be allowed to begin; there will be no 'cherry picking' by the UK on access to the Single Market (that is, there will be no especially favourable sectoral agreements); and the UK will not be permitted to enter formal trade talks with non-Member States until it leaves the EU.

This seemingly firm and united line has arisen in large part from the high levels of support for Eurosceptic parties and movements in many Member States. To avoid giving Euroscepticism further encouragement, which could threaten the very existence of many EU governments and, in turn, the EU itself, the EU cannot risk letting the UK be seen to have won a deal that results in it being materially no worse off, let also potentially better off, than it was pre-Brexit. As Emmanuel (now President) Macron said during his 2017 election campaign: 'I don't want a tailormade approach where the British have the best of two worlds. That will be too big an incentive for others to leave and [will] kill the European idea, which is based on shared responsibilities' (quoted in Slawson 2017).

However, notwithstanding this seemingly common resolve, during the EU's crises Member States have shown a firm determination to pursue and defend their particular national interests and policy preferences. They have, of course, always looked carefully to these, but during the eurozone and migration crises in particular they showed themselves to be more than usually resolved to 'dig in' – as, for example, when most Central and Eastern European states refused to accept the Commission's proposals (even though they had been backed by a qualified majority vote in the Council) to distribute migrants between Schengen states on a compulsory basis. In a similar vein, during the Brexit negotiations the EU27 will doubtless disagree on countless specifics that are particularly important to them and will seek to defend or advance their own positions with vigour.

Conclusions

As has been shown in this chapter, Brexit is far from being the only major crisis the EU has experienced in recent years. The eurozone and migration crises are the best known of these other crises, but they are very far from being alone. In varying ways, many of these other crises have had, are having, and will continue to have impacts on differing aspects of the Brexit process.

6
The implications of Brexit for the future of Europe

Michelle Cini and Amy Verdun

Introduction

The result of the UK's referendum on EU membership came as a shock not only to UK elites, but also to the rest of the EU. The outcome hit the EU, its Member States and its institutions, hard for many reasons – but perhaps for three in particular. First, it was the first time (barring the exceptional cases of Greenland and Algeria, for which see Kiran Klaus Patel's Chapter 12 in this volume) that the EU would diminish in size. Second, EU actors recognised that the political implications of the UK's decision would reverberate across their domestic political arenas. Third, the outcome was extremely puzzling. Few could figure out exactly why UK voters wished to leave, why the UK government would accept the decision when there was such a slim majority in favour of leaving, why the popular support was against what most experts and leading politicians advocated for, and what the UK would put in its place. Furthermore, the referendum results varied significantly across the UK, suggesting that any new relationship the UK might end up having with the EU (what became known as a 'soft' or a 'hard' British exit from the EU) could alter the UK's constitutional settlement. Despite numerous concerns about how the UK and the EU would sort through the many issues involved in only two years, Prime Minister Theresa May invoked Article 50 on 29 March 2017 by notifying the EU Council President Donald Tusk of the UK's intention to leave the EU (HM Government 2017b).

While the domestic debate on Brexit has mainly focused on the implications for the UK, it is important to reflect on the possible implications of Brexit for European integration more generally. The challenge comes from the fact that Brexit is not 'the only game in town', but rather one of several 'crises' that have been ailing the EU, and which will also affect European integration (Cini & Pérez-Solórzano 2016; Nugent, Chapter 5 in this volume). As such, Brexit has to be considered as part of a broader package of uncertainties determining the direction of travel for the EU. On that basis, we view successive EU crises (e.g. the eurozone crisis, the migration crisis, and the crisis associated with Brexit) as contextual factors that open windows of opportunity and generate sources of motivation for actors who seek to take advantage of the instability and uncertainty that crisis provokes. They do this by pushing their own agendas. These agendas, whether or not they deal explicitly with European integration, have repercussions for the EU. These repercussions are not so much final outcomes as processes of change: they either fragment the EU or make it more cohesive. With that in mind, in addressing the possible impact of Brexit on European integration, we distil two broad trajectories, the first of which leads to the fragmentation and weakening of the EU (the centrifugal trajectory); and the second, which leads to greater EU cooperation, and the strengthening of the European integration process (the centripetal trajectory).

The UK: an influential EU Member State

The premise on which the argument rests is that the UK has been, until now, an influential member of the EU. Ever since joining, in 1973, what was then the European Communities, the UK, as one of the larger Member States, has more than most helped to shape European integration. It has done so in two ways: first, by constraining EU initiatives; and second, by supporting and promoting EU initiatives.

In its constraining role, the UK often sought to veto or limit EU initiatives. An example of such behaviour can be found in the negotiations on the Maastricht Treaty. These negotiations led to the creation of the EU with its important new policy of EMU and its Social Chapter. The UK managed to restrict integration in these areas and eventually negotiated special arrangements for itself in both cases (but only having first made sure they were restricted in their scope and not overly 'federal') (Verdun 2000). More recently, the UK exerted its veto against the reform of the Lisbon Treaty. Other Member States were keen to strengthen the rules on budgetary and fiscal governance, in the light of the eurozone crisis, so as to firm up the Stability and Growth Pact (SGP). As there was no unanimous agreement on the matter, the other Member States signed the Treaty on Stability, Cooperation and Governance (often known as the 'Fiscal Compact') as an intergovernmental treaty in 2012, which subsequently came into effect in 2013.

The UK has not always been successful in its attempts to limit EU initiatives, however. As UK Prime Minister Thatcher discovered in the early 1980s, for example, the national veto, preventing the operation of qualified majority voting, was already something of a chimera. To this day, more often than not, the Council takes decisions by consensus. On those occasions when the Council actually votes, in the vast majority of cases the UK votes *with* the majority. Having said that, recent research by Simon Hix and Sara Hagemann suggests that this situation has recently changed. Their research on formal voting outcomes shows that although the UK failed to vote the same way as the winning vote in only 2.6 per cent of the cases in the period 2004–9, in the more recent period (2009–15) it was deviating from the winning vote in 12.3 per cent of cases (Hix & Hagemann 2015).

Second, in its supportive role, the UK itself promoted various initiatives, from the introduction of regional and cohesion policy in the 1970s, to the relaunch of the internal/Single Market in the 1980s, and even, though it ultimately never became a full member, the design of the architecture for EMU and Justice and Home Affairs. It also was often an advocate of 'widening' over 'deepening', that is, in favour of expanding the EU, so as to include new Member States, rather than supportive of deeper integration in the areas in which the EU was already involved. Its policy influence is perhaps most clearly identified in the UK's shaping of Enlargement Policy and in its impact on Common Security and Defence Policy, where the UK became a core EU player – not least because of the size of its armed forces and defence sector.

Successive UK governments have thus been fairly successful in shaping EU initiatives in line with what they conceive to be in the national interest. Of course, there are many instances where 'red lines' were crossed and compromises agreed – even if they were not always presented as such back home. Standing back from the specifics, the UK's influence has promoted, first, a particular form of European integration, and second, a particular ideological agenda. In the case of the former, UK governments have tended, more than other governments, to favour intergovernmental solutions to institutional reform. The instigation of the pillar system at Maastricht, which failed to integrate internal affairs and foreign policy into the EU's supranational 'European Community' pillar, is a notable case in point. With regards to the latter point, UK governments have advocated a more liberal economic agenda within the EU, irrespective of the party in power.

The impact of Brexit

Based on the premise that the UK has been an influential Member State of the EU, what then might be the implications of UK withdrawal for European integration? While the two perspectives – a centrifugal and a centripetal one – oversimplify the options available, and do not cover all potential implications, they do serve as a useful heuristic device in highlighting the ways in which Brexit might be used by different actors to advance their own political agendas on the future of Europe.

The centrifugal trajectory

Arguably, the EU has never been more fragmented than it is today. Divisions over policy preferences have become bitter. European solidarity has been undermined as a consequence of both long-term problems and more recent crises. Growing distrust of European elites has been exploited by nativist groups and parties, often allied with anti-immigration sentiment, to propose populist solutions to Europe's problems. Euroscepticism has sometimes driven these agendas, though on other occasions it has simply become a supplementary agenda. Important substantive policy differences often lie at the source of these divisions. The political cleavage that opened up during the eurozone crisis, based on an economic split between creditor states, such as Germany, and debtor states, such as Greece, saw the countries directly involved in the crisis take opposite sides in a bitter blame-game. A similar phenomenon was witnessed at the height of the migrant crisis, where the absence of effective burden-sharing exacerbated already fragile relations between North and South, and between East and West. The citizens and governments of numerous Member States began to disengage from European integration, turning in on themselves. Collective institutions, such as the border-free Schengen system, were suspended, ostensibly for a limited time, but flagging up the possibility of total collapse. While policy differences may be resolved – once solutions are found and the crisis passed – the more fundamental differences that shape them, differences in assumptions about social and economic liberalism, whether from the left or the right, seem more intractable.

Where does Brexit and the UK fit into this analysis of the EU? It is paradoxical that the UK was always on the outside of these issues. It looked on while the crises were in full flow. But these high-profile crises hide the fact that where the more pro-European governments of the EU, perhaps supported by a Franco-German vanguard, would be inclined to seek deepened integration (as in areas such as fiscal policy, police cooperation, and immigration and border control), the UK was typically the voice providing opposition and scepticism, and advocating greater caution. Although there were occasions when the UK was in a minority of one, it was often speaking out loud the private thoughts of other Member States. Where Central and Eastern European governments were reluctant to appear anti-European, they were often content with the UK's more subdued vision of integration. With this voice gone, others will have to take over this role, and their vision will be a different one than the liberal-market-oriented, Atlanticist view that the UK typically represented. These other states, moreover, do not have the same political clout that the UK managed to conjure up – the product of its seniority in the EU, its democratic track-record, the size of its economy and population, and its long experience in diplomacy and foreign affairs. Nor do they necessarily possess the skills of UK statesmen and diplomats, or hold the natural advantage of being native speakers of the English language. This could mean that calls for less integration will have weaker backers. Or, given that even without Brexit, Central and Eastern European states, such as Hungary and Poland, have become more vocal in their resistance to supranational and regulatory EU initiatives, it could mean that anti-EU sentiment persists, but in more statist form, and without a clear articulation that reaches the citizens and political leaders of other Member States. Even though many Europeans are appalled at the British tabloid press, it has offered a language for others elsewhere in the EU to emulate. The national media in Eastern Europe do not reach other Europeans as easily.

Likewise, there are numerous political groupings within Member States, both parties and more diffuse social movements, which reflect popular concern over the deepening of integration in the EU. Without the constraints that UK membership represents, those groups may see an opportunity for further mobilisation of support, resulting from the fear that the EU without the UK could push ahead to integrate further in certain areas. The same arguments used to justify a Leave vote in the UK referendum could also hold sway in other European states (Cini and

Pérez-Solórzano 2016). Anti-immigration, anti-globalisation and anti-elite political positions are hardly exclusive to the UK. While Hobolt (2016, 1273) argued that there was no evidence of short-term contagion effects, in the sense of other Member States planning on holding referendums, she admits that 'the Brexit vote nonetheless poses a serious challenge to the political establishment across Europe' and that such effects might thus emerge in the months and years ahead.

The centripetal trajectory

However, without the UK, the EU might be better equipped to move into crisis resolution mode. The Brexit negotiations, if handled well, could help the process of rebuilding solidarity among the EU27. The German government has itself pushed this line (Duff 2017, 1). There is nothing more unifying than having to show a common front. The EU demonstrated this unity early on, during the Bratislava European Council meeting of September 2016, and it was also evident in the run-up to the agreement of the negotiation mandate in April 2017. Indeed, even if relations between the two sides remain relatively cordial, the Member States entering into negotiations with the UK will be aware that the effectiveness of the EU's negotiating strategies will be carefully examined by their own domestic constituencies and that they will need to demonstrate their toughness. The argument often made in the weeks following the UK referendum, that EU Member States will want to ensure the UK does not get too 'good' a deal in order to deter Eurosceptic forces in other Member States' domestic constituencies, still carries some weight – at least in some quarters. The European Council, led by European Council president Donald Tusk and the head of the Brexit taskforce of the Council, Didier Seeuws, is especially important when it comes to bringing the Member States together, since it is responsible for the EU's common negotiating stance (European Council 2017a).

While solidarity has been sorely lacking among the EU Member States in recent years, this has not prevented the emergence of new initiatives. The eurozone crisis has already led to new institutional initiatives, new legislation, a new treaty, and even new institutional mechanisms to deal with the sovereign debt crisis and to prevent further financial meltdown (Verdun 2015). One can easily argue therefore that one of the consequences of the eurozone crisis has been to open the door to further European integration. Brexit may make further steps in this direction even more likely. While the UK neither joined EMU, nor prevented the introduction of the euro, it has since the early 2000s argued vehemently for recognition that the EU comprises more than one currency. It has stressed that the EU's (read: eurozone's) policies should not be prejudicial towards Member States using currencies other than the euro. For the UK, this position most often took the form of a defence of the interests of the City of London, and of a more 'facilitative and liberal approach to financial regulation' (Moloney 2017). This matter was of such importance to the UK government after 2010 that it featured as one of the issues dealt with in David Cameron's pre-referendum negotiations. With the UK leaving the EU, and the other EMU 'outs' much weaker, the stage is set for the euro to become, once again, the flagship policy of the EU – and perhaps for further post-crisis steps towards a fiscal (or economic) union. As Sapir et al. put it: 'Brexit also involves opportunities for the EU27. It may generate momentum towards building more integrated and vibrant capital markets that would better serve all its Member States' economies, improve risk sharing to withstand local shocks, and make the Union a more attractive place to do global financial business' (Sapir et al. 2017).

In other policy areas, too, there is some indication of the development of a new pro-integration agenda. Indeed, in the second half of 2016, following the Bratislava European Council in September, France and Germany announced that they were considering strengthening cooperation on security matters. Some might argue that the expected departure of the UK from the Common Security and Defence Policy (CSDP) makes little difference, since the UK has been something of a half-hearted member since at least 2010, and because the North Atlantic Treaty Organization (NATO) is more important for European defence. But from a centripetal perspective, with the UK's departure, the EU loses half of its Franco-British defence axis, which has been at the heart of the CSDP. Thus, in order not to weaken EU defence policy, something needs to be proposed to fill the gap left by the UK. The fact that US President Donald Trump appears less committed to the Western Alliance means that the development of a more robust European defence policy seems more important than before. German leader Angela Merkel seems fully to have grasped this fact, when announcing at the end of the G7 Meeting in late May 2017 that the EU will need to take charge of its own defence (*Politico* 2017).

Even if these integrative initiatives go ahead, the EU cannot simply return to a business-as-usual approach to integration, but must learn from the experience of Brexit and other EU crises. The March 2017 Commission White Paper on the Future of Europe indicates that there are some important decisions to be made. Without considerable resources (competences, funds) at the EU level, the EU cannot be everything to everyone. While it is a system that is based on the rule of law and a large *acquis communautaire*, the EU is struggling with various Member States that do not always respect the founding principles of the EU. Moreover, the protest votes witnessed in the 2016 Italian referendum, as well as the lessons learnt from Brexit and the election of Trump, indicate that citizens are disgruntled with the way globalisation has treated them (Blockmans & Weiss 2016, 3).

Yet, with national elections in Western Europe in late 2016 and spring 2017 (Austria, the Netherlands and France) having generated more pro-EU than anti-EU populist leaders, there may be more scope for unity among Member State leaders in the coming months and years. Having had a chance to vote explicitly with European integration in mind, and with more clarity after the UK referendum about the challenges involved in being outside the EU (*Financial Times* 2017a), there might even be more support from European citizens for deeper European integration. Yet the EU is well advised to ensure that with any deepening comes some sort of increase in democratic accountability to its citizens.

Conclusions

Brexit is one of several crises to have hit the EU in recent years. The implications of Brexit on European integration are, therefore, also the consequences of those other crises. We view crises as windows of opportunity and sources of motivation for actors who take advantage of instability and uncertainty to push particular agendas. Those agendas are not necessarily pro-integration, in the sense of unconditional transfer of national powers to supranational institutions (*supranational* integration), but they are associated with EU-level reform. They may, as such, seek to push European integration in a non-supranational direction, by promoting new forms of intergovernmentalism, by institutionalising a multi-speed, differentiated model of European cooperation (Cini & Pérez-Solórzano 2016), or by further enhancing mechanisms that advance coordination and fine-tuning, as has been the case with social policy coordination (Verdun & Wood 2013). In his contribution to the Brexit debate, Ferrera (2017) for example makes the case for the establishment of a European Social Union, one that is 'capable of combining domestic and pan-European solidarities'. Alternatively, other agendas pushed by actors in times of crisis may seek to promote disintegration. Actors working for the collapse of the EU and a return to exclusively national, or even nationalist, politics will also see crises as an opportunity for them to push their own vision of the future. It remains to be seen which of these competing agendas will be successful. There are no clear indicators as to which agenda will win, as there is no mechanism that will at all times push forward the pro-cooperation agenda. But the political winds that are blowing through the EU27 seem to have produced fertile soil for another attempt at deepening integration. Provided that both the EU and national leaders remain committed to European integration, the event of Brexit may very well mark another bout of centripetal activity, bringing the remaining EU Member States closer together.

7
Decentralised federalism

A new model for the EU

Simon Hix

The EU is facing multiple crises. Brexit. Refugees crossing the Aegean and Mediterranean. Putin's shadow over the Baltics. A possible new eurozone debt crisis. President Trump threatening to undermine NATO. Growing support for populist anti-European parties. Challenges to liberal democracy in Hungary and Poland. And so on, and so on.

The EU has faced profound challenges before, such as the French National Assembly's rejection of a political union in the 1950s, President De Gaulle's 'empty chair' policy in the 1960s, the oil price hikes and 'stagflation' in the 1970s, the battle over the UK's budget contribution in the 1980s, and the various rejections of treaties by the publics of Denmark, Ireland, France and the Netherlands in the 1990s and 2000s. In the face of each of these challenges the European integration project has found a way to muddle through; perhaps never as quickly, elegantly or efficiently as many would have liked, but the car has been kept on the road, the bicycle has continued to move forward, or whatever other metaphor you prefer.

As with these previous challenges, a common response to the current challenges is to advocate 'more Europe'. Most visibly, in March 2017 the Commission presented its White Paper on the Future of Europe, which set out five 'scenarios' for the EU27 by 2025 (European Commission 2017b). Of the five scenarios, it was clear that the Commission favoured the fifth, where: 'The EU decides to do much more together across all policy areas'. This would include *inter alia*: deeper integration in the eurozone, such as genuine fiscal union and more coordination of national tax, expenditure and social policies; a European Defence Union, with integrated military command structures; greater cooperation in the management of external borders of the Union and more integrated asylum and refugee policies; new policies within the Single Market on energy, digital and services; and a new budgetary structure for the Union, including a new EU 'own resource' (for example from a carbon tax or a Europe-wide sales tax).

However, this time, this sort of ratcheting forward of integration is unlikely to work. There are simply too many current challenges, and they cover many more areas of EU action than any previous challenge: from macro-economic policies, to security and defence, to justice and interior affairs, and even social cohesion and integration. Add Brexit to the mix, and the political and institutional foundations of the EU are also now open to question. The extent of policy integration that addressing all these challenges at once would entail – for example in the Commission's 'scenario five' – would mean the most significant step forward in European integration certainly since the Single European Act, and perhaps even since the Treaty of Rome.

Such a major step forward is now impossible. First, it is more difficult to achieve policy integration in any one area, let along across a whole range of areas, amongst 27 states than it was amongst six, nine, 12 or 15. More Member States means a greater divergence of interests and preferences and, as a result, invariably at least one Member State who will prefer 'no deal' to any options on the table.

Second, and above all, unlike in any previous period of European integration, the public cannot be ignored, and the public is heading against the EU. Until the early 1990s there was a 'permissive consensus' towards the European project (e.g. Inglehart 1970). This consensus came to an abrupt end in the early 1990s, with the Danish and French referendums on the Maastricht Treaty and the sudden emergence of anti-European parties in the 1994 European Parliament elections. Mark Franklin and his collaborators characterised this period as the 'uncorking' of popular opposition to European integration, with the idea that once the cork of public opinion was out of the bottle it could not be put back in (Franklin et al. 1994). The public had woken up to the new reality: that a 'political union' of sorts had been created by their political leaders without this being clearly mandated or noticed much by voters.

Until the mid-2000s, though, this popular opposition to the EU was mainly expressed in European Parliament elections and in EU referendums, which were the two main arenas where (some) voters could express their opposition to European integration at the same time as 'punishing' governments and mainstream parties. Yet, the issue of 'Europe' remained largely absent from the main political contests that mattered: elections to national parliaments. As long as national elections focused on the standard fare of domestic politics, of national taxes and spending policies, and as long as anti-European parties did not win many votes or seats in these elections, mainstream parties on the centre-left and centre-right could ignore growing popular opposition to European integration.

This changed dramatically in the 2010s. The eurozone crisis, and the consequent 'austerity' packages in debtor states and 'bailouts' in creditor states, meant that Europe now encroached directly on national tax and spending debates. Similarly, the refugee crises, and the sheer volume of people moving across borders, affected domestic debates about immigration, social cohesion, crime and even terrorism. Added to this was growing opposition in many North Western European societies (such as the UK, Denmark, Sweden and the Netherlands) about the volume of immigration from Eastern Europe. Few concerns about migrants from Central and Eastern Europe had been expressed while the economies had been growing, but economic downturns and public spending cuts combined with mass immigration led to greater competition for low-skilled jobs and greater competition for declining public services.

Together these factors produced growing support in *national* elections for parties that combined anti-EU positions with anti-austerity and/or anti-immigration policies and anti-establishment populism. This is shown in Figure 7.1. The data are the percentage of total votes for left and right populist parties in the most recent national Parliament elections. This is a good indicator of the influence of populist parties in EU politics, as there are no compositional changes over time and the overall support levels are weighted by the size of each country.

The figure clearly shows a growth in the support for anti-European populist parties in the wake of the eurozone sovereign debt crisis, which began in 2008, and then a second jump in support following the refugee crisis, that first hit in the spring of 2015. Between 2000 and 2016, support for populist parties on the radical left (such as Syriza in Greece, Podemos in Spain and Sinn Fein in Ireland) grew by about 4 per cent, while support for populist parties on the radical right (such as UKIP in the UK, the Front National (National Front) in France, the Alternative für Deutschland (Alternative for Germany), the Partij voor de Vrijheid

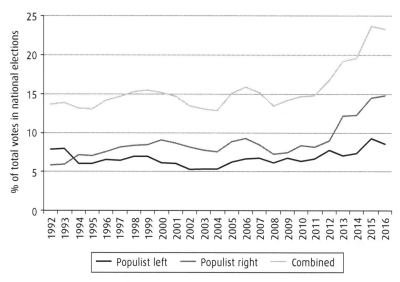

Figure 7.1 Support for populist parties in national elections in EU Member States (Hix & Benedetto 2017)

Note: The figure shows the percentage of total votes for populist left and populist right parties in national parliamentary elections in each year in the 28 countries that were either EU Member States in 1992 or that joined the EU since 1992. In other words, these data are weighted by the size of a country.

(Party for Freedom) in the Netherlands, the Dansk Folkeparti (Danish People's Party), the Sverigedemokraterna (Sweden Democrats) and Prawo I Sprawiedlowość (Law and Justice in Poland) jumped by about 8 per cent. So, together, populist anti-European parties of various stripes now command the support of almost one in four voters across Europe, and this support has grown dramatically following the eurozone and refugee crises.

It may be too early to conclude that European integration is finished and that the EU is doomed. What is clear, though, is that the standard EU response to crisis, of 'more Europe', is not going to work this time. It is simply not going to be supported by 27 Member States and their increasingly sceptical publics.

What other options are there? Table 7.1 presents one way of thinking about this question. In any multi-level political system there

Table 7.1 Institutional design options for the EU

Degree of policy centralisation	Decision-making mode	
	Consensual	Majoritarian
Centralised/harmonised	Intergovernmentalism	Supranationalism
Decentralised/flexible	Loose union of states	Decentralised federalism

are two main dimensions of institutional design. The first dimension relates to how decisions are made at the centre. At one extreme, decisions are by unanimous agreement ('consensus'), usually at the highest political level. At the other extreme, decisions are made by a simple majority of states. But no multi-level system operates through pure majoritarian rules, as a union could not survive simple majority 'dictatorship'. So, in practice, the alternative to unanimity is majority rule with significant checks and balances ('veto players'), where decisions require the support of majorities in multiple legislative chambers, as well as an independent executive and an independent judiciary. For example, the German federal system is more 'majoritarian' than the US system, because the parties in the German government usually control a majority in the Bundestag (and the Bundestag is more powerful than the Bundesrat), whereas the US president does not have a right of legislative initiative and is forced to build legislative coalitions issue by issue across two powerful legislative chambers (the House and Senate) (cf. Tsebelis 2002).

The second dimension relates to the degree of centralisation or decentralisation of policymaking power. This dimension also relates to whether common rules require a high level of harmonisation of local policies or whether states are allowed a degree of discretion and flexibility in the application of central rules. For example, across federal systems there is significant variation in the level of centralisation of policymaking power, where the states in some systems (such as Switzerland and the US) have considerable independent tax-raising power and legislative autonomy.

This gives us four ideal types of designs, which characterise various options for the EU. Most international organisations, such as the World Trade Organization or NATO, are 'loose unions of states': where few powers are centralised, and all major decisions are reached by unanimous or near-unanimous agreement. This may not seem a realistic option for the EU, but it is the direction of travel supported by many right-wing populists in Western Europe as well as some more mainstream conservative parties in Central and Eastern Europe, particularly in Poland, Hungary and the Czech Republic.

The current design of the EU combines both 'intergovernmentalism' and 'supranationalism'. Intergovernmentalism, via consensus agreements between governments (usually at the level of heads of government in the European Council), is the main EU decision-making mode for treaty reforms, multi-annual budgetary packages, foreign and security policies, some aspects of refugee and asylum policies (such as refugee burden-sharing), and most aspects of EMU and the emerging mechanisms for the coordination of national macro-economic policies. Supranationalism, with agenda-setting by the Commission and legislative action by majorities in the Council and European Parliament, is the standard mode for governing the Single Market and the flanking policies (such as social and environmental policies), for justice and home affairs policies (although not refugee burden-sharing), and for the regulatory framework governing EMU and the emerging Banking Union.

Within both of these decision-making modes, the EU has become increasingly centralised, with little discretion for the Member States once decisions are made. Within the Single Market, for example, directives were originally envisaged as 'framework rules' within which Member States would have some discretion. But directives have become indistinguishable from normal 'laws', which require extensive harmonisation and adherence to the detailed articles in any directive. This may be the optimal legal and economic strategy for governing the Single Market, as harmonisation ensures regulatory compatibility and legal certainty, but this significantly reduces Member State discretion. And, as the policy competences and legislative rules of the EU have expanded, centralised decision-making and harmonisation has increasingly become a policy straightjacket for domestic publics.

One implication of this centralisation is that policy competition between mainstream political parties has become severely restricted (Dorussen & Nanou 2006). Parties cannot compete on social and environment policies, market regulation, international trade policies and. increasingly too, on immigration and asylum policies. And, for Member States of the eurozone, choices over taxing and spending have increasingly been removed from domestic political contestation. This is not healthy for European democracy. If voters would like to significantly change policy status quos – either in a leftward or rightward direction – then they must also support anti-European positions. More interventionist economic and tax policies are not possible within the design of EMU, while more discretion in the application of regulatory standards or in immigration policies is not compatible within the current design of the Single Market or EU justice and home affairs policies. In other words, centralisation of the policy powers of the EU inevitably pushes even moderately left-wing or right-wing voters into the arms of radical left and right populists.

But, there is another option, which I call 'decentralised federalism'. This model of a multi-level polity requires two things: 1) granting policy competences to the central institutions in a restricted set of policy areas, and allowing majority decision-making over these policies; and 2) granting a high degree of flexibility and discretion to the states in the application of central rules. Decentralised federalism implies an alternative 'grand bargain' for all Member States: where some policies are further integrated (such as new fiscal instruments, military command structures and refugee burden-sharing) in return for more decentralisation and flexibility in other policy areas (such as macro-economic policies within the eurozone, in expenditure policies such as agricultural price support, or in regulatory policies in the Single Market for all Member States).

So, for example, within the eurozone, states would be allowed to run higher public deficits, but in return there would be no obligation on the more fiscally stable states to bail out states that run into difficulties with their debts. Contrast, for example, the EU's imposition of severe austerity on Greece in return for repeated bailouts with the US government's decision to allow the City of Detroit to default on its debt. Fiscal hawks will immediately complain about potential contagion or free-riding in such a system. But, a genuine banking union and more independent fiscal capacity of the EU, via eurozone bonds for example, would counterbalance the greater independent fiscal autonomy and responsibility of the states that make up the monetary union.

Similarly, in the services sector, greater flexibility and discretion could be a way of liberalising services markets. In the mid-2000s the Commission proposed a Services Directive based on 'mutual recognition' in the services sector, which would have opened up services sectors across Europe to greater competition. The Services Directive was eventually watered down, and the result (which entered into force in 2009) has not achieved much in terms of opening up services markets to new providers. The problem is that the strategy for the services sector so far has been based on the principle of a common set of rules – mutual recognition and harmonisation – for all sectors and all Member States. With so many conflicting interests between and within Member States, a comprehensive reform of services is impossible, even via the EU's supranational decision-making mode.

An alternative would be a decentralised federal model: to allow groups of states to liberalise their services sectors, or parts of their services sectors, on a bilateral or multilateral basis within a common EU-wide legal and regulatory framework. So, for example, Germany and Austria could agree to mutually recognise each other's service providers, as could Sweden and Denmark, the Benelux states, the Visegrad states, Spain and Portugal, Bulgaria and Romania, the Baltic states, and so on. In time, this patchwork structure could gradually be linked up, with cross-agreement rules, perhaps coordinated by the Commission. This may sound fanciful to some European policymakers, but is exactly how the liberalisation of the US services economy has evolved, with bilateral and multilateral agreements between states to recognise each other's services providers.

One aspect of such an architecture may be some forms of 'asymmetric integration', where sub-sets of states voluntarily choose to integrate policy competences in some areas. This is called 'flexible' or 'multi-speed' integration in the EU context. Several of the larger Member States have raised this form of cooperation as a possible way of enabling further integration of refugee and asylum policies. This might be consistent with decentralised federalism, but asymmetric integration also has the potential of establishing a permanent two-tier design – with an 'inner core' and an 'outer periphery' – which would undermine the cohesion of the EU as a whole. In contrast, decentralised federalism would be a way of keeping the EU27 together within a single institutional framework, although with some flexible integration, such as the euro and Schengen.

Overall, the EU is at a turning point in its history. Never before has it faced so many crises on so many fronts. The standard crisis management response in the EU is to push for further policy integration. This may have worked in the past, but is unlikely to work now. The EU27 are simply too heterogeneous. And, above all, there is growing public opposition towards deeper economic and political integration, and the further restrictions on domestic policy choices that this would inevitably entail.

There are alternatives to deeper integration, one of which I have called 'decentralised federalism'. This model would enable some new policies to be centralised, to establish genuine fiscal union in the eurozone, or common European refugee and common defence command structures for example, but in return for greater decentralisation and flexibility in other areas, such as macro-economic policy choices and some regulatory policy choices within the Single Market. This might be anathema to many Euro-federalists, who see the Single Market and EMU as great achievements of the European integration project. But more decentralisation and flexibility may be the only way to save the European integration project from either permanent gridlock or slow collapse. Furthermore, decentralised federalism may foster greater policy innovation and economic growth, which in turn should erode public support for populist anti-European forces.

8
Seven Brexit propositions

Towards a Union that protects

Luuk van Middelaar

After the UK referendum, there was a palpable temptation in Brussels to dismiss the result as insular British doggedness, in the hope that a marginal readjustment of a few policies or symbols would suffice to keep the voters of the other countries of the Union on board.[1] A dangerous illusion. The EU urgently needs to strike a new balance between the freedom and the protection that it endeavours to provide. Voters will not be fooled by empty, meaningless slogans like 'A Europe of results', 'Better Europe' or 'Big on big things, small on small things'. The distinction between freedom and protection offers a better tool for fashioning a political response. This distinction reveals real dilemmas, and as a result forces a search for a sincere political language, a sincerity that could only benefit the Union's political life. There are some signs this adjustment is taking place, but more must be done.

1. Starting point: British voters have not gone mad

It would be a mistake to attribute the victory of the Leavers on 23 June 2016 to the campaign's often baseless claims against 'Brussels', or to the 'irrational' behaviour of the British voters voting against their well-understood economic interests, or to the fact that Rupert Murdoch or other powerful enemies of the European project are laying down the law to the British media. Nor should we understand the result of the referendum as purely the result of 'fact-free politics', where feelings of prejudice run rampant. In a country like Great Britain, one cannot win a vote with lies and propaganda alone. It is impossible to convince 52 per cent of voters to vote against their personal interests (even if lies may have made the difference between winning and losing). The British people, it must be said, have expressed something else beyond this vote, something that could very well be 'rational', once the perspective is broadened beyond the analysis of economic self-interest alone.

2. First message: identity politics trump economic interest

It is of little importance whether the British voters refused to believe the economic warnings of 'experts',[2] or whether they did believe them but simply did not care because of other priorities. Evidently, the result of the British referendum is part of a larger phenomenon in the Western world: on both sides of the Atlantic, more and more voters are rejecting the rationale of globalisation and its corollaries, such as open markets and borders. The left is primarily targeting the economy (the Transatlantic Trade and Investment Partnership, the EU, the euro), while the right is concerning itself with migration (of Muslims, Mexicans, Polish, Romanians, depending on the context). The net result is the same, as we saw during the American presidential primaries with the success of outsider candidates Bernie Sanders and Donald Trump, as well as in the French 2017 presidential elections, with the high scores for leftwing anti-capitalist Jean-Luc Mélenchon and nationalist Marine Le Pen. The battle was between the 'centre', in the broader sense (as represented by 'Remain', Hillary Clinton or Emmanuel Macron), and the 'fringes', verging on the 'extremes'.

3. Second message: Brexit weakens Brussels doctrine

For the EU in particular, the possibility that identity politics trump economic interests amounts to an existential crisis. A choice like this will, of course, have an adverse effect on Brussels doctrine in general, and on the two central elements of European integration in particular. Since the time of the founding of the Coal and Steel Community, the entire system has been based on (1) the postulate that economic interdependence creates grateful populations and (2) the idea that integration is a one-way street towards 'ever closer Union'. Only the membership of new Member States and the addition of new competences are envisaged. In this vision, there is no place for Member States to quit the club, neither is there space to repatriate competences to the national level. In this sense, the result of the Brexit referendum was unthinkable. Now that it has taken place, it is necessary to change the doctrine.

4. Battlefield: national elections

The battle between the fringes and the centre represents a real danger for the EU. The Union is a large democratic sounding board and this struggle is one of the principal issues in each election. In reality, 'European elections' do not take place once every five years (as only a Brussels-centric point of view could see things), but rather several times a year.

Since the Brexit vote, a number of national elections have taken place in Europe confirming the pattern. One can think of the rerun of the final round of the Austrian presidential election in December 2016 (for which neither traditional governing party qualified and in which pro-European Green candidate Von der Bellen beat the anti-European FPÖ-candidate Hofer) or of the Dutch parliamentary elections of March 2017, where the biggest winners were the pro-European centrist-liberal and green-left parties on the one hand, the extreme-right PVV of Geert Wilders on the other. But without denying the strategic interest of these battlefields, the real post-Brexit test for the Union was always going to be the French presidential election of April–May 2017. France is where the front line between the forces 'for' and the forces 'against' Europe is starkest. The country's systematic importance is due to its weight within the Union, its political system that favours polarisation, as well as the state of shock in which it finds itself following a series of terrorist attacks. The final round between pro-European centrist Emmanuel Macron and National Front leader Marine Le Pen, who campaigned for a 'Frexit' from the EU and the eurozone, electrifying as it was, crystallised the same cleavage observed in the UK and Austria; it may even restructure the party-political landscape, since in France too, the traditional governing parties of the moderate right and moderate left suffered defeat. Although Macron secured a large victory on 7 May, this expressed just as much a vote against Le Pen and her party in the name of the Republic as a vote in favour of Macron's pro-European and liberal agenda (for 43 per cent of those voting for him, stopping her was their main motif). Telling in this respect were the results of the first round: both the pro-European camp (Macron, Fillon, Hamon) and the anti-European camp (Le Pen, Mélenchon, Dupont-Aignan and some smaller candidates) arrived at added totals of about 49 per cent. Just as in post-Brexit UK some observers see 'two nations', French commentators speak about 'les deux France'.

Although the immediate outcome in France was a relief to the EU, it would be premature to speak of a 'European spring'. The pro-European camp will need to increase its voter base to more solid majorities. This means that in France, as elsewhere, Europe must win back the centre and the undecided voters, with a new strategy.

5. The answer: a new balance between freedom and protection

In order to win back the centre, the EU must find a new balance between its efforts to promote economic freedoms, and its role as a social protector. The British referendum, along with evidence from other national elections, reveals a divide among the populations. It is a divide between, on the one hand, voters who generally appreciate the EU for its freedom, openness, and the opportunities it offers and, on the other hand, those who ultimately fear the disorder and disruptions that the EU creates in terms of migration, competition for jobs, or the loss of national sovereignty. This divide may be informed by, even though it may not directly map onto, the divide between the 'mobile', often the entrepreneurs, the young, students, the well-off, or those who have nothing to lose when leaving their country, and the 'sedentary', who are fine staying home. As we know, '[t]he European order gives the benefits of equal treatment only to the footloose' (van Middelaar 2013, 255).

Two nuances: this divide cannot be reduced to an opposition between 'the elite' and 'the people', because this revolves around a 50–50 ratio, as we have seen in the case of the British referendum and the Austrian and French presidential elections. Similarly we cannot slide into sociological determinism: millions of the 'poor' and the 'elderly' voted for Great Britain to remain in the EU, and a number of the 'rich' and the 'youth' voted to leave. In the end, it is of course the free choice of each individual, based on their interests, experiences and values, for which only they themselves are responsible.

6. Policies: the importance of borders

It is crucial, therefore, that the EU works and is seen to work, not only for half of the voters, its own freedom-loving 'clientele' as it were, but also addresses the other half. Failing this, we risk a 'civil war', in which the European side will be quickly beaten by the strength in numbers of the hostiles. This disastrous outcome may yet come to pass in but a few short years.

The key message should therefore be to express that, alongside the old 'Europe of opportunities', European leaders and institutions must work for a 'Europe that protects'. If this message has been first heard in France – when in 2007 French presidential candidate Nicolas Sarkozy asked for *'une Europe qui protège'* – by now it resonates across the Union as a whole. At the same time, it must be recognised that achieving a better balance between freedom and protection can mean two different things: either minimising the negative effects of freedom, or producing more order.

The first is fundamental with regard to social and economic security. Because the EU cannot credibly replace the national welfare states without becoming the 'super-state' that the voters clearly refuse, it must at least stop sapping the national and local institutions of their protective and healthcare systems. In terms of policies, two priorities stand out here. First, to retain the elements of the agreement between the EU and Great Britain of February 2016 (the 'new UK settlement'), if not in their UK-specific legal form at least in their political substance, in particular those aspects of the agreement concerning the possibility of an 'emergency brake' procedure in relation to freedom of movement (Pisani-Ferry et al. 2016). Second, to find a solution for the Posted Workers Directive, above all for the purpose of confronting hostile and Eurosceptic climates in other Member States.[3]

A better balance between freedom and protection can also mean providing order. Since the Brexit vote, the themes of internal and external security have finally received the necessary attention: defending Europe is no longer a taboo. The regulation of September 2016 concerning a new European body of coast guards and border guards is useful and important, and it is the implementation of this decision that now matters most.[4] Enlargement is the other major issue when it comes to a discussion of borders – not the 'physical' but the territorial border. In this regard, it falls to the European leaders to decide how long they want to continue their game of hypocritical diplomacy (of which both parties are guilty, incidentally) around the status of the candidate-country Turkey (unless the ever more pronounced authoritarian slide of the Turkish state under president Erdogan decides the issue for them before). At the very least, leaders must realise that an eventual Turkish membership would not only have considerable (and very real) 'external' geopolitical consequences, but also costs in terms of the 'internal' capacity of the EU to regain the trust of its citizens, without which it cannot survive.

After a summer where the shock of post-Brexit denial gripped Brussels, later signs were more promising. In the letter of invitation for the informal summit of Bratislava on the 16 September 2016, the president of the European Council Donald Tusk wrote, without hesitation: 'People quite rightly expect their leaders to protect the space they live in ... It is therefore crucial to restore the balance between the need for freedom and security, and between the need for openness and protection.' Those who know the realistic liberalism of the Pole, quite visible in his role in the migrant crisis during the winter of 2015–16, would not have been surprised. More remarkable, however, was the 'State of the Union' speech by Jean-Claude Juncker, delivered on 14 September 2016 in Strasbourg. What the president of the European Commission said, among others, about border guards, border patrol and Chinese dumping was just as remarkable as what was not said – not a word about the TTIP in the nearly 50-minute speech (Juncker 2016). More recently, in his speech after the first round of the French presidential election, on 23 April 2017, Emmanuel Macron called for 'a Europe that protects', keenly aware that he needs to reach out to those voters who are angry or frustrated with the EU. Denial is clearly a thing of the past. In the months and years ahead, European leaders must solidify the implementation of this new balance between freedom and protection. It is a matter of survival.

7. The 'We are Europe' policy

As long as European citizens consider Brussels as a threat to their constitutional, political or cultural identity, the Union will remain in murky waters. Even if a real response emerges to force the creation of a Union that is to care for and protect its citizens, there will remain an important role for communication. It is particularly incumbent upon the heads of state and of government before, during and after each summit meeting, to show and explain to their respective voters that Europe cannot be reduced to 'Brussels' alone. Rather, whatever our nationality, at the heart of the Union, Europe belongs to us all.

III: The Member States

9
Britain's singular other
Germany and the Brexit crisis

William E. Paterson

The road to Brexit

The Fall of the Berlin Wall in 1989 was arguably the key event in post-war British politics. The UK's role in the allied victory and its role in post-war Germany gave it an enhanced status and removed the rivalry that had scarred British–German relations in the preceding century. This privileged role for the UK was swept away by German unity, where Germany achieved full sovereignty and territorial expansion. It is this sense of loss that explains Prime Minister Thatcher's hostility to German unification (Campbell 2004, 32–41).

German unity turned out to be a critical juncture and took Germany and the UK along different paths. The German government under Chancellor Kohl opted for the path of deeper integration in the Maastricht Treaties, while the UK made ever more frequent use of 'opt-out' provisions to escape the embrace of deeper integration. Until the onset of the eurozone crisis, these divergent paths did not appear to be an immediate existential threat to the EU, though the complete failure of the UK government to inform the British public about the EU obviously carried grave risks in the event of a crisis. With the breaking out of the crisis, the status quo no longer looked like an option for Germany and members of the eurozone and it was clear that at some point further steps would need to be taken to safeguard the eurozone. Within the UK, the eurozone crisis emboldened the Eurosceptics, who now perceived the EU as a failed enterprise, which they sought to exploit to effect a British exit, and the defenders of British membership of the EU could not draw on a reservoir of public knowledge and support. The decisive blow however was probably Chancellor Merkel's decision to allow Syrian refugees to proceed from Austria to Germany in August 2015, which was quickly exploited by the Eurosceptic press and politicians to give the (wholly mistaken) impression that Britain would be threatened by waves of refugees. Ironically both the eurozone and the issue of migration were covered by 'opt outs', but the low level of information about the EU in Britain allowed them to be used as an argument in favour of leaving.

David Cameron and renegotiation

Under pressure from Eurosceptics inside the Conservative Party and electoral pressure from UKIP, Prime Minister Cameron decided to hold an 'in–out' referendum on the UK membership of the EU, though it was labelled as an 'advisory referendum'. This was to be preceded by a renegotiation of the terms of the UK membership where it was hoped that Britain would be granted major concessions in relation to 'freedom of movement of labour', the area where the Conservative government felt under most pressure from UKIP. In the renegotiation, David Cameron had hoped to secure concessions through relying on the 'good offices' of Germany to move other Member States to support sufficiently dramatic concessions so as to allow him to triumph. In taking this option, Cameron assumed that Germany occupied a hegemonic position. This calculation failed for a number of reasons. Whilst Germany operates as a 'reluctant hegemon' (Paterson 2011) in the eurozone, it lacks hegemonic power across the EU as a whole. Almost no attention was paid to other Member States whose agreement would have been necessary. Cameron also assumed a convergence of priorities between the UK and Germany, failing to understand that Germany was above all concerned with maintenance of the eurozone and of the EU as a whole. Ultimately, the UK's 'transactional' approach to its EU membership clashed with a German approach that reserved significant space for fundamental values, freedom of movement being one of the more important. The British approach of demanding bespoke 'opt-outs' and its policy of promiscuous differentiation, which had been so successful in the past, would therefore have its limits. In the Brexit post-mortem, many in the UK continue to argue that, had there been one more concerted push, German Chancellor Angela Merkel would have conceded on free movement. There is no evidence for this view and even if she had conceded some ground, it would not have been accepted by other Member States.

After the referendum

The balance of UK policy towards Germany changed sharply with the arrival of Theresa May as prime minister, who reversed the policy and personnel choices of her predecessor. There was a perception that David Cameron over-invested in Germany, and after an initial visit to Berlin by Prime Minister May no great effort was made to court Germany or any other major Member States. With the arrival of President Trump, attention has been concentrated on Washington and potential trade partners rather than European partners. A 'Remainer' in the referendum campaign, May subsequently positioned herself at the head of a 'hard Brexit' course and appointed three pro-Brexit ministers (Boris Johnson, David Davis and Liam Fox) to key ministerial posts. One of the assumptions of the 'hard Brexit' position is that the negotiating advantage lies with the UK and that the correct course is to press the British position strongly (whilst being prepared to leave if progress does not result). This highly risky position which reflects a visceral dislike of the EU rests, to some extent, on the view that Cameron's renegotiation failed largely because he had indicated a strong preference to remain and had not stressed that he would be prepared to exit if the renegotiation failed.

For the German government, Brexit has slipped sharply down the list of priorities. Chancellor Merkel's first priority, especially after a temporary surge in support for the Social Democratic Party's candidate, Martin Schulz, was to secure re-election. The second priority was maintaining the unity of the remaining EU members post-Brexit, since a special responsibility is seen to fall on Germany in this regard. A third priority was to deal with the threats to the EU posed by Putin in Russia and Trump in the US, and a fourth was dealing with the eurozone and migration crises. Only then was Brexit considered a priority.

The economics of Brexit

In Cameron's premiership there was a widely held view that Germany, and particularly Merkel, would throw its weight unequivocally behind the British negotiating position. This was always an unrealistic position which ignored the fact that Merkel had to take account of the preferences of other Member States and that 'freedom of movement' was a core EU value. Nevertheless the failure of Merkel to meet British expectations in this regard led to deep disappointment in the UK.

Post-referendum, attention has shifted in the direction of German business. Germany is the exporting nation *par excellence* and the interests of export-oriented business could be expected to weigh heavily. Moreover, German businesses are heavily invested in Britain. In 2016, Germany exported €86 billion worth of goods to the UK, while German imports from the UK were only half of that. Germany is also a major investor in the UK car industry with a very healthy trade balance in pharmaceuticals, machine building and electronics (Turner & Green 2017). In recent years a number of authors, notably Hans Kundnani (2014), have argued that German external preferences are essentially set by its export-oriented firms.

Although these factors might be expected to lend credence to the primacy of economics argument, in actual fact the evidence points the other way. Trade with Britain is much smaller than trade with the rest of the EU. Merkel's priority, accepted by German business, is to keep the EU together and the Single Market flourishing (Savage 2017). Hans Kundnani's view that business is becoming more dominant in preference-formation seems to be the reverse of what is happening. Traditionally, the German export industry indeed shaped German preferences, but in a series of recent decisions the relationship has been the other way around. Merkel overruled the objections of business, for instance, in order to press sanctions against Russia in the Ukraine crisis. Even more strikingly, the support that German business gave the proposals for a TTIP gained no traction whatsoever, and on Brexit German firms were forced to bow to the wider interest. There is an obvious symmetry here with UK businesses, which have also been unable to make their preferences in favour of British Single Market membership count.

The politics of Brexit

If the view that the economic interests of Germany will be enough to secure a favourable outcome for Britain in the Brexit negotiations is misplaced, it is reasonable to ask whether the political environment will be any more benign.

The clouds gather

The starting point is the feeling of annoyance generated by Brexit. Germany had taken the lead in offering Britain concessions in successive negotiations since the UK's original entry into the EEC in 1973. These concessions were often made against strong resistance from France. The German government felt it had gone as far as it could in the negotiations with Cameron, and was therefore surprised and disappointed that Cameron was unable to sell the deal to the British public despite continually assuring them that victory was inevitable. They were further irritated by post-referendum British claims that this was the fault of the Germans, who had been unreasonable in not making concessions on freedom of movement. This charge ignores the fact that limitations on free movement would have received even less support from the other Member States. The harsh tone employed by Prime Minister May towards the EU, and her identification with President Trump, also succeeded in further alienating German opinion.

Germany's lonely position

A British exit from the EU leaves Germany with a number of unwelcome problems. The UK is a major contributor to the EU budget and its departure raises awkward questions in relation to financing, with a number of Member States entertaining expectations that Germany – as the richest and largest Member State – will fill the gap. The financing issue also explains the firmness of the German insistence that Britain must settle its debts before the negotiation of any future trade deal can begin. In relation to the EU27, the focus of the German government will be on containing expenditure and exporting its brand of austerity. This was an area where Britain was a dependable ally. Germany thus also stands to lose its most powerful ally against (economic) statism. The departure of the UK also leaves Germany even more exposed as the dominant power in the EU. A great deal now hinges on the recovery of France under Emmanuel Macron.

Germany's position as 'reluctant hegemon' is also likely to come under more pressure after Brexit. The term applies especially to Germany's role in the eurozone crisis. In the past, Germany would have sought to deal with the crisis through the Franco-German relationship but France's weakening economy meant that it became clear quite quickly that it was not a viable partner in this regard. Germany's ever-strengthening economy and principal creditor status placed it in the driving seat in relation to setting the rules in the eurozone.

Germany's historical past and the costs associated with a hegemonic role meant that it was one it accepted with some reluctance. By some measures the largest economy, it is now even more obvious that Germany is the dominant Member State, a role that comes with increased expectations and responsibilities. This is at its most obvious in relation to the migration crisis where the Eastern European Member States continue to benefit from substantial EU funds while refusing to play their part in a fair distribution of incoming refugees. In that context, demands from Britain that it be afforded a bespoke Brexit deal are especially irksome.

Changing geopolitics

These added burdens have arisen at a time when the political sands are shifting around Merkel's feet. Geopolitically, she is the first German Chancellor to face a challenge from a US president. Barack Obama had been a staunch ally of Chancellor Merkel whilst in office, but Donald Trump's cry of 'America First' has made enemies of the liberal world order generally – and China and Germany specifically – because of their large trade surpluses with the US. Things started to normalise after the Chancellor's visit to Washington, and Trump became somewhat less hostile, but he is still a long way from being a supporter of Germany and made a number of statements critical of Germany at the G20 Conference in Hamburg (Gathmann & Wittrock 2017). The fact that the UK continues to support the position of President Trump, despite its oft-proclaimed support for global free trade and the Paris Climate Accord, is a source of bafflement and annoyance to many Germans. Merkel is further pressured by the actions of President Putin in Syria and the Ukraine. Whereas her Social Democrat coalition partners offer strong support in her dealings with the US, they have continued to privilege engagement, not containment, in her dealings with Russia. The emergence of illiberal governments in Hungary and Poland is a source of further pressure on Chancellor Merkel.

The envisaged departure of the UK has not led to the contagion effect some predicted, although in truth this was a view that was only really held by the British. Nevertheless, the EU remains fractious, with southern Europeans attacking Germany's austerity policy and Eastern Europeans opposing Merkel's refugee policy. Faced with these challenges, Merkel's priority has to be to focus on keeping the EU together, rather than spend time and political capital on the Brexit negotiations.

The election of Emmanuel Macron to the French Presidency has transformed the mood and reduced the German sense of isolation;. Macron is a pro-European who is keen to revive the Franco-German alliance, although French economic weakness will mean that Germany remains the indispensable and dominant partner in this relationship, with all the attendant responsibilities. Nevertheless, the Franco-German relationship represents the future and policy attention will be centred on that relationship rather than pandering to the British as they vanish in the rear-view mirror.

In relation to the negotiations themselves, one immediate problem arising is the relative readiness of the respective negotiating teams. The German team, despite still coping with the migration and eurozone crises, is formidably well prepared. They have, in turn, been shocked by the ignorance and lack of preparedness on the part of the UK. The British coordination mechanism on the EU was traditionally regarded with great admiration by other Member States, with the UK's Permanent Representation to the EU (UKREP) in Brussels considered formidably well briefed. The resignation of the hugely respected Sir Ivan Rogers as UK Permanent Representative on 7 January 2017 and his replacement by Sir Tim Barrow, a non-EU security specialist without any of Sir Ivan's vast knowledge, has gravely weakened UKREP. Moreover, the new ministries established to deal with Brexit – the Department for Exiting the EU and the Department for International Trade – are headed by ministers with no recent experience of dealing with the EU, and are seriously understaffed. This leads to myriad difficulties. The UK government's desire for a quick deal on the rights of EU nationals in the UK, seen as essential for the operation of the British labour market, ignores many of the legal and technical complexities involved. The insistence on abolishing the jurisdiction of the CJEU while aiming for the best possible access to the Single Market is viewed with confusion in Germany. If Britain were to secure favourable terms of access to the Single Market, it would need to be on the basis of equivalent regulation, for which there would have to exist some process to monitor divergence and resolve conflicts. An alternative to the CJEU would be cumbersome and extremely difficult to agree upon.

Whilst the area of trade policy is of the greatest interest to the two governments, the 'red lines' set out by the UK government in Prime Minister May's Lancaster House speech (May 2017a) will make agreement very difficult. The area of security and counter terrorism should be much easier to resolve given the UK's acceptance of Europol and the obvious common interest both countries have in this area. Here too the 'red line' on the oversight of the CJEU would create obstacles in the technical details of cooperation in areas such as data protection, which is extremely sensitive in Germany for historical reasons.

Cooperation in the area of foreign policy, which has always been intergovernmental and is outside the jurisdiction of the CJEU, will be easier. The danger here is that the UK regards security as its 'get out of jail' card, able to produce large concessions on the trade front. The German view is that security is best understood as a common good that is in the interests of both countries and should therefore not be used to extract leverage in other areas. Although cooperation with the UK is seen as desirable, the German government is stepping up defence cooperation with France, including the joint development of a fighter aircraft and increasing spending on Germany's own defence forces to ensure continued security after Brexit.

Conclusions

The future is uncertain, more so than usual, and the outcome of the Brexit negotiations are unclear. What is clear is that the result of the UK referendum marks a deep caesura in UK–German relations. After an awkward initial start under Margaret Thatcher, the post-German unity relations between Britain and Germany have been unprecedentedly close. This closeness required the exercise of tact and restraint on both sides, but especially on the German side. A united Germany inevitably reduced the importance of the UK, even in regard to relations with the US, traditionally a cornerstone of British self-regard. Although they diverged on integration issues, the two countries were close on trade and security. Under David Cameron, who relied totally on Germany in his renegotiation bid, relations were probably closer than at any time in recent history.

Theresa May began her tenure as prime minister with a successful visit to Berlin, but since then relations have rapidly worsened. The German government has been dismayed by May's uncritical support for President Trump and her jettisoning of the more traditional UK role acting as a 'bridge' between the US and Europe. A series of veiled threats on security and the possibility of the UK adopting a low-tax 'Singaporean' model in the event of talks breaking down have been received poorly in Germany, where it is pointed out these would harm the UK more than the EU.

The decision by Theresa May to attempt to strengthen her majority by calling a snap election on 8 June 2017 turned out very badly for her, resulting in a 'hung parliament'. Prime Minister May was forced to strike a deal with the Democratic Unionist Party of

Northern Ireland to secure a majority. It is quite difficult to establish what the voters intended but at the very least it indicates a lack of support for Prime Minister May's 'hard Brexit course'. It was not at all clear that Prime Minister May would be able to survive as prime minister beyond the initial weeks. The weakness of the British government has provoked some alarm in Germany and Foreign Minister Sigmar Gabriel in an interview with *Welt am Sonntag* indicated that the German government might be prepared to make concessions to encourage a 'soft Brexit'; in particular he floated the idea of a joint court rather than the CJEU to arbitrate disputes (Maidment 2017). The Chancellor has been extremely sparing in any comments in the run-up to the Federal Election of 24 September.

Whatever option finally emerges, Germany will not, and cannot, act as a comfort blanket for the UK in the future. The British hope that the US might fulfil this role also looks unlikely, after President Trump indicated that a trade agreement with the EU will take precedence over a similar deal with the UK. For Germany, the departure of the UK will be regrettable on trade and budgetary issues, but it will not make a significant dent on Germany's upwards rise, either politically or economically. For Britain the results will be economically and psychologically very painful.

10
France, Britain and Brexit

Helen Drake

2017: a year of disruption

Brexit, and the election of Emmanuel Macron, have galvanised the political environments in Britain and France, respectively. Each development is, in its own way, highly disruptive of the status quo. If the mantra of disruption is 'to move fast and break things' (BBC Radio Four 2017), then the election of Macron to the French presidency and the wholesale success of his political movement La République en Marche (LREM) in the French National Assembly fits the bill entirely. Macron and his party sped to power in little over 12 months and the French political landscape is, for now, littered with the debris of the political parties that he – and LREM – outwitted. In the business world, disruptive change involves stealing a march on one's incumbents whose customers initially deem the new product to be inferior (Christensen et al. 2015). Substitute Macron for 'product' and voters for 'customers', and here, too, the analogy is not so far-fetched (if unpleasant).

In the case of Brexit, the process can hardly be described as 'fast' but as time goes on, finding evidence that Brexit will *not* be inferior to EU membership is becoming harder and harder. Moreover, the UK's withdrawal from the EU is by definition a matter of 'breaking things', and the Franco-British relationship will certainly not be left undisturbed by the separation. At the same time, Brexit in fact fits perfectly into a cross-Channel friendship that for centuries has been marked by competition, collaboration, rivalry and change. No one should have been surprised that the UK's shock decision by referendum to withdraw from the EU was greeted in France in part as an opportunity for French competitive advantage. 'Let the expatriates return!', exclaimed French Prime Minister Édouard Philippe when presenting his government's legislative programme to the National Assembly (Philippe 2017). The French leader was making a general point about France's future, but on the specifics of Brexit, such overtures have been just as common as expressions of regret. Given that 'Year One' of Brexit (from the referendum of 23 June 2016 to the UK general election of 8 June 2017) coincided with the French electoral marathon – culminating in the presidential and parliamentary elections in May and June 2017 respectively – it was particularly likely that Brexit would serve as electoral bait across the French political spectrum.

Brexit and the EU in the 2017 French elections

According to Édouard Philippe, the results of those elections can be taken as evidence that the French remain firmly attached to the EU and the euro, since they voted for a candidate – Emmanuel Macron – who openly embraced France's European identity (Philippe 2017). 'Frexit' was certainly averted in the 2017 elections, despite being on the electoral ticket. One candidate, François Asselineau, had openly campaigned for Frexit but scored less than 1 per cent (0.92 per cent) of the votes in the first round of the presidential elections. Two other presidential candidates – Marine Le Pen and Jean-Luc Mélenchon – fought highly Eurosceptic campaigns and achieved significant scores: in the first round the two candidates between them won just over 40 per cent of the votes combined (a total of over 14 million votes); and in the second round, Le Pen broke through the barrier of 10 million votes with a score of 33.9 per cent of the total (against Macron's 66.1 per cent).

The entire thrust of Mélenchon's campaign was to rail against the idea of a 'submissive' France. Applied to the question of Europe, this translated into a Plan A: to radically reform the EU treaties along with other Member States wishing to free themselves (as Mélenchon saw it) from, in particular, the rigours of eurozone governance. If Plan A failed, then Plan B was for France to unilaterally 'leave' the EU's treaty framework ('the EU: change it or leave it'). In the case of Marine Le Pen, the horrors of the EU, as she portrayed them, were both central to her platform and a factor in her loss of the second-round presidential vote to Macron. Her number one proposal (out of 144) was to 'recover France's national sovereignty in a Europe of independent nations at the service of its peoples' (Le Pen 2017), much as proponents of Brexit aim to 'take back control'. She would negotiate this recovery of France's 'monetary, legislative, territorial and economic sovereignties' (Le Pen 2017) with her EU counterparts, and put the result to the French people in a referendum. For Le Pen, Brexit was inspirational, representing, in her eyes, nothing less than the liberation of the British people. Unfortunately for Le Pen, she performed badly when debating these issues on live TV, especially in the head-to-head debate with Macron between the first and second rounds of the presidential elections. Apparently unsure of her technical ground, her visceral emotions were laid bare for anyone who chose to see.

Sixty years of French engagement with the EU: at what cost?

Nevertheless, were the French to hold an 'in–out' referendum of its own on the subject of its EU membership, we would be unwise to predict the outcome. 'Frexit' was evidently no longer unthinkable by the time of the 2017 elections in France. Previous referendums in France on EU affairs have seen either narrow victories for further integration (as with Maastricht in 1993) or rejections (the Constitutional Treaty in 2005), and French public support for EU membership remains shaky (Eurobarometer, 2017). Generations of French politicians since 1945 have proclaimed their commitment to European integration in the form of a promise 'to make Europe without unmaking France' (see Bossuat 2006; Drake & Reynolds 2017, 111), but France's relations with the EU are problematic for domestic French politics, and have been for some time. In this respect, France and the UK are not so dissimilar in their quandary over what it means to be an EU Member State.

In 2011, the Economist's Intelligence Unit downgraded France from a 'full' to a 'flawed' democracy on the specific grounds that its response to the eurozone crisis – agreeing to more stringent oversight of national finances by Brussels – was undermining national democracy (Drake & Reynolds 2017, 113; Economist Intelligence Unit 2011). By the time of the 2012 presidential elections, the extent to which France was integrated into the EU was made more explicit by the leading presidential candidates than was typically the case; they could hardly do otherwise in the context of the EU's ongoing crises (financial and migratory, to name but two). That election, it has been argued, was an unprecedentedly 'Europeanised contest' whereby candidates joined the dots between national political competition (the presidential election) and EU-level policy orientation (Dehousse & Tacea 2012, 16). They did so overwhelmingly to oppose the EU in some shape or form. The appeal of the two leading Eurosceptic candidates of 2017 seen above – Mélenchon and Le Pen – was certainly established in this 2012 contest (between them they won almost 30 per cent of the votes in the first round). But front runners François Hollande and Nicolas Sarkozy were also critical of the EU's handling of the crises, and raised expectations that they would be the president to improve EU affairs.

Constitutionally speaking, French presidents do have considerable leeway over European policymaking. Institutionally, they also have far more of a free hand than, say, the UK prime minister has: as Rozenberg (2016) has demonstrated, they are simply not held to account by their parties in Parliament in the same way. (We have seen how unwelcoming UK Prime Minister Theresa May has become to her parliamentary opposition on the matter of Brexit.) But to bring their party to power in the first place, French presidential candidates have to clear the hurdle of the two-round voting system of the presidential election. They have to 'catch all' in their electoral camp, Europhiles and Eurosceptics alike, by means of a 'synthetic vision of Europe' (Rozenberg 2016). This is a vision that papers over the cracks in their own parties and in the camp that delivered 50+ per cent of the national vote, and stores up problems for the next elections. President Macron, as we saw above, came to power by creating a new political camp entirely. In so doing, he neatly side-stepped the previous 'laws of nature', and created an opportunity (however ephemeral) for French-led disruption on the EU stage.

Towards a 'political Europe'?

It would seem from President Macron himself that the plan is to secure a 'political Europe'. This is anything but original. For Rozenberg (2016, 2), '[t]he solution of a 'political Europe' is so regularly put forward that the idea has become polymorphous and even meaningless'. It certainly is a mainstay of French discourse on the EU, and it does arguably have some shape, at least conceptually. In Macron's own words, a political Europe is a 'voluntary and realistic association of states' that have agreed upon 'useful policies' on matters such as the freedom of movement of goods and people, and especially young people, security, monetary and fiscal affairs, and culture (Macron 2017). Macron differs little from his predecessors here in rationalising European integration as a matter for national states and governments (over and above free markets, and in theory favouring the long term and the strategic); as a project defined by fundamental values (freedom, peace, progress); and as an expression of Europe's potential as a global actor.

This is a vision that is airily dismissive of the EU's actual nature as an intensely rules-based system of governance and, true to French form, Macron mocks the EU for its 'tyranny of agendas and calendars', likening the EU to neighbours in crisis-management mode, no longer trusting each other to run their communal assets and instead devising ever more rules to govern their interactions (Macron 2017). He attributes Euroscepticism in general, and Brexit in particular, to such distractions, as he sees them. He, in contrast, is impatient to get back to basics. By the end of 2017, says Macron, he will initiate 'democratic conventions' all across Europe to get the continent back onto this political footing – a Europe that unites people. Member States can sign up or not, as they wish, he breezily announces. This, he claims, is a job for a new generation of political leaders, and perhaps here he has a point. Brexit, we should note in contrast, is being handled in the UK by an existing generation of leaders, many of whom appear unable or unwilling to escape the shadow of the past when it comes to the UK's relations with the EU, and many of whom are seeking, if anything, to go backwards not forwards. With reference to both the EU–UK Brexit negotiations and Macron's plans for a political Europe, Kuper's (2017) argument against relying on rhetoric rather than a gritty engagement with the rules seems timely.

In the case of France there is some sense of more concrete priorities, and Brexit is towards the bottom of the list. It features as one of three EU-level negotiations that Prime Minister Édouard Philippe has identified as 'crucial', the others being the 'redefinition of our project as 27 with Germany and those of our partners who want to move ahead'; and the EU's financial perspectives for beyond 2020 (Philippe 2017). Above and beyond this triad of talks come two broader priorities for France. The first is to 'reconcile' the French with the EU; the second is to build a 'Europe that protects' (via improved eurozone governance; progress on EU defence policy and 'social convergence', and the development of a commercial policy based on reciprocity). These two ideas – restoring public confidence in the EU and in French leaders' ability to lead it, and re-orientating EU policy – are not remotely new, and flow from the 'political Europe' goal outlined above. As such, Macron's best hope for results lies in French engagement on the ground. By way of example, the Franco-German Council in July 2017 ended with an announcement of plans for a joint ('European') fighter jet. Whilst this signalled shared intentions to bolster the EU's autonomous defence capacity, the initiative for now raises far more questions than answers (*Le Monde* 2017).

Negotiating change ...

Will France will be any more successful at re-engaging with the EU under Macron's leadership than the UK will be at disengaging via Brexit? To succeed in either case implies productive negotiations with the other EU Member States and with the EU's own institutions. Productive negotiations, in turn, require the primary parties (in the case of Brexit, the EU Commission and the UK government) to be both properly constituted and fully functional (see Crump 2006). Year One of Brexit has already provided much food for thought in these regards and could be instructive by comparison for the French case.

By properly *constituted* we mean they must have clearly defined roles and cohesive and predictable support from supporting parties (such as junior partners in a government coalition). Taking the example of Brexit once more, the parties to the negotiations and their roles are highly structured on the EU side by dint of Treaty provision and the negotiations guidelines and directives that have flowed from them (European Commission 2017c, European Council 2017a). On the UK side, the cohesion and predictability of the primary party – the UK government – has been weakened since the UK general election of 8 June 2017, in which the Conservative government lost its majority in the House of Commons.

Second, to be *functional* means at the very least to be able to own the problem or the opportunity, to identify it as such; to take decisions; and to communicate those decisions as required (Crump 2006, 2). The EU party to the Brexit negotiations is for now fully functional: agreed on what Brexit means for the EU, agreed on how they want to talk about it with the UK government, in what sequence and by which deadlines. To date, they have communicated their interests coherently, and speak with one voice. The solidarity of the EU27 may well fray when it comes to decision-making time, but they have entered the talks in good shape. In contrast, the UK party is dysfunctional. Rhetorically, the government has defined Brexit as an unrivalled and unprecedented opportunity for the UK, but this has yet to be translated into a negotiations script and is contested, even within the government. In term of its decision-making capacity, the UK government has explicitly bound itself by the 'will of the British people' as expressed in outcome of the 23 June 2016 referendum. Since that referendum, the courts and Parliament have predictably entered the decision-making arena since even the 'will of the people' must be implemented via due democratic process. Owning and communicating these facts – that the UK is a weak and dysfunctional negotiations party at a Brexit negotiations table where the power is stacked against it – is understandably challenging.

... Or change through disruption?

For France and in contrast, negotiating its way back in to a position of power and influence within the EU27 should be far less fraught. France is well constituted as a negotiating partner following Macron and LREM's victories at the 2017 elections. Moreover, it is functional: Macron 'owned' Europe from the night of his election victory on Sunday 7 May onwards, by appropriating symbols such as the EU anthem and the EU flag; Macron and his government have identified the EU as an opportunity; and to communicate all this, France's current leaders are deploying a familiar rhetoric of 'political Europe' with the intention of disarming the Euroscepticism that has taken root in French political parties and public opinion alike. On the other side of the table are individual Member States and the EU institutions. There is no joint bloc to face France down, nor are France's partners brandishing a ticking clock. The complex and heightened emotions that characterise the Brexit negotiations are less of an issue in France's relations with the EU.

But there are time pressures on Macron and his government to deliver on their electoral promises (and not only on EU affairs). The presidency is 'fast' – a short five years (Cole 2012); expectations are high and the political climate is troubled. The very nature of Macron's disruption of the status quo creates conditions in the political environment that threaten France's ability to negotiate change at the EU level. We saw above that he is supported politically by a new camp that is untried and untested, and this potentially weakens the constitution – the coherence – of France as a negotiating partner. Indeed, the first weeks of the new government witnessed numerous ministerial resignations and reshuffles. Then there are threats to the functionality of France as an EU partner, and would-be leading partner at that. In particular, the risk of domestic distractions is high, given the controversial agenda of socioeconomic change and the several false starts already made in this regard, and this will drain attention and decision-making resources (including political capital) away from the French executive.

Conclusions

We have seen above that in the case of both France and the UK, 2017 will have been a year of some reckoning. In particular and for both countries, EU membership came to dominate the political agenda and capture people's emotions. In neither case was the status quo deemed sustainable. Accordingly, and on either side of the Channel, political leaders are engaged in challenging conversations with their domestic and EU constituencies. The end game is change, and the method is disruption. Strictly speaking, disruption is not negotiated change. It is a method of challenging the status quo that relies on creativity, speed and luck. Its intent is positive in the sense of growth: of markets, market share and consumer choice. But 'moving fast and breaking things' is a high-risk strategy in the business world, and in the political environment may well come at very high cost. Brexit and the Macron effect have broken their respective moulds, and we await the outcomes with much interest.

11
Brexit and Ireland

Collateral damage?

Nicholas Wright

Introduction

Nowhere are the complexities of Brexit more apparent than in the challenge they pose to Ireland, North and South, and particularly in the issue of the border between the Republic and Northern Ireland, the UK's only land border with a neighbouring state. The European Council guidelines identify the 'unique circumstances on the island of Ireland' as one of the three main issues to be dealt with in the first stage of the Brexit negotiations which are focused on the actual withdrawal (or 'divorce'), along with citizens' rights and the UK's financial obligations (European Council 2017a). Only once sufficient progress has been made on each of these – a determination to be made by the European Council based on a recommendation by the EU's chief negotiator, Michel Barnier – can discussion of the post-Brexit UK–EU relationship, including the nature of their new trading relationship, begin.

Brexit has, though, begun against a backdrop of increasing tension in Northern Irish politics, partly but not only as a consequence of the fallout from the referendum result which saw a 55.8 per cent vote in favour of Remain. Following the referendum, the first minister and deputy first minister wrote to the prime minister in August 2016 calling, in essence, for the status quo in terms of freedom of movement of people, goods and services to be maintained (Doherty et al. 2017). However, the subsequent collapse of the Northern Ireland Executive in January 2017 brought 10 years of power-sharing to an end and led to elections to the Northern Ireland Assembly in March (less than a year after the previous elections). While the two main parties dominated once more – the pro-Remain Sinn Fein won 27 seats, only one fewer than the pro-Leave Democratic Unionist Party – the results mean that for the first time Unionist parties no longer have an outright majority, while overall 70 per cent of Northern Irish voters backed 'parties opposed to Brexit' (Murphy 2017).

Since then, negotiations between Sinn Fein and the DUP have made little progress. Moreover, the results of the UK general election in June 2017 have caused further complexity, with the DUP agreeing to support a minority Conservative government through a 'confidence and supply' arrangement. This has led some, including former Conservative Prime Minister Sir John Major, one of the architects of the 1993 Downing Street Declaration,[1] to question the capacity of the UK government to act as an honest broker in Northern Irish politics, an important element of the Good Friday Agreement (Syal & Walker 2017). The key point, though, is that as long as power-sharing remains in abeyance, Northern Ireland lacks an independent voice representing both communities in the discussions that will determine how Brexit will impact them.

This chapter explores the political ramifications of Brexit for the two parts of Ireland in greater detail. It begins by examining the role played by the EU both in supporting efforts at peace in Northern Ireland but also in facilitating the remarkable improvement in the Anglo-Irish intergovernmental relationship in recent years. It then considers the challenge Brexit poses to Northern Ireland's political settlement, as well as to Ireland and Anglo-Irish relations in the context of the border. In doing so, it seeks to highlight the inherent tension between the UK government's broader stated aims regarding the return of sovereignty and desire for control of borders on the one hand, and its declared commitments and legal obligations to sustain Northern Ireland's political settlement on the other. While these tensions are not easily resolved, failure to do so is likely to place even greater pressure on devolution and the broader peace process.

1. The EU and Northern Ireland

In the almost two decades since the Good Friday Agreement was signed (HM Government 1998), Northern Irish politics have transformed, as has 'Northern Ireland' as a political issue both in the UK and internationally. Although currently suspended, the devolved administration in Belfast, the Northern Ireland Executive, has seen Unionist and Nationalist politicians working together as equals despite ongoing and sometimes significant tensions. Meanwhile, North–South engagement between Belfast and Dublin has become normalised to an extent barely imaginable only a few decades previously. Finally, Anglo-Irish relations have never been closer, as symbolised by the state visits of Queen Elizabeth II to Ireland in 2011 (the first by a British monarch in a century) and the Irish President Michael D. Higgins to the UK in 2014 (the first ever by an Irish head of state). The House of Lords European Union Committee described this relationship as having been 'turbocharged in recent years by an unprecedented degree of friendship as the Northern Ireland peace process has advanced' (House of Lords 2016, 3), while the UK government considers that it 'has never been better or more settled than today' (HM Government 2017d, 21). Much of this has been down to the many years of hard work and commitment of politicians, officials and activists from all sides.

However, the influence of the EU both directly and indirectly has also been vital in facilitating a sea change in relations. Indeed, the UK government acknowledges the EU's 'unwavering support for the peace process' in its recent position paper on Northern Ireland (HM Government 2017d). The EU's engagement with Northern Ireland can be seen both technically/financially and politically – or as 'context and agency' (Hayward 2017a). In technical terms, EU membership has been expressed primarily through the access the UK and Ireland have to a number of EU programmes and the funding they disburse. The most obvious example of this is the Common Agricultural Policy (CAP). EU subsidies provided through the CAP currently represent 87 per cent of income for Northern Irish farmers compared with 53 per cent for the UK overall (Burke 2017). In 2014, the then Department of Agriculture and Rural Development for Northern Ireland noted that Northern Irish farmers received almost £300m in annual subsidies which they considered 'essential support … sustaining farming communities' (HM Government 2014a, 40).

Funding and support has also been provided through the EU's regional policy, designed to help the EU's most economically disadvantaged regions through the pursuit of a range of Union-wide cohesion objectives (European Commission 2017a). Northern Ireland has thus benefited from the EU's *INTERREG* programme, as well as the dedicated *PEACE* programme, launched in 1995 'as a direct result of the EU's desire to make a positive response' to the peace process (SEUPB, 2017). This has supported projects in Northern Ireland and the border counties of Ireland focused primarily on improving economic and social stability and increasing cohesion between communities affected by the conflict (European Parliament 2017b). In 2014, the UK government's Review of the Balance of Competences reported that more than 100,000 people had gained qualifications through PEACE II funding, and more than 800,000 people on both sides of the border had participated 'in cross-border activities and reconciliation projects' (HM Government 2014b, 52). The PEACE III (2007–13) and PEACE IV (2014–20) programmes, meanwhile, have contributed, or are scheduled to contribute, €225 million and €229 million respectively, with objectives including community reconciliation, economic development and education (Special EU Programmes Body 2017).

Underlining this financial commitment, in 2007 the Barroso Commission established a special Northern Ireland Task Force 'to examine how Northern Ireland could benefit more from EU policies', particularly in terms of encouraging and sustaining economic growth (European Commission 2016). The creation of the NITF is the first time the Commission has created 'a close partnership specifically with one region' in this way (European Commission 2014, 10). These mechanisms have been intended to support the peace process and help drive reconciliation and collaboration. What has made them particularly important is the perception of the EU as being 'neutral' in a way the UK or Irish government cannot be (Bell 2016). In essence, the EU is uniquely positioned to offer a friendly, outside and 'apolitical' hand.

This neutrality has been especially important at the political level. Here the EU's core contribution has been to help depoliticise a range of complex issues including justice and policing, identity, equality and human rights by enabling cooperation between national governments and local communities in the context of broader EU membership. Thus, while the difficult negotiations that have brought about and sustained the peace process over more than 20 years have focused on, and been driven primarily by Belfast, London and Dublin, the institutional framework and normative environment provided by the EU – described by former *Taioseach* Enda Kenny as the EU's 'intangible role' – has been crucial in creating the space for the different sides to move forward (Flanagan 2015, 4).

This indirect facilitation can be discerned in a number of ways. For example, we have seen a dramatic change in the dynamic of relations between London and Dublin which really began their upward trajectory with the 1985 Anglo-Irish Agreement (Tannam 2017). One senior Irish diplomat attributes this in part to the two countries having joined the then EEC at the same time (1973), and since then having spent so long 'sitting around the table together'. Thus, Irish governments have recognised they have 'more in common with the UK than they thought', a view reciprocated in London.[2] For another former Irish *Taoiseach*, John Bruton, the two countries being part of the EU has seen the transformation of a 'bilateral unequal relationship' into 'an equal membership of something bigger than either of them' (House of Lords 2016, 42). If the close intergovernmental cooperation that has developed since 1985 has been 'a fundamental cause of the peace process' (Tannam 2017), for Bruton it is their common EU membership that 'made all the progress that followed possible' (House of Lords 2016, 42).

The EU's institutional contribution, meanwhile, can be seen in the 1998 Good Friday Agreement. Thus, while it is a bilateral treaty, the 'status of the UK and Ireland as EU Member States is woven throughout' (Douglas-Scott 2015, 4), for example in how sensitive issues related to human rights and identity are both framed and addressed. The political settlement established in 1998 is finely tuned, carefully balancing a range of issues of concern to the communities involved. The EU's contribution is to provide what is essentially outside adjudication and a common system of protection based on European law and the principle of equality, something that can be accepted by all parties within the context of EU membership.

One of the clearest expressions of this can be seen in how, prior to the 2016 referendum, the border had largely ceased to be 'an issue of contention' (Bell 2016). Thus, whilst the Good Friday Agreement enshrines Northern Ireland's status as part of the UK until such time as its population decides otherwise, the border itself has softened to the extent that it essentially no longer matters in terms of communication, mobility and trade. Crucially, it has enabled 'Nationalists in Northern Ireland to develop a sense of common identity with fellow EU citizens' in Ireland whilst also addressing Unionist concerns (House of Lords 2016, 43). This 'de-emphasising of state sovereignty' has come about as a result of Europeanisation and the peace process (McCall 2015, 158), with the EU acting as an important 'enabling factor' for peace. Not for nothing, therefore, did Charles Flanagan, Ireland's former foreign minister, suggest that it is in Northern Ireland that 'the EU's positive influence has been most keenly felt' (2015, 4).

2. Northern Ireland's 'hard border' conundrum

Northern Ireland is, of course, not alone in facing challenges from the UK's departure from the EU – all parts of the country will be affected to some extent. However, its unique position and circumstances – not least the current lack of a functioning Northern Ireland Executive to give it a voice – mean there are very specific concerns about the consequences for its economy and political situation, both of which are closely interlinked. While all sides have made clear their commitment to ensuring that the interests of Northern Ireland are properly considered in the negotiations, the region remains 'particularly vulnerable to the potential negative effects of Brexit' (House of Lords 2016, 13) while the Irish government has warned of 'profound implications' for the whole island (Irish Government 2017, 6). For its part, the UK government emphasises that political stability 'is dependent on the continued operation of the Good Friday Agreement's institutions and constitutional framework, effective management of the security environment, and economic prosperity' (HM Government 2017d, 3). The importance of and linkages between each of these are clearly reflected in the issue of the border.

The problem in this regard is clear. Under EU law, the establishment of a hard border would be consistent with the UK government's commitment to withdraw from both the EU's Single Market and Customs Union (and in the event of a 'no deal' scenario, would likely be inevitable). However, this is an outcome that all are seeking to avoid. The UK government has called for 'flexible and imaginative solutions' to the border issue in the context of broader discussions about future UK–EU customs arrangements (HM Government 2017c, 2–3). For its part, and using identical wording, the EU had also previously made such a call 'with the aim of avoiding a hard border, whilst respecting the integrity of the Union legal order' (European Council 2017), and the Irish government has made clear its rejection of any 'visible, "hard" border on the island of Ireland' (Irish Government 2017, 7). The challenge, though, is how to turn these shared aspirations into reality.

As always, the devil lies in the detail, and particularly in how to manage the issues of freedom of movement for people and goods that will have such economic and political significance. Of the two, the movement of individuals is more straightforward. Neither the UK nor Ireland is a member of the Schengen area, with free movement of people across the islands governed instead by rules agreed under the Common Travel Area (CTA) (encompassing the UK, Ireland, Isle of Man and Channel Islands). Alongside these, a range of reciprocal arrangements guarantee rights to residency, voting, health, social welfare and work. The CTA pre-dates by many years both countries' membership of the EU, is recognised in the EU treaties, and is acknowledged in the European Commission's negotiating guidelines as being in conformity with EU law (HM Government 2017d). The UK government's proposal is therefore to continue with the current CTA arrangements, which is relatively uncontroversial.

More difficult, however, are the proposals regarding the movement of goods. Here, the UK is seeking 'as seamless and frictionless a border as possible' (HM Government 2017d, 14), and one involving no form of physical infrastructure. However, it is difficult to see how this will work if the UK is ultimately outside the Customs Union and Single Market. While there is a range of potential options in terms of the UK's future relationship with the EU,[3] these show that the desire to maintain an 'invisible' border is incompatible with the pursuit of an independent international trade policy (e.g. Hayward 2017b) or the avoidance of a costly additional regulatory burden, unless the UK government is willing to countenance some form of special arrangement for Northern Ireland. Doherty et al. (2017) have suggested, for example, that Northern Ireland could join the European Economic Area in its own right. While Simon Coveney, the Irish foreign minister, has suggested that a 'unique political solution' will be required (Cooper & Marks 2017), a development along those lines currently seems unlikely.

Thus, the risk remains that a hard border will be the ultimate outcome. This would result in immediate and significant economic consequences. The economies of Northern Ireland and the Republic are 'deeply interdependent' (House of Lords 2016, 17), with Northern Ireland exporting £2.7 billion of goods to Ireland in 2015, representing 36 per cent of its total goods exports (HM Government 2017d). Indeed, in some sectors it is feasible to talk of an 'all-island market and … and all-island economy' (Doherty et al. 2017, 2), two examples being the Single Energy Market and the aforementioned agricultural sector (House of Lords 2016). Estimates by Ireland's Economic and Social Research Institute are of a potential 20 per cent overall reduction in bilateral trade as a consequence of Brexit, with small companies bearing the brunt of this (Economic and Social Research Institute 2015). Such a contraction in economic activity could be expected to have a major impact on Northern Ireland's economy, which has already suffered significantly and, according to Oxfam, 'disproportionately' from austerity (BBC News 2014). Indeed, given the British government's current economic policy direction, it is unlikely that HM Treasury would be either willing or able to make up the consequent financial shortfalls, for example in funding to agriculture. It has, though, raised the possibility of the UK continuing post-Brexit to participate in the funding of specific initiatives such as the PEACE programmes discussed above (HM Government 2017d). For its part, the Irish government believes Brexit poses 'very significant and serious challenges to its economy'

(Irish Government 2017, 9) and is seeking support from the EU to manage and mitigate the risks to trade with the UK, its largest bilateral trading partner.

The political ramifications of such a development are even less appealing. Northern Ireland's fragile and fractious political settlement, Anglo-Irish intergovernmental relations, and the UK's longer-term post-Brexit relationship with the EU would all be at risk in the event a hard border is re-constituted. The dismantling of physical barriers between North and South was an important element in securing nationalist support for the political process (Gilmore 2015) and has been both 'a symbol of and a dividend from the success of the peace process', transforming the daily lives of people in Northern Ireland and in Ireland's border counties (Irish Government 2017, 20). The practicalities of re-bordering would be hugely complex. Dozens of farms and rural communities sit astride the border and some of the suburbs of Derry/Londonderry now extend across it (Bell 2016). It is hard to see, therefore, how the establishment of a new frontier could avoid their division. It would also entail the building of a physical infrastructure including customs checkpoints, a border security regime, etc. (McCall 2017). In a region still highly sensitive to political symbolism, there would be significant negative associations with such developments. Indeed, McCall warns that Nationalists and Republicans are both likely to interpret this as 'an abrogation' of the 1998 agreement (McCall 2015, 158). Regardless of the fact that such re-bordering would simply be fulfilling the legal and technical responsibilities for managing a frontier between the EU and a non-Member State, it would mark a stark reversal in a political process that has gone a long way to detoxify complex questions surrounding British and Irish sovereignty and identity.[4]

Conclusions

This chapter has sought to provide a brief examination of the potential impact of Brexit on Northern Ireland, and the huge difficulty involved in balancing the Province's unique political and economic circumstances with the UK government's commitment to withdraw the UK from the EU. While the issue of the border is only one aspect of the story, it is nevertheless reflective of the wider problems that need to be considered, particularly: how to sustain Northern Ireland's political settlement and the peace process; how to protect the Anglo-Irish relationship; and, ultimately, what kind of post-Brexit relationship the UK wishes to establish with the EU. It is in the context of Northern

Ireland more than anywhere else that the interlinkages and tensions between UK domestic politics and its Brexit aspirations are thrown into sharpest relief. There remains the risk that Northern Ireland will be used for leverage in the negotiations, with the 'moral imperative' of safeguarding the peace process presented as necessitating a special arrangement for the UK in its future trading relationship with the EU. However, it is hard to imagine that the EU27 will collectively sanction any agreement that weakens the integrity of the legal and regulatory structures upon which the EU is constructed and through which it trades with the wider world. This could potentially leave both Northern Ireland and the Republic paying a significant price for the UK government's pledge that 'Brexit means Brexit'. As the Irish *Taoiseach*, Leo Varadkar, declared in August 2017, this is indeed 'the challenge in our generation'.

12
Something new under the sun?
The lessons of Algeria and Greenland

Kiran Klaus Patel

The UK is the first fully fledged Member State ever to decide to withdraw from the EU. But it is not the first country to do so. While the case of Greenland – an autonomous part of Denmark which left the European Community (EC) in 1985 – is sometimes mentioned in Brexit discussions, other cases are largely unknown. Only five years after the Treaty of Rome, in 1962, Algeria took the same step as part of its assertion of independence from France. And despite all the debates about Brexit, Grexit, and other scenarios in our own times, even among EU experts, few know that the Caribbean island of Saint-Barthélemy, a French overseas collectivity, changed its status in 2012 from an Outermost Region of the EU to that of an Overseas Country or Territory.[1]

This chapter discusses the lessons that can be learned for Brexit from the 'Algexit' of 1962 and the 'Greenxit' of 1985, these being the two cases for which the medium- and long-term effects of withdrawal can be assessed, and for which archival records are available (Patel 2017). It argues that important lessons can be learnt from these earlier experiences, despite the obvious differences from today's situation with the UK. Most importantly, it highlights the complex relationship between processes of integration and disintegration as a more permanent feature of the European integration process than existing research has had it.

Taking (back) control

The stakes were high and the message was clear. The leading representative of the leave camp argued that his island was very special 'in terms of language, culture, economy and social structure'. Moreover, he stressed the islanders' intention of 'developing on the basis of locally generated values.' For all these reasons, it was vitally important to sever the ties with Brussels 'in order to preserve the peculiarity of the country.'[2] While that might sound like Nigel Farage, these were in fact the words of Greenland's Prime Minister Jonathan Motzfeldt, speaking on behalf of Greenland's government prior to the 1982 referendum. On the world's largest island with a population of some 50,000, dissatisfaction with the EC had been gaining momentum for quite some time. Economic arguments centring on the EC's Common Fisheries Policy as a challenge to the island's most important sector coalesced with debates about identity. Already in 1972, when Denmark held an EC membership referendum, 70 per cent of Greenlanders opted against accession, but their vote was overruled by the majority in the country as a whole. Back then, there had been little Greenland could do. After Denmark granted home rule in 1979, however, Greenland held a membership referendum in 1982, which ultimately led to its withdrawal from the European Community three years later.

Sovereignty, self-determination and the desire to take back control played an even bigger role in the Algerian case. The country entered the EC as part of France. When the Treaty of Rome was signed, France still had vast colonial possessions, and the link between metropolitan France and Algeria was particularly strong. Article 227 therefore stipulated that most of the Treaty's regulations also applied to the North African country, which thus became a part of the original community of six Member States. The Algerian War of Independence, waged for eight long years with hundreds of thousands of deaths and many more eventually forced to flee the country, was fought mainly to shake off the yoke of French rule. But, unsurprisingly, the Front de Libération Nationale (FLN) also wanted to cut the connection with the EC. Looking back a few months after independence had been won, Algeria's first president Ahmed Ben Bella deplored the '300 years of colonial domination' and heavily criticised the EC, particularly its nascent Common Agricultural Policy (Ben Bella 1963, 7).

Europe's colonial past is therefore central to explaining why Algeria and Greenland became part of the EC; in both cases, integration into the

European Community did not result from a sovereign decision by the people of the country, but was determined by the will of the motherland. Obviously, the situation of today's UK is markedly different: it first formally applied in the early 1960s, was admitted in 1973, and has since enjoyed all the rights and obligations of full membership. Still, the mix of economic and identity arguments that drove the Brexit campaign has certain parallels in the Algerian and Greenlandic cases. In all three countries, the specific history, values, forms of economic and political governance, and the social fabric all turned into key arguments for withdrawal. The EC/EU was accused of not accommodating these differences. The desire to (re)gain control therefore unites all these cases. This also distinguishes all three of them from the debates about the option of a Greek withdrawal from the eurozone, which was much more about a state's inability to live up to the commitments of membership.

Undoing and reconnecting

Some three months after his aforementioned speech, Ben Bella wrote a letter to the president of the European Commission, Walter Hallstein. Given his public announcements, his request might have come as a surprise. He requested that despite Algeria's withdrawal from the EC, existing rules and regulations should remain in force. Algeria was thus to be treated as if it was still part of the European Community.[3] And what did Greenland's Motzfeldt do in parallel with his leave campaign? As the island's prime minister, he quickly negotiated an association agreement with the EC (Patel 2017). Both countries thus opted for a paradoxical double move. On the one hand, they sought greater sovereignty, control and independence. On the other hand, they were highly interested in maintaining close ties to the EC, mainly for economic reasons.

And, surprisingly, close ties continued to exist in both cases even after withdrawal. Given that Ben Bella wrote his letter on 24 December, one might be tempted to speak of a Christmas miracle since, in fact, the European Community basically accepted Algeria's request. Half a year later, in June 1963, a secret document of the EC Council of Ministers noted that Algeria was treated 'de facto as a Member State of the Community.'[4] Greenland also quickly obtained its association agreement. Several Member States were highly interested in close links with the island, not least due to its rich fishing waters. This holds particularly true for the Federal Republic of Germany, whose fishing lobby pressed Bonn to push this point. Denmark's position was particularly awkward: since

Greenland continued to be part of the Danish Realm (*Det Danske Rige*), it was the Danish government that had to submit the withdrawal proposal in Brussels – despite strongly disliking the islanders' decision. Copenhagen therefore also supported the association deal in an attempt to limit the damage (Patel 2017). The role of the British government is particularly interesting: during the referendum campaign, the Foreign and Commonwealth Office enquired informally in the Danish capital whether it could help positively influence public opinion in Greenland, as London was afraid that the Arctic example might unleash disintegration tendencies elsewhere. Ironically, it was the government of Margaret Thatcher – the nightmare of every Brussels bureaucrat – that was especially concerned about the repercussions of Greenland's exit and worked to avert it.[5]

The situation of the UK today bears both similarities and differences to these processes in Algeria and Greenland. Worlds separate the scope and depth of European integration today from the pre-Maastricht and pre-Lisbon realities of the 1960s and 1980s. Economically and geostrategically, the UK is a giant in comparison to Algeria or Greenland. The international system has changed markedly too, with the end of the Cold War and a new era of insecurity challenging core pillars of governance in Europe and the wider transatlantic context. In the British case, Prime Minister Theresa May has declared that she was prepared to accept hard Brexit and has stressed that she did not want the UK 'half-in, half-out'. She also stated that it was her 'priority' to pursue a 'free trade agreement with the EU' (May 2017a). Negotiations might thus lead to comparably loose ties between the remaining EU and the UK – in the context of the range of relationships the EU has with states such as Norway, Iceland and Switzerland. Still, it reveals that even a large trading and military power such as the UK relies on keeping some close ties with the EU, and that the populist idea of regaining full sovereignty and autonomy is partly impossible.

Incremental solutions

As the cases of Algeria and Greenland reveal, there has never been a default mode for leaving the EC/EU. Today, the Lisbon Treaty's famous Article 50 has created a procedure for withdrawal, although it also leaves a lot of room to decide on the details of the deal. How, then, did Algeria's and Greenland's relationships develop after pulling out? The following assessment will not judge whether the deals were beneficial for one side or the other – for that, much more space would be needed. Instead, it will examine the intensity of the formal ties to the EC/EU – as the more straightforward yardstick that reflects the chapter's interest in the political and legal dimensions of withdrawal.

Algexit can be summarised as a trajectory from 'super-soft' to 'super-hard' and from there again to a softer constellation. For several years in the 1960s, the country retained a precarious special status that kept lawyers awake at night. As late as 1968, an internal EC document maintained that its close relations with Algeria still lacked a clear legal basis. With regard to trade, the country continued to float in an undefined twilight zone, almost as if it was still part of the common market.[6] Gradually, however, Algeria's privileged position crumbled. The EC's Member States started to apply different rules in their trade with the North African country. And as the common Market was established and the common organisation of the market for more and more specific commodities agreed on, the former colony increasingly found itself on the wrong side of the fence. The common organisation of the wine market, established in 1970, was the hardest blow. Around 1960, Algeria had been the globe's fourth largest producer of wine. Domestic consumption was small in the mostly Muslim country, but it was the world's biggest exporter. Wine accounted for half the country's exports, and it mainly traded with EC countries. With the 1970 market organisation, the EC's protectionist Common Agricultural Policy created insurmountable trade barriers, which had a deleterious effect on Algerian wine exports. Algiers complained bitterly about these measures, but to little avail. Meanwhile, wine producers in the Member States were happy to be rid of competitors from the southern shores of the Mediterranean. Today, Algeria produces hardly any wine at all, and this had much to do with its relationship with the EC/EU. In a nutshell, therefore, 'Algexit' also led to 'Alcexit', at least in the longer term (Meloni & Swinnen 2014).

From this low point in the 1970s, EU–Algeria relations slowly improved over the past four decades. Building on several smaller agreements, the two partners concluded an association agreement in 2002 and later added further steps. Still, it has long lost the special status it held in the years immediately after 1962. In many ways, it is now treated as any other North African country; the special ties from a colonial past that impacted on the first decade after independence having withered away.

In contrast, Greenland's exit was consistently soft. Despite the concern about foreign fishermen plundering its rich waters, Greenland agreed to a series of protocols to the association agreement, which granted the EC extensive access to its fisheries, a point insisted on by the West Germans in particular. Since then, relations have intensified further. Today, Greenland is one of the EU's Overseas Countries and Territories, where primary and secondary EU law applies automatically, though with some derogations. Trade relations are so intense that Greenland has, ironically, started to move closer to the EU compared with the situation in 1985. In contrast, devolution within the Danish context has continued, with some activists in Greenland now demanding full independence from the Danish Realm.[7] This could lead to a reversal of the dynamics of the 1980s, when Greenlanders wanted to remain part of the Kingdom, but rejected EC membership.

At this stage, it remains unclear what kind of deal the UK and the EU will ultimately agree on. It is rather unlikely that this question will be answered as quickly as some Brexiteers would like, or within the two-year period stipulated by the Lisbon Treaty. The experience of Algeria and Greenland is a reminder that a new settlement will only be the basis for the next phase, and not the once-and-for-all, clear-cut solution that the exit camp likes to imagine.

Colonial legacies

Taking stock of the historical experience also highlights a dimension that has long seemed obsolete: Europe's colonial past. This was clearly at the core of Algeria's and Greenland's experience, and also impacted on the recent decision of Saint-Barthélemy, an island 'discovered' by Christopher Columbus and, with some interruptions, a French colony since the seventeenth century. Brexit also conjures up a colonial past. Theresa May's optimism, in her 17 January 2017 speech, that the idea of deepening links to 'India, Pakistan, Bangladesh, America, Australia, Canada, New Zealand, countries in Africa' will be met by similar feelings in these former British colonies has yet to prove itself. Moreover, she had a good point about the need to 'strengthen the precious union between the four nations of the UK' (May 2017a): Northern Ireland, whose past some historians consider to be principally colonial history, is obviously a case in point, where one can only hope that the peace agreement will hold. And it is worrying that as soon as the Brexit referendum's results were made public, Spanish Foreign Minister José Manuel García-Margallo declared that the day had come closer when the Spanish flag will fly over Gibraltar (Amón 2016). Disintegration in the EU has the potential to reopen the door to seemingly remote chapters in Europe's unsettled past. Most Europeans have never heard about the 1713 Peace of Utrecht that forced Spain to cede Gibraltar to Great Britain, and a UK withdrawal would obviously ignore the 96 per cent of voters in Gibraltar who opted for 'remain' in the referendum. Not only Northern Ireland and Scotland, but also Gibraltar thus has the potential of turning into a key stumbling block in the Brexit negotiations. So while exit decisions are seemingly about a country's future, they are also closely related to the continent's haunted past.

Conclusions

The cases of Algeria and Greenland demonstrate that withdrawal from the EC/EU is not completely unprecedented. Admittedly, the integration process has changed massively since the 1960s and 1980s, as have the wider European and global contexts. Moreover, the UK is a power of a different calibre than the two earlier 'exiteers'. Still, their trajectories are quite revealing, especially with regard to the motives leading a majority to opt to leave the EC/EU. In addition, in both cases the complex renegotiation process at the moment of exit did not lead to a complete unwinding of ties, and the long-term trajectories after withdrawal were of great importance.

History reveals that the details of the deal, and the historical context informing it, both impacted massively on the eventual outcome. Very often, negotiators on both sides of the table shared an interest in maintaining close ties, at least initially, regardless of public rhetoric. While the exit settlement matters a lot, of course, the substantial minority that opted for 'remain' in the Brexit referendum might yet find some consolation in history. Any deal will be a precursor to the next deal, as this chapter shows, and in that sense, hardly any decision is fully irreversible – for better or for worse.

Finally, examining instances of withdrawal from the EC/EU conveys an important message concerning the history of the European integration process. A careful historical assessment challenges the logic of the 'ever deeper union', as a powerful narrative the EU itself has forged and helped to disseminate. In this standard story, there is no place for phases and processes of disintegration; that is why Brexit is perceived as such a fundamental challenge to the EU. As shown here, however, Brexit would in fact not be the first moment of disentanglement and disintegration in the EU's history. This reminds us how little attention EU history has attracted so far, and that even some basic facts have no impact whatsoever on the public debate. For all the talk about crisis, the European integration process has mastered difficult moments with astonishing resilience. In doing so, it has undergone fundamental transformations, and the multiplicity of crises it presently faces are most worrying. Still, the stakes for the UK are certainly higher than for the EU.

Part Two
Issues and policies

IV: The political economy of Europe

13
What impact will Brexit have on the euro area?

Waltraud Schelkle

A major consequence of Brexit is that the financial centre of the euro area (EA) – the City of London – has decided to cut regulatory ties with the euro area as a whole. The City's role in banking and investment finance in the EA was always an anomaly, made possible primarily by the creation of the Single Market in financial services. The UK government shaped EU legislation in favour of banks that reside in London and use the City as a gateway to the Continent. This was not economic nationalism, since it favoured above all transnational banks, and it was not protectionist since the idea was to foster financial liberalisation in all EU Member States. Rather, it was an exercise in 'economic patriotism' (Clift & Woll 2012, 308–9, Morgan 2012): the idea was to champion free trade in a sector in which the national economy has a comparative advantage. However, economic nationalism has fought back, notwithstanding the rhetoric of 'Global Britain'.

This chapter focuses on the likely effects of Brexit on the EA. What changes are in the offing for a currency area that is abandoned by its major financial centre? The chapter makes three claims in particular: (1) some of the business currently transacted in London will go to the EA, which is a mixed blessing; (2) the EA's regulatory approach will become more attuned to the financial institutions and political preferences prevalent in Continental Europe; and (3) the euro will remain permanently stronger vis-à-vis the British Pound.

Relocation of financial services

The City will certainly lose in relevance for European finance and seems to be resigned to this, although not without lobbying the government for favours. A study by Bruegel assumes, at this stage inevitably arbitrarily, that about 30 per cent of wholesale banking in Europe will relocate from the City to the continent, which would leave London still hanging onto a sizable share of 60 per cent of the European banking industry (Sapir et al. 2017, 5–6). Both the British government and officials in continental Europe have threatened one another with 'competitive' taxation and regulation of banks if they stay or move, respectively. It beggars belief that such open threats of a race to the bottom should be issued on both sides of the Channel: not even ten years have gone by since the biggest financial crisis in post-war history broke out, caused, inter alia, by lax standards and regulatory enforcement. The only silver lining in this is that supervisors, like the member of the Bundesbank's Executive Board responsible for financial supervision, and the Governor of the Central Bank of Ireland, have come out publicly against such archaic offers to transnational finance (Dombret 2017; Sapir et al. 2017, 6).

The reason for the declining relevance of London as a gateway to mainland Europe is that banks stand to lose their 'passporting' right. This is the ability to use a banking licence issued in one Member State to do financial business anywhere else in the EU. Passporting could be substituted by so-called equivalence, by which a bank proves that the jurisdiction from which it has its licence covers all the areas and is as strict in its regulation of the various areas as the EU. But such equivalence decisions cover only the wholesale business, not retail. And they are not permanent: they come under scrutiny each time there is legislative change in one of the two jurisdictions. Besides, the EU has been reluctant to afford US banks such equivalence, which makes it unlikely that it will treat UK banks any more leniently ten years down the line.[1] '[T]he prospects for EU market access through the UK look rather dim', as Andreas Dombret (2017) from the Bundesbank put it.

It is unlikely that the EU-related parts of the City's business and the accompanying jobs will all relocate to a single new centre inside the euro area, such as Amsterdam, Dublin, Frankfurt or Paris (which are the four most frequently mentioned). In fact, some financial business may not go to the EA at all. There is anecdotal evidence that some US banks may relocate to places like Warsaw instead, because they do not trust that the

EA will survive;[2] again, this is made possible by the Single Market and the passport it gives to any and all banks that are incorporated as headquarters or subsidiaries in another Member State. Other US banks may reduce their presence in Europe altogether and relocate to New York, the City's old rival in international finance.

Anglophone observers are always quick to portray any change as yet another nail in the coffin of the euro project. But such speculation demonstrates a rather short memory of the history of European monetary integration. At the height of the crisis in 2008–9, there was a consensus, reaching the echelons of high finance, central banking and supranational regulatory bodies, that financial markets had become too prolific in generating phony assets and that they had become too interconnected and too self-absorbed for their own good, let alone for the good of the rest of the economy (e.g. Bernanke 2016; Turner 2015). If Brexit can contribute to the shrinking of an oversized financial system in the EA, then it may well turn out to be a net benefit for every economy. Political and market pressure will make this hard to resist, though, proving again how hard it is to contain boom–bust cycles and 'excessive financial elasticity' at the national level (Borio 2014).

Relocation of the financial sector to the EA is a mixed blessing from another point of view. It reduces the scope for risk sharing. The Irish bailout in 2011 illustrated how this worked when the UK was still a member of the EU. Banks headquartered in the UK were the largest creditors of Ireland; according to the Bank for International Settlement they were exposed to the tune of around €160 billion on an ultimate risk basis and also held large claims on Spain (around €98 billion). The UK government offered to guarantee €3.8 billion of the €85 billion rescue package for Ireland. A meeting at the Treasury came to the conclusion that this was the best and cheapest insurance it could get for banks for which the British taxpayer would otherwise have been potentially liable. This implicit insurance premium of around 4.5 per cent looked particularly attractive after the UK had performed three years earlier the biggest single bank bailout in history. The rescue of the Royal Bank of Scotland had cost the British taxpayer £113 billion (around €138 billion) by 2013 (HM Government 2014c: para 3.14), costs that were still accumulating by 2017. It was in the EA's interest that the UK financial system was not destabilised even more, as this could have unleashed flight from the pound, a flight that only various central bank swap arrangements would have prevented from turning into a full-on currency crisis, and which would have contributed to the nervous breakdown of markets. The risk sharing also works the other way round. To the extent that British banks with international exposure were rescued by the British taxpayer, the bailouts also stabilised banking systems across the continent. Any relocation of banks will reduce such risk diversification. To make up for it, the overall risk level needs to be brought down by ensuring a smaller, less leveraged and better regulated financial system.

Refocusing the regulatory approach

With the creation of the banking union that came into effect in 2014, the ECB has become the developed world's largest financial supervisor, measured by the banking assets under its purview.[3] The Single Supervisory Mechanism has the responsibility for the licensing and supervision of all euro area banks, but supervises directly only around 130 'Significant Institutions', representing 85 per cent of all bank assets in its jurisdiction. For the rest, it delegates supervision to national authorities and merely supervises their practices. Since financial regulation is no longer national, or even European, the ECB will in future make its voice heard through international fora, such as the G20 and the Basel Committee. Even before the banking union was agreed in June 2012, the European Commission was pro-active in pre-empting US financial regulation and opted for setting standards so as to prevent having to follow standard setting by others (Moloney 2010, 1342–3). To the great dismay of hedge fund managers, it regulated their business. Some of them subsequently became the biggest funders of the Leave campaign.

Even before the crisis, financial re-regulation set the EU on a collision course with the UK. Some of this seems to have been a chosen path: indeed, the Cameron administration apparently preferred litigation to negotiation, as these examples attest to.

- The UK challenged the Financial Transaction Tax (C-209/13 *UK v Council*): the UK wanted the Court to annul the introduction of the tax under enhanced cooperation because it deemed it to be costly for non-participating countries, since the tax would be levied on any transaction in which one party is from any of the 11 participating countries. The UK lost the case.
- The UK government also took other EU legislators to court (C-270/12 *UK v European Parliament and Council*) regarding the prohibitions of short-selling and other aspects of credit default swaps. The UK disputed whether the newly created European Securities Market

Authority had the authority to conduct interventions in financial markets that would suspend, temporarily, the short-selling of financial instruments or buying of credit default swaps if the orderly functioning of markets so requires (notably a downward spiral of asset prices). Again, the UK lost the case.

- The UK government wanted the capping of bankers' bonuses annulled (C-507/13 *UK* v *European Parliament and Council*). It disputed that the EU has the right to restrict the variable element in the remuneration of 'material risk takers' in financial institutions. The UK dropped the case after the Advocate General delivered his opinion that the case should be dismissed by the Court.

The dilemma for the UK government is now stark: as soon as the UK wants to act on its preferences, or has to give in to the lobbying of hedge funds and bonus-seeking bankers, equivalence of UK and EU financial regulation becomes a distant prospect.

A test case may soon arise, namely that regarding the jurisdiction of central counterparties.[4] This multi-billion currency business is to clear claims and liabilities arising, mainly, from trillions of derivatives. These clearing houses emerged as a consequence of financial re-regulation after the crisis of 2008–9. The international regulatory community at the G20 level agreed to reduce shadow banking and the risk of over-the-counter derivatives, the latter being the main activity of central counterparties. Over-the-counter means that these financial instruments are not traded on an exchange but between two market parties; so if one side fails to meet the contract this may trigger a liquidity crisis for the other party, and because the sums involved are so huge, this can easily spread across the market. Clearing houses can reduce this risk since only net payments have to be met by each party, and the central counterparty itself acts like a mutual insurance fund in that it can meet the obligations of the failing party out of the 'margins' it requires each party to pay. An additional problem may arise, however, if the clearing house – that tends to hold open positions overnight that are in the order of one billion euros – has a currency mismatch (i.e. not enough funds in the currency that the failing party was supposed to deliver). Hence, central bank cooperation is required.

In 2011, the ECB announced that central clearing in euros has to happen in its jurisdiction. The UK government challenged this requirement as discriminating under Single Market rules. The Court case T-496/11 *United Kingdom of Great Britain and Northern Ireland* v *European Central Bank (ECB)* was decided in the UK's favour: the Eurosystem Oversight Policy Framework was annulled on the ground that the ECB referred to 'securities' for which the central bank has no mandate. This wording can easily be changed. The ECB kept a brave face and sent a signal of cooperation shortly before the referendum, entering immediately into a formal swap agreement with the Bank of England that would give the latter unlimited access to euros. But it is not clear that this is the last word. Andreas Dombret, the Bundesbank's supervision tsar, was quoted as saying that euro-clearing can stay in the UK only if its authorities comply with the European Market Infrastructure Regulation (Marsh 2017).

Strengthening of the euro vis-à-vis the pound

The breadth and depth of the financial system are vital determinants of an exchange rate. We should expect the euro to strengthen permanently vis-à-vis the pound sterling as the role of the City of London diminishes and international financial regulation reflects continental European preferences more strongly, as argued above. This may help to recalibrate trade (im)balances between the two currency areas, although UK services exports to mainland Europe will likely be adversely affected by Britain exiting the Single Market. The negative effect on UK's export of services will be muted by the fact – well-established in the economics of intra-industry trade between advanced economies – that the competitiveness of core export industries in advanced economies depends less on costs (as determined by the exchange rate) than on strong brands, innovation and logistics.

It is hard to say how this will play itself out when it comes to the euro area's internal imbalances. The following table shows the UK's main trading partners and the UK net trade balance in goods and services for 2014.

As Figure 13.1 shows, the UK has a deteriorating trade balance with the EU as a whole. At the beginning of 2016, the main EU trading partners of the UK were, on the import side (and in order of magnitude): Germany, China, the US, the Netherlands and France; and on the export side: the US, Germany, France, the Netherlands and the Irish Republic.[5] Three out of five main importers, then, and four out of five main export destinations, are in both the EU and the euro area. A strengthening of the euro vis-à-vis the British pound would rebalance trade with strong trading nations in the euro area. On the whole, this would be unproblematic and arguably beneficial for both sides.

A further consideration, however, is whether the transition to a stronger effective (trade-weighted) euro will have an additional disinflationary effect on the EA economy.[6] This would be problematic, since

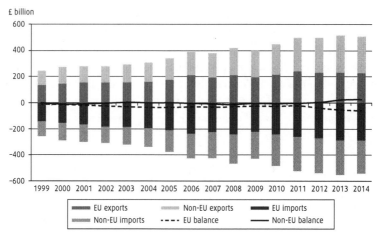

Figure 13.1 UK exports, imports and trade balance to EU and non-EU countries

Source: Office for National Statistics

it is the opposite of what the euro area economy needs to bolster its recovery. Low growth and low inflation (even deflation in some sectors) make already onerous debt burdens more difficult to serve leading to a surge of non-performing loans. The plight of Italy, with its conservative banking system that had not financed a bubble that burst, is a warning sign of how debt may become unsustainable in an environment of low growth and low inflation.

Unlikely changes

Having enumerated the three most likely changes that will follow British withdrawal from the EU, it is worth pointing out two possible changes that are not very likely. The first concerns the potential for a breakdown in central bank coordination. While central bank cooperation may be affected by the UK's withdrawal, the crisis management of 2009–10 showed that central banks have become quite accustomed to coordinating their rescue operations effectively. Indeed, this has been the case ever since the breakdown of the Bretton Woods system in the 1970s. In 2009–10 a network of swap lines prevented currency attacks on Eastern European currencies, while a swap line between the Bank of England and the ECB supported Irish banks exposed to net claims in pounds sterling. These were made into a standing arrangement between six central banks in October 2013: the US Federal Reserve, the ECB, the Bank of England, the Bank of Japan, the Swiss National Bank and the Bank of Canada (also called the C6). The cost-effective prevention of currency crises in open economies is in the interest of all countries trading with, and investing in, each other; this will not change with the UK's withdrawal from the EU.

A second unlikely scenario is a wholesale decline in the perceived value of EA membership. The threat of currency crises makes it unlikely that other countries' desires to seek or maintain euro area membership will be affected by the UK's withdrawal. Even at the height of the crisis, Baltic countries joined the EA: Estonia in January 2011, Latvia in 2014 and Lithuania in 2015. This was, moreover, not because there existed overwhelming popular support for membership or pressure on them to join. Rather, policymakers in these countries realised that EA membership would make their economies less exposed to current account crises and less dependent on the goodwill of foreign central banks. The cross-border payments system, TARGET, eliminates foreign exchange constraint and provides insurance against a sudden stop of trade finance (Schelkle 2017, Chapter 9). Furthermore, the Single Supervisory Mechanism now protects them against the ring-fencing of liquidity by supervisors in other euro area countries.[7] For these small economies, giving up the exchange rate does not mean losing a policy instrument, since they would have to follow the moves of the ECB anyhow. The peripheral Member States of the EU do not have the advantages of the UK, which is an old financial power with an established reputation that it will not default on its foreign debt, and hence they are unlikely to take any cue from the UK's withdrawal.

In sum, Brexit is likely to have negative effects on the EA. Contrary to what some policymakers seem to think about those trying to attract parts of the City into their jurisdiction, the relocation of financial services into the monetary union may well turn out to be a cost for these jurisdictions. Contingent liabilities for this crisis-prone sector will increase and the relocation will reduce risk sharing between the two currency areas, although by how much is hard to predict. Other effects, such as that on financial regulation in the EA and on trade with the UK, are more ambiguous and probably of second-order relevance.

14
The Brexit iceberg

Chris Bickerton

There is a way of thinking about Brexit that has proven popular because it is of comfort both to the UK and to the remaining 27 Member States of the EU. This is to view Brexit as a curiously British affair, important in the short term for the EU but of limited wider significance. Those who think this way within the UK see Brexit as an affirmation of the country's distinctive traditions and as a means by which the UK can regain its rightful place in global politics – in Europe, but not a direct part of it, and a bridge between Europe and the US (Rachman 2016).[1] The continental version of this view welcomes Brexit as the first step towards deeper European integration. As a prominent French journalist put it, a day after the 23 June EU referendum vote, 'My English friends, thank you for your sacrifice' (Quatremer 2016).

Far from being a unique or isolated event, however, we should think of Brexit as an iceberg: merely the visible portion of a much larger and more powerful mass below the surface that needs to be properly studied and understood (Bickerton 2017b). This is not to suggest that European disintegration is just around the corner but rather to draw out from Brexit some points of connection with wider trends that are affecting Europe as a whole. Three such points of connection are discussed below: political contestation after Brexit; economic growth models and their interaction with the EU's Single Market; and the relationship between Brexit and the structure of the modern European state. In effect, what follows is analysis of the political, the economic and the constitutional spheres as they relate to the UK's decision to leave the EU.

An EU of discontent

Critics of the British press believe it has fuelled a nationalistic anti-Europeanism that has few parallels elsewhere in Europe. In fact, the UK is representative of a growing division in Europe on the matter of European integration. Politicians and political scientists alike frame this as a more general struggle between the winners and losers of globalisation, of which the EU is a symptom rather than a cause.[2] By virtue of its openness to trade and its flexible labour market, the UK has done better in some ways than other EU Member States in dealing with the effects of globalisation. In France, the combined vote for Marine Le Pen and Jean-Luc Mélenchon – two explicitly Eurosceptic candidates – in the first round of the country's presidential election was 14.5 million votes, around 40 per cent of French citizens who voted. Elsewhere in Europe, Eurosceptic parties and movements have become key political players at the national level. In Italy, the Five Star Movement (M5S) regularly tops opinion polls. The M5S has fudged its position on the euro but has made the issue of 'monetary sovereignty' a central part of its platform. The other leading opposition party in Italy is the Northern League, a long-standing Eurosceptic voice in Italy.

The precise meaning of Euroscepticism differs across national contexts and there is a marked difference between eurozone and non-eurozone Member States. The EU's critics find it hard to win support for exiting the eurozone, as Marine Le Pen has discovered. However, far from being popular it is common to hear people say that they regret having joined the euro but that now they are in the eurozone they are stuck with it. The expectation that membership of the euro would translate into a political and social community – widely held by all those who lauded the project in the course of the 1990s and early 2000s – has proven unfounded (McNamara 2015; Streeck 2016a, Chapter 7). The euro has brought forth greater heterogeneity than before and structural differences between national economies (so-called 'supply-side factors') are the basis of powerful intra-eurozone forms of competition. Accepting that the euro is a 'trap' (Offe 2015) from which it is very difficult to escape is quite different from a positive sense of belonging, though interpreters of polling data tend to confuse the former with the latter.

The mainstreaming of Euroscepticism does not mean other countries will follow the UK in leaving the EU. Many contingencies produced the Brexit outcome, including the poor pro-EU campaign and political rivalries within the British Conservative Party (Cummings 2017b). Other institutional factors – such as being outside the eurozone – made the UK's exit relatively easier to contemplate than for most other countries.

Moreover, what we are really seeing in Europe is not so much a deepening antagonism between Member States and the EU. It is rather a widespread crisis in state–society relations, where national party systems find themselves convulsed by the forces of popular disaffection and disenchantment with mainstream politics. These forces overwhelmed the UK's EU referendum and they are exerting powerful effects elsewhere in Europe. The EU may appear shielded from direct criticism, but if Member State governments are unable to rule authoritatively because of a hollowing out of their national political life, then this leaves the EU as a weak and ineffectual regional body.[3]

One market, many growth models

Brexit had many causes and it would be wrong to single out economic factors. However, if one looks at the political economy of Brexit then there are clear lessons for the rest of Europe. The nub of the matter is that national growth models mediate heavily the experience people have of European economic integration. In the British case, this interaction produced results that helped push the UK out of the EU. In other countries, the results are different but the lesson is the same: there may be one European Single Market, but there are many different national growth models. Each model has its strengths and weaknesses but the Single Market makes it very difficult to reform these models, leading to a build-up of pressures.

In Britain's case, the economy grows by expanding the labour market. This has the effect of boosting aggregate demand and injecting life into the country's service sector-dominated economy (Baccaro & Pontusson 2016). This model delivers low levels of unemployment – even outside the booming Southeast of England – but is associated with low productivity and low wage growth, both of which are prominent features of open labour markets (Giles 2017).[4] The only way the labour market can grow, in the absence of significant domestic population growth, is through high levels of net immigration. For this reason, the free movement of labour is at the heart of the UK's experience of the Single Market. This aspect of the British growth model has received much less attention than the other, more fashionable part, namely the very high reliance on credit as a way of compensating for stagnant real wages, what Colin Crouch calls 'privatised Keynesianism' (Crouch 2009). Commentary around Brexit and immigration has focused on the themes of xenophobia and racism but the core of the matter lies in the nature of the British growth model.

This mediation of Single Market rules through national growth models produces very different results in other parts of Europe. In some countries, such as Romania, Bulgaria and in the crisis-hit economies of Spain, Greece, Italy and Ireland, net emigration is the great worry and criticisms of the EU focus on fears of a 'brain drain'. Elsewhere, in countries with heavily regulated labour markets such as in France and Sweden, protest has centred on 'posted workers' and the clash between national labour codes and the rules regulating EU migrant labour.

The German growth model is fundamentally different from the British one. The focus is on building export surpluses, with little consideration given to aggregate demand. Indeed, Germany's huge balance of payment surpluses exists only because of a long-standing policy – supported by the German trade union movement – of wage and price suppression. Whilst Germany has been an economic success story from an aggregate perspective, when one looks inside the country the results are more mixed (Bickerton 2017c). The euro-equivalent of Poundland shops dominate the high streets in many ostensibly wealthy German cities. Labour market and welfare state reforms in Germany have created a large group of people who have seen their incomes stagnate since the mid-2000s. If we add to that the effect of negative interest rates on a country with a high savings rate we can begin to understand why there is so much opposition in Germany to the idea of a European fiscal transfer union. 'We've not had it easy', goes the argument, 'so why should we help out the Greeks and the Italians?' The political consequences of this interaction between the German growth model and European economic integration are not as dramatic as Brexit but they are shaping the EU in profound ways. They go a long way to explaining why Germany took the line that it did during the eurozone crisis and why further integration of the eurozone is politically off the agenda.

The Single Market radicalises the differences between national growth models whilst at the same time making it harder to change the models themselves. The pressures this produces go well beyond the Brexit result in the UK's 2016 EU referendum.

The endurance of Member Statehood

A final way in which Brexit unites the UK with the rest of the EU is that it has been an exemplary lesson in what it means for a 'Member State' to leave the EU. The term 'Member State' refers to a distinctive form of statehood and not just a legal title referring to formal membership of the EU (Bickerton 2012, 2017a). The UK underwent its own transformation from nation-state to Member State. As a result, Brexit poses more than just juridical and regulatory challenges. As a process, Brexit makes demands upon the British state that presume it to be and to act like a nation-state, when in fact it has become a Member State. This puts the British state under acute constitutional, administrative, political and social pressures. As Ross McKibbin observed, the EU has become 'as much a part of the structure of the British state as the Union with Scotland once was' (McKibbin 2014).

The characteristics of Member Statehood shape the Brexit process in manifold ways. The European orientation of the administrative British state was on show throughout the referendum campaign, with major British institutions – such as the Bank of England and the Treasury, and the 'deep state' of the higher education sector – openly backing the Remain campaign. The lack of planning around Brexit, itself a symptom of the deep Europeanisation of the British state, has placed a huge post-referendum burden on the civil service, which is now struggling to manage.

Brexit has challenged another feature of Member Statehood, namely the orientation towards problem-solving and consensus-building within institutional settings where all parties share the same basic political outlook.[5] In effect, Brexit has obliged British diplomats to act in ways that are quite alien to them, in particular with regards hard bargaining and assessing important trade-offs. Rather than accepting the costs of leaving as a price worth paying, we have seen prolonged equivocation on the part of British officials about whether there will be any cost associated with Brexit at all. 'Having your cake and eating it', a phrase that was the butt of many jokes in the media, points directly to this inability to think in terms of costs and benefits. An earlier example was David Cameron's letter to the president of the European Council. Setting out the UK's various 'baskets' of demands; the language used suggested that the goal was not to defend the British national interest but rather to transform the EU for the better. It was very difficult to tell if the prime minister saw himself as defending the national or the European interest, as the boundaries between the two had become, by that point, quite blurred.

It is also noteworthy that there has been a great reluctance to accept that Brexit means the UK is 'going it alone' in any meaningful way. Nationalist histories of the past – including that of the UK – have made much of the ability to 'stand alone' but in the UK's case even confident Brexiters have sought the comfort of wider communities such as the 'Anglosphere' or the Commonwealth (Bell, 2017). The referendum campaign itself never addressed directly the issue of the UK's status as an outsider. Even discussions about leaving the Single Market or the Customs Union were muted. Instead, there was an extensive debate about which 'model' the UK would adopt. Critics of this discussion talked of a 'bespoke arrangement' for the UK, which had comforting echoes of receiving special treatment and of not being left out in the cold. This refusal to consider Brexit as the state transformational challenge that it is continues into the post-referendum period. British civil servants currently working within the Department for Exiting the European Union (DExEU) are, for instance, only seconded – for a term of two years – from their original ministries, the implication being that their services will only be needed for this short interim and transitional period. This is clearly a dramatic under-estimation of the administrative challenges posed by Brexit.

The relevance of the British experience for the other EU Member States is clear. As Member States rather than nation-states, they also constitute themselves as discrete political communities through their participation in wider networks of rule, from the EU through to the G20, the United Nations (UN) and the WTO. Self-government and the ability to construct a national will that stands apart from other national wills is as alien to these other EU Member States as it is to the UK. The Greek example is telling here. It was only the eccentric and self-absorbed person of Varoufakis who could attempt to stand up to the Eurogroup, the Greek state as a whole being unable to contemplate life outside of either the eurozone or the EU. Opposition to the Troika was thus limited to mere grandstanding, with the Greek people left to pick up the pieces.

Brexit raises the fundamental issue of representation and the capacity of a state to represent to the outside world the collective and popular will. Member statehood is premised on a horizontal understanding of power and legitimacy where it is being a part of the wider community that matters most. The authority of governments is the borrowed authority of this wider group. Brexit thus reveals in a dramatic fashion the way in which Member States struggle to fulfil even their most basic functions of self-government associated with the model of the sovereign state. This is by no means only a British affair. It is also an urgent issue for all European citizens who believe in the capacity – and duty – of governments to represent the will of their citizens.

Conclusions

This chapter has argued that Brexit should not be treated as an exceptional and standalone phenomenon, isolated from the rest of the European continent. Though it is unlikely that other countries will follow suit in the near future, Brexit nevertheless expresses some fundamental tensions present within the project of 'ever closer union'. It is something of an irony that it is precisely in its decision to exit the EU that the UK has identified itself as a European state, whose trajectory and fate have many lessons for the EU's 27 remaining Member States.

15
The new crisis of ungovernability

Abby Innes

The Brexit vote represented, in the most part, a public reaction against radically increased material insecurity, frustration with political elites seen to collude with international business at the public expense, despair of public services wreathed in regulatory red-tape and perverse decisions and, finally, austerity. And yet the root of these phenomena with which the EU became associated can be traced back not to Britain's accession to the then EEC in 1973, but to the state reforms initiated at the national level within liberal market economies over the past 30 years. Indeed, within Europe, Britain has been at the forefront of these reforms, initiated by Margaret Thatcher's Conservative governments during the 1980s. To the extent that the case for Brexit was built on the claim that the EU alone was the root of these evils it should be understood as a tragic exercise in misdirected blame, particularly since, insofar as the EU became increasingly supportive of these reforms, it did so directly at the behest of successive UK governments. If the Brexit vote was largely based on opposition to these policies then it is diagnostically important that these phenomena be traced back to their original source in the state reforms of the past three decades, which is the aim of this chapter.

Over the last 30 years liberal market economies have transformed the character of their states through privatisation, outsourcing, internal managerialism and agencification, and through the rejection of interventionist industrial policies and the development of 'quasi-markets' in welfare provision. These changes have been pursued in parallel to increasingly 'competitive', market-conforming tax and regulatory regimes that at the same time reduce the social requirements on corporate capital. These measures have been driven by the dominant

New Right diagnosis of the economic and state crises of the 1970s, justi-
fied by the analysis of the public choice or 'supply-side' school of economics aligned with the Chicago School. This diagnosis said that the
self-aggrandising and bureaucratic 'Leviathan' state was essentially to
blame for these crises, rather than other factors such as technological
change, the Nixon shock, the end of Bretton Woods, the oil crises or conflicting craft unions. However, far from producing better government for
less money, these pro-market state reforms have caused a new crisis of
ungovernability that is far more profound than the original.

The problem is that very few supply-side reforms have worked on
the terms by which they were publicly validated. Instead they have created new organisational pathologies that have served to aggravate rather
than reduce the social polarisation resulting from de-industrialisation in
the 1970s and the liberalisation of capital movement after the 1980s.
Capital mobility and technological change spurred the growth of multinational companies and these have in turn found increasing scope for
deploying regulatory and tax arbitrage between newly competing, rather
than coordinating, states. Not only have state reforms failed to deliver
a more efficient state and more socially inclusive economic growth, but
the unprecedented increase in the porosity of these states to business
involvement has enabled more political corruption and conflicts of interest. This has created the most damaging possible scenario for democratic
capitalism. In this situation the mainstream political elites are seen to
instrumentalise the powers of the state for party political or even private
gain while simultaneously withdrawing its protections from the public.

If we look back through the last 30 years we have a history of
increasingly bi-partisan efforts towards the marketisation of the state
in accordance with supply-side orthodoxies that hold most of the modern functions of the state to be suspect. New Labour reversed multiple Thatcherite reforms but critically, over successive governments, it
opened up welfare services to taxpayer-funded private providers on an
experimental basis while moving more wholeheartedly towards regulatory and tax competition, leading a social democratic shift in the same
vein in much of the rest of Europe. New Labour saw in the creation of
a mixed-market state the possibility of combining wealth creation with
greater efficiency and responsiveness in public service provision: that
consumer choice would keep the middle classes attached to the welfare
state. But with the end of the social democratic veto on private provision for public goods the route was opened for the massive extension of
these reforms by subsequent right wing governments in which supply-
side thinking increasingly dominated.

Unfortunately the assumptions behind supply-side criticisms of the modern state are fundamentally flawed for at least two reasons. Firstly, this critique of the state is based on an abstract, super-reductionist understanding of really-existing states. Supply-siders see the state as equivalent to a monopoly business firm or cartel, with radically dispersed and hence inattentive shareholders (read: voters!). In this approach the monopoly or cartel has become the presiding stylised fact in deductive modelling of the state and its sins (Brennan & Buchanan 1980; Niskanen 1973; Tullock 1965; Dunleavy 1991). With these extreme normative working assumptions the state is depicted as being doomed to operate with all the negative tendencies of a monopoly, such as exploitative price-making, parasitic rent-seeking and general budgetary greed and institutional complacency and inefficiency. Clearly, if you conceive of the state in this narrowly economistic way then the only rational solution is to break up the monopoly wherever possible and subject it to market forces, but the argument is circular rather than empirically founded.

The second flaw in supply-side reasoning, even if you find purchase in the diagnosis, is the failure to anticipate the practicalities of marketising the really-existing state. As a different body of economic theory – namely, of contract and property rights – warns, the higher the complexity of a good or product the higher the risk of 'asymmetrical' contracts in which the seller has more information than the buyer and hence has built-in opportunities to exploit that buyer (Barr 2015; Hart et al. 1997). Transaction cost theory, which considers the 'friction' costs of contractual negotiation and compliance, shows that trying to manage such contracts leads to massively increased costs (Williamson 2002). These costs can hardly be rendered efficient because of the intrinsically unbalanced nature of the original contract (Baker et al. 2002, 41). The analogy between state and firm also elides the fact that a failed firm reallocates labour and capital resources in a way that is painful in the short term, whereas a failed state collapses the main mechanism for social integration and public order *per se* (Shaxson & Christensen 2016).

The vast majority of the tasks and goods provided by modern states violate most of the preconditions for efficient markets, such as perfect information between buyers and sellers, no external effects not priced in the original transaction ('externalities') and no interdependencies between buyers and sellers. As Hans Werner Sinn remarked of regulatory and tax competition between states, 'since governments have stepped in when markets have failed [historically], it can hardly be expected that a reintroduction of the market through the backdoor of systems competition will work. It is likely to bring about the same kind of market failure that brought about government intervention in the first place' (Sinn 1997, 249). And indeed it has, but in the meantime the now profoundly 'hybridised' UK state has developed distinct pathologies of its own.

The supply-side theory of the state as a scheming Leviathan anticipated nothing about what would happen when marketisation of the state necessarily failed to produce a competitive market as a result of the nature of the goods and services it provides. After 30 years the evidence suggests that introducing choice and competition into the state and between states produces the worst, rather than the best, of both public and private regimes. In the case of tax and regulatory competition, the largest, wealthiest firms in particular have increasingly escaped their share of the fiscal contract via a race to the bottom on rates, standards and enforcement. They have also pushed the burden for continuing taxation onto less mobile factors such as labour and small- and medium-sized enterprises, while producing no evident compensatory dividend in greater productive investment or increased growth (Shaxson & Christensen 2016). In the meantime, the evidence for the profound market and regulatory failures behind the global financial crisis is comprehensive. In the case of welfare, the norm has become one of profit-seeking firms engaged at the tax-payers' expense but in thoroughly non-competitive conditions which force the state into Kafkaesque games of regulatory catch-up because of its ongoing statutory responsibility for outcomes. These are textbook scenarios for 'moral hazard', in which private providers have few incentives to avoid risky or perfunctory behaviour because of *de facto* (publicly funded) insurance. And of course such hazards existed in theory in the vertically integrated state, but with fewer transaction costs, minus the profit motive and (whisper it) offset by a vocational sense of public service.

Today's taxpayer-funded quasi-markets in welfare and public service provision are characterised either by highly fragmented systems, such as the poorly regulated private trusts with low economies of scale seen in Academy schools, or by public service industry oligopolies, with the necessary conditions for efficient competition a rarity. Public service companies like G4S, SERCO and Capita have a proven tendency to sweat the guaranteed public funding while only producing 'satisficing' – that is to say perfunctory, low-quality – performance within hard-to-monitor contracts, which explains the higher costs, lower service quality and increased regulatory oversight of the services in question. Moreover, this oversight is largely doomed to ineffectiveness because the most important activities in schools, prisons, hospitals, etc. cannot be codified, and attempts to codify them increase transaction costs whilst incentivising behaviour towards box-ticking at the expense of the core but uncodified tasks. Even the quickest study of Communist central planning would have warned supply-siders that overbearing regulatory control and sanction creates multiple systemic informational and organisational distortions and contributes to professional demoralisation.

The problem, which is relatively hidden from the service-using public, but which is equally serious, is that the increasing role for private businesses is replicated throughout the entire state administration. This has caused extensive administrative and informational fragmentation and hence, again, those increased transaction costs. After a sabbatical in the Cabinet Office, Matthew Flinders argued that institutional fragmentation and the bureaucratic Taylorism of agencification had ended the capacity of UK central government to operate 'meta-governance' over state authority (Flinders 2008). But this process of disintegrating state capacity has only intensified after 2010 and 2015 under the supply-side policies of the Conservatives. The process of Brexit is going to reveal how critically weak the capacity of the UK state has become.

According to one of the very few studies that evaluates these reforms over the long term, Ruth Dixon and Christopher Hood find that reported administration costs in the UK have actually risen by 40 per cent in constant prices over the last 30 years, despite a third of civil service numbers being cut over the same period, whilst total public spending over the same period has doubled. Most significant of all, they find that running costs have been driven up the most in the outsourced areas. Service failures, complaints and judicial challenges have at the same time soared (Dixon & Hood 2015). This is in no respect the 'better government for less money' heralded across the political aisles.

The UK is now experiencing a crisis of supply in social care and in the NHS and an unprecedented recruitment and retention crisis for doctors and teachers. Indeed, one recent YouGov poll showed that over half of the UK's teachers contemplate leaving the profession within the next two years (Boffey 2015). These shortages are exacerbated by the new ambiguity surrounding the immigration status of EU nationals and the rate of EU nationals leaving the NHS has already accelerated sharply since the referendum. UK trains are roughly six times more expensive than those on continental Europe (Khan 2017). The UK recently saw the worst prison riot in decades at the G4S-run HMP Birmingham. UK prisons now have the highest suicide rate since records began (BBC News 2017). But not only do these reforms repeatedly fail to deliver on their promises, they have also undermined the democratic accountability of the state by undercutting the government's ability to reverse failing or unpopular policies. State autonomy is undermined when authority is given to unaccountable and poorly regulated private business actors on long-term and highly informationally asymmetric contracts. The National Audit Office, for example, has declared the financial statement of the Department of Education to be unsafe and unsound for the second year running (National Audit Office 2017). At the same time, via the creation of Academy Schools, parents have lost their legal rights of redress in a system that performs more poorly on the gaming of league tables and on exclusions and attainment for disadvantaged students compared with Local Education Authority (LEA) maintained schools, because the legal contract now stands between the Secretary of State and the legally private institution of individual Academy Trusts, of which there are now thousands. In the meantime, supply-side reforms have created major business interests in the perpetuation of these policies and increased the structural dependence of the state on individual businesses. It is hard to imagine a system more productive of a popular perception that political elites collude with business at the expense of the public interest. But since the leading Brexiteers are also the strongest exponents of these already failed state reforms, that sense of public disillusionment may actually worsen once they deepen these practices and the EU is no longer available as the target of frustration. However, there is a serious risk that other more xenophobic and less potentially constructive narratives will be brought into play first.

So why isn't there a public debate about the systemic crisis of the state, as occurred in the 1970s? One reason is that this crisis does not fall neatly between party lines as it did in the 1970s. The expressive function of the main parties is not aided by the fact that all the most powerful actors in this system, from the political parties to large public industry corporations and the City, are implicated in its creation. Nor is an effective party political debate encouraged by the fact that business representatives now form some 30 per cent of senior civil service appointments, constitute the majority of non-executive board directors in every department, and can be brought in as special policy advisors through a revolving door that now spins – without serious regulation or sanction – both in and out of government. The system of party political finance in this context has become a political economy of its own.

The double standards are stark if one compares the relentless criticism of Britain's failing industrial corporatism in the 1970s to that of the corporatist relationship between the City of London and the UK Treasury, though the City's neglect of national developmental needs is an entrenched historical tendency (Crouch 2005, 146–7). If warring UK craft unions were a restraint on UK productivity in the 1970s, then why is there no equivalent outcry today over the fact that tax and regulatory competition have contributed more evidently to the financial crisis and the financialisation of firms than to either their improved productive capacity or innovation potential? And why are the City and the Treasury not deemed unhealthily close when this relationship produces a dystopian vision of the UK as a tax haven (Withnall 2017)? Even if supply-side reforms had not built so powerful a constituency for their extension it would be politically awkward for mainstream parties to call for actively rebuilding the state after so many years of insisting on its comparative inefficiency. But that criticism was only ever coherent in the light of the analogy between state and firm: an analogy that not only ignores the historical role of the state in making and sustaining markets but also the entire body of behavioural economics regarding the theory of firms that questions their profit-seeking efficiency, and understands them as complex institutions prone to internal opportunism and contractual failures.

Is it any wonder, then, that those with the poorest life chances in this economy in particular despair of mainstream parties? It is the populists alone who have said 'we feel your pain'. The trouble is that the UK's populists argue that the voters' problems have been caused exclusively by the EU. The more glaring truth is that many voters are disappointed because mainstream UK parties – sometimes aided, sometimes countered by EU policy – have, over the last 30 years, made the state both an inefficient public regime and a poorly performing market. Indeed, they have succeeded only in creating a chaotic hybrid state that is now prone to all the rent-seeking and exploitative behaviours, along with byzantine and bureaucratic attempts at regulatory catch-up, which supply-siders are supposed to abhor. But on these failures the supply-siders have had nothing consequential to say. As for the main opposition party, in the continuing absence of a coherent analysis of why supply-side reforms have failed, Labour leader Jeremy Corbyn looks like a time traveller from the state crisis of the 1970s, while the Blairites just look guilty.

One of the most remarkable ironies of Brexit is that it is the supply-siders who are now in the driving seat who have done so much to discredit the efficacy of the state and, by extension, its executive, while passing the blame largely onto the EU: if we were looking for appropriate culpability then *exactly* the wrong faction won. If you consider the politics of Michael Gove, Iain Duncan Smith, David Davis or Boris

Johnson in the UK, these are supply-side militants still determined to disintegrate the institutions of the state and rent out its authority to the private sector.

The persistence of supply-side reforms in the face of their demonstrable failure is consequently profoundly politically dangerous as well as socially damaging. Ironically, though predictably, these failures will be intensified under any Brexit outcome engineered by the chief exponents of supply-side reform. In the short term, it is hard to be optimistic. It is not clear how this trend to political polarisation can be reversed without a radical shift in the political economic paradigm, since the UK production regime, like that in the USA, offers up an increasingly divergent set of social interests. The knowledge economy encourages a dramatic shift in the producer coalition landscape and the welfare regime that it favours. There were distinct patterns in the Brexit vote and the 2016 US election of divergent voting preferences between the centres of the new knowledge economy – rooted in ICT and services – and those of the rural, industrial and mid-range technology economies. These trends support a worrying thesis (Schwartz 2017), which is that there are deepening structural divisions in advanced capitalist economies between those higher educated voters who feel able to self-insure in minimal or failing state conditions, and therefore prefer the dynamism of highly liberalised economies, versus those with little hope of achieving a stake in that system. Such massive social polarisation, particularly in a majoritarian electoral system, is inimical to compromise, consensus and democracy.

V: Law and justice

16
The ties that bind

Securing information-sharing after Brexit

Deirdre Curtin

Introduction

The history of European integration has for many decades been one of
unity and, at the same time, one of differentiation. As the EU has moved
into areas that were previously exclusive to the nation-state, such as
criminal law and border control, a preference by some Member States for
'outsiderness' over full membership has progressively come to the fore.
The UK – in common with Denmark – has never been a full participant
in the Area of Freedom, Security and Justice (AFSJ). During the Treaty
of Amsterdam negotiations in 1996, the UK acquired the right to opt out
of various EU initiatives in the field of police and judicial cooperation. It
never joined the Schengen Convention and maintained the right to opt
out from the Schengen border control system, which enabled the UK to
continue exercising controls at its borders.

The Treaty of Lisbon in 2009 merged police and judicial cooperation in criminal matters into the main structure of the EU, making initiatives in this policy domain subject to qualified majority voting and
the supranational institutions of the EU. In response, the UK negotiated
a block opt-out, giving it the option to opt out of pre-Lisbon police and
criminal justice measures (around 100 measures) or to remain bound
by them. The UK exercised this block opt-out in 2014, but rejoined 35
measures – including participation in EU agencies such as Europol and
Eurojust – later that same year. During the scrutiny that took place in
2014 in the House of Lords assessing whether the UK should rejoin these

35 measures, Baroness Prashar highlighted that the measures were 'thoroughly assessed', 'judged to be in the national interest' and deemed 'vital' (European Union Committee 2016, 9). The UK opted not only to join a considerable number of police and criminal justice measures, but also the Passenger Name Record (PNR) Directive. All these measures were substantively judged – fewer than three years ago – to offer crucial benefits to public safety and national security. As Home Secretary, Theresa May emphasised their necessity in order to 'stop foreign criminals from coming to Britain, deal with European fighters coming back from Syria, stop British criminals evading justice abroad, prevent foreign criminals evading justice by hiding here, and get foreign criminals out of our prisons' (European Union Committee 2016, 9).

One of the top four overarching objectives of the Brexit negotiations for the UK has been 'to keep our justice and security arrangements at least as strong as they are'.[1] This is in the UK's own interest and is indeed acknowledged as such by UK law enforcement agencies. The EU tools and capabilities the UK would like to see retained or adequately replaced include Europol, Eurojust, the second generation Schengen Information System (SIS II), the European Arrest Warrant (EAW), the European Criminal Records Information System (ECRIS), the Prüm Decisions and PNR. The UK's future relationship with Europol has been identified as 'a critical priority' (European Union Committee 2016, 20). The form that this might take has not been given much consideration but there are some sources of inspiration for a future relationship that is both inside and outside, with some variations in between. As Denmark is the first EU Member State to negotiate an agreement with Europol with the status as a third party, the negotiations may very well set a precedent for the those conducted by the UK. Norway has also negotiated a bilateral international agreement with the EU as a third country, and the trajectory of both the negotiation process and the result will be explored below. As a former Member State, Britain will definitely require more than third-country status (in all its existent permutations) after Brexit, in order to avoid a surgical severing of an integral part of a well functioning organism. That is, at least, the perspective of the cooperating law enforcement agencies themselves. Severing an artery, thereby cutting off a much needed security relationship within Europe cannot be considered in the public interest either. As Bruce Springsteen (1980) expressed it lyrically: 'now you can't break the ties that bind'. A panoply of alternative nautical-knot metaphors are on offer to help understand how the various parts might be kept together after Brexit. This chapter discusses several of these – the Danish 'adjustable bend', the Norwegian 'anglers' loop' and bespoke Brexit–Europol 'tangles' – to shed some light on the options for the UK's post-Brexit participation in AFSJ. The chapter will examine how an 'in between' solution will affect the rule of law and the protection of fundamental rights and which courts will ensure justiciability in the last instance.

A Danish 'adjustable bend'

The possibility of a UK cooperation agreement with Europol being conditioned on continued cooperation in other EU policy areas, such as the Single Market, is not entirely unrealistic, particularly in view of recent discussions on Denmark's future relationship with Europol. In a referendum that took place in December 2015, the Danish electorate rejected a proposal to transform the Danish opt-out system into an opt-in on EU matters on Justice and Home Affairs. The Danish public also voted to opt out of the new Europol Regulation, and Denmark is thus no longer a member of Europol as of 1 May 2017. To ensure future cooperation between Denmark and Europol, on 17 February 2017 the Council added Denmark to the list of *Third States* with which Europol may conclude agreements (Council Implementing Decision 2017a). The Commission considered it 'vital to provide for cooperation between Europol and Denmark on key matters', particularly given that it is 'one of the key contributors to the Europol database' (European Parliament 2017c). The intention was to construct Denmark-specific arrangements that amounted to less than full membership of Europol. In essence this is a type of 'associate' membership of Europol (while – oddly – Denmark remains a full Member State). It is explicitly conditioned on Denmark's continued membership both of the EU and of the Schengen area, its full implementation of the Directive on cooperation in police matters, its acceptance of the jurisdiction of the CJEU and its acceptance of the competence of the European Data Protection Supervisor (EDPS).

The obligation for Denmark to remain bound by the Schengen acquis was strongly disputed by the Danish People's Party (Dansk Folkeparti) which had been adamant during the referendum process in its support for reintroducing border controls and exiting Schengen (Garulund Nøhr 2016). Prior to the referendum, the Danish People's Party had promised voters that a 'no' vote would still ensure full membership of Europol but withdrawal from Schengen. The new agreement certainly does not meet this promise. The Agreement on Operational and Strategic Cooperation between Denmark and Europol entered into force on 30 April 2017 after being approved by Council decision

(Council Implementing Decision 2017b). The Agreement emphasises the 'urgent problems arising from international crime' and the wish to ensure cooperation between Europol and Denmark. Article 8 allows a representative to be invited to the Europol Management Board and for its subgroups to act as observers, but does not grant it the right to vote. On the experience of other Agencies, the deprivation of the formal right to vote is not to be seen as a crucial stumbling block to effective cooperation in practice.

The concern that Denmark may lose access to Europol information is well-founded given that the Agreement does not include any provisions on this matter. Following the Agreement, Denmark will lose the possibility to directly search in Europol databases, following the principle of interoperability. Denmark will however have the possibility to designate up to eight Danish-speaking staff to handle Danish requests, and to input and retrieve data from Danish authorities in the Europol processing systems (Europol 2017). What this will mean in practice remains to be seen but Denmark as a voluntary Europol outsider may in practice and informally be granted (much) more liberal access to relevant data, also from other Member States, than its legal position would warrant. The agreement between Europol and Denmark (Europol 2017) may be a template for the UK after Brexit, but many of the conditions imposed on Denmark, alone or together, may prove problematic for the UK in future arrangements with Europol, including subjecting the UK to the jurisdiction of the CJEU, and requiring its participation in Schengen.

A Norwegian 'anglers' loop'

Within the UK it is felt that in the Brexit context, there is not only the Danish 'precedent' but that the UK should look at 'something more than that' (European Union Committee 2016, 60). What that 'more' designates in this context is unknown and arguably does not (yet) exist. Something 'less than' the Danish knot is a Norwegian one: an anglers' loop. The bilateral agreement concluded with Iceland and Norway on the surrender procedure between the EU Member States and Iceland and Norway provides that disputes be resolved through a meeting of representatives of the governments rather than through recourse to the CJEU (Official Journal of the European Union 2006). This bilateral agreement states that the contracting parties shall consider 'the development of the case law of the Court of Justice' as well as the development of the case law in Iceland and Norway to achieve uniform application and interpretation of the Agreement (Article 37). In this way the case law of the CJEU may play a role in the interpretation of provisions. The practicalities of this influence are unclear as yet, particularly considering that the Norway/Iceland agreement has not yet entered into force.

One thing is certain: since the new Europol Regulation entered into force on 1 May 2017 future agreements between Europol and third countries are formal 'international agreements' negotiated on the legal basis of Article 218 TFEU and entailing a veto power by the European Parliament. This is a quite different legal and political situation to that prevailing when Denmark was (with considerable haste) entered onto the list of third countries with which Europol could make agreements and when the agreement was subsequently made. A further practical issue concerns the actual time it may take for the UK to negotiate an agreement with Europol. The average negotiation time for operational agreements that allow for the exchange of data is around nine to 12 years (European Union Committee 2016, 58). The UK is unlikely to accept this lengthy period of negotiation, particularly as it has played such an 'active role in the development of EU policy on police cooperation and access to data for law enforcement purposes' (Carrera et al. 2016, 4).

Bespoke Brexit–Europol 'tangles'

The UK has been a member of Europol since its creation in 1998. It also included the 2009 Council Decision as one of the 35 measures that it rejoined following its block opt-out arrangement after the Treaty of Lisbon (Carrera et al. 2016, 43). In November 2016, the UK announced that it would opt in to the new Europol Regulation (Home Office 2016). The government highlighted the timing of this opt-in in the context of Brexit by stating that, whilst the UK is leaving the EU, 'the reality of cross-border crime remains'. The UK considers Europol to be a 'valuable service to the UK and opting in would enable us to maintain our current access to the agency, until we leave the EU' (Home Office 2016). The National Crime Agency (NCA) has listed a UK opt-in to the new Europol regulation as an 'immediate priority' and has classified membership of Europol or an alternative arrangement as its most important priority (European Union Committee 2016, 51). Whilst some EU agencies allow for non-EU Member States to enjoy a level of participation in the workings of the agency, which may be used as a precedent for future UK relations with Europol, these non-EU states do not always enjoy voting rights. For example, the new Europol Regulation states that the Management Board is to be composed of 'one representative from each Member State and one representative of the Commission', with each representative having a voting right. The Management Board can also invite non-voting observers to its meetings (Official Journal of the European Union 2016, Article 14(4)). Given that Europol merely allows EU Member States and the Commission to be represented in the management board, the UK must negotiate an agreement with Europol to remain connected in order to retain some form of influence. Europol may establish and maintain cooperative relations with third countries, but the Council must first publish a list of third states with which Europol may conclude such agreements (Official Journal of the European Union 2009, Article 26(1)).

Before any agreement can be concluded with the UK on its future cooperation with Europol, the Council must, therefore, first add the UK to the list of countries with which Europol may conclude agreements. Europol furthermore recognises two types of agreements with third parties, namely, strategic and operational agreements. Strategic agreements are 'limited to the exchange of general intelligence whereas operational agreements allow for the exchange of data' (Europol 2017). For example, Norway signed a strategic agreement with Europol in 2001, thereby removing obstacles to the exchange of data. Norway's position is limited, however, in comparison with full membership, and also with regard to the Danish version. Norwegian police cannot search Europol's database directly and must go through Europol's operational centre to ensure compliance with Europol rules before being granted access to the analysis forums.

According to Adler-Nissen (2015b, 195), Norway 'has failed to secure agreements with the EU on matters such as the transfer of sentenced prisoners and has yet to reach an agreement on common rules on documents in legal proceedings and evidence gathering'. Hufnagel (2016, 175) furthermore argues that Norway's agreement with Europol is conditioned on its being closely associated with law enforcement cooperation in the EU 'through its association with the Schengen cooperation mechanisms' and as a member of the European Economic Area. A UK agreement with Europol will therefore be much more problematic if the UK moves toward a hard Brexit, with no participation in Schengen or in the Single Market. Of course, it will always be an option – unlikely though it is – that the UK as a non EU Member State joins the Schengen area in the future, a status that would then be shared with Iceland, Switzerland, Norway and Liechtenstein. The crucial difference is that the UK has never been part of Schengen and as such is unlikely to now join (given that Schengen is now an integral part of the EU, as opposed to when the agreement with Norway and other EEA states was concluded).

There are in any event no non-Schengen states outside the EU with which the EU engages in anything comparable to its cooperation with Member States or Schengen states. Nor has there ever been an existing Member State that exited before, so a further bespoke arrangement in specific regards cannot be ruled out, provided that there is no hard Brexit. In such circumstances it would be difficult to envisage – or justify – a cherry picking bespoke arrangement with the UK in AFSJ.

'Now you can't break the ties that bind'

The House of Commons Justice Committee (2017, 11) considers the security and safety of the UK's residents as 'too precious to be left vulnerable to tactical bargaining'. Where there is a will, however, there may yet be a way. The highly pragmatic solution adopted – at the very last moment before the new Europol Regulation entered into force on 1 May 2017 – of Denmark being added in an unprecedented fashion, as a Member State, to the list of third countries with which Europol may conclude agreements, bears witness to the desire of the EU to find solutions that would enable ongoing cooperation and access to databases, even if this is not the same as full participation in Europol. But we should recall that that fundamental political willingness to engage in these kinds of legal and temporal knotting arrangements was for Denmark as a 'full' Member State, and not for a genuine (future) third country, which is what the UK is about to become, albeit from the position of having been a Member State partially 'opted in' to the system.

The likelihood of considerable 'bits and pieces' looms large in particular as the UK struggles to maintain already existing levels and choices of cooperation. The reason may not only be the need to do what is necessary for the security and well-being of the citizens and residents of the UK, but also the considerable sunk costs incurred by the UK in setting up the existing arrangements (e.g. on implementing the Prüm decisions) as well as the likely costs of replicating capabilities outside the EU (e.g. on the EAW or a Europol-type agency or database). The UK clearly faces a future different from that which has gone before. It will move from being an engaged insider in which it operated, in practice, as a leader – in its own words, the UK was 'a leading protagonist in driving and shaping the nature and direction of cooperation on police and security matters under the auspices of the EU' (European Union Committee 2016, 10) – to a disempowered outsider. The vista thus beckons of the UK having to formally prove 'adequacy' arrangements prior to any data-sharing agreements just like any other third country – a bitter pill for the UK given the manner in which its own personal data protection for law enforcement purposes preceded – and provided a model for – that of the EU itself.

The leadership role of the UK has undoubtedly been instrumental in designing the very foundations of AFSJ as well as constructing some important pillars (for example, on data retention and recent EU rules on PNR). The UK has the highest number of seconded officers at Europol headquarters in the Hague; it was a major advocate of the European Arrest Warrant and the PNR Directive and the (subsequently annulled) Data Retention Directive. But emancipation is nigh for the EU27. There is no reason to believe that we will see anything but further intensification of the role and powers of the agencies in this field and their steering 'management' by national administrations on the ground. Information-sharing, and in particular the further development of the principle of inter-operability across the supranational–national divide, will gain ever more importance and accrued practical content in the years ahead. The role of the CJEU will become more and more pivotal in ensuring the balance with fundamental rights and the issue of access to justice for individuals will remain as challenged and difficult as it is today.

Opt-outs and other differentiation processes may actually reinforce the integration process, through the 'stigmatization of transgressive states' (Adler-Nissen 2015b, 2). Whatever was the case with regard to the existing British (and Danish) opt-outs from borders, asylum, migration and justice policies, the position of the UK as a stigmatised outsider will greatly intensify after Brexit. Yet there is a paradox as the UK will almost inevitably be forced to 'mimic' rules and regulations in the future, without any formal democratic participation in defining their content and without contributing towards the ongoing, and at times fundamental, debates on core issues before the CJEU. Mimicry of 'bits and pieces' of AFSJ, along with continued application of CJEU interpreted case law, seems to be the bespoke Brexit antidote in this field at any rate. The AFSJ is a space to be closely watched as the negotiations unfold – both in terms of law and in terms of the ongoing practices below the political radar. Yet the peculiar saga of how Denmark was legally enabled to remain part of Europol in spite of the fact that a national referendum specifically decided it would not may provide some indications how elites can construct legal and pragmatic ways out of clear political dilemmas. Where there is a will, it seems, there may well be a way, in particular in areas that are more under the political radar than others (e.g. police cooperation and information-sharing). You cannot, after all, break the ties that bind.

17
Citizenship and free movement in a changing EU

Navigating an archipelago of contradictions

Jo Shaw

Introduction

One result of the UK's referendum on EU membership on 23 June 2016 has been to leave behind a situation of considerable legal and personal uncertainty for EU27 citizens and their families resident in the UK, and UK citizens and their families resident in the EU27 Member States.[1] It has also struck a blow against the viability of much of the UK economy, where a 'high employment–low wage–low productivity' triangle has largely been kept in place by a ready supply of labour from elsewhere within the Single Market, especially since the post-2004 enlargements. It is the putative impact of this supply of flexible and arguably cheaper labour on domestic labour markets which means that calls to end free movement come not just from those who oppose immigration *per se*, but also from those on the political left who profess an international-ist outlook yet who argue that free movement makes it harder to pur-sue domestic policies that push the UK towards being a 'high wage–high productivity' economy.[2]

The focus in this chapter is on the individual rights and status con-sequences of the ending of free movement as a result of leaving the EU, rather than wider questions about either the principles (Parker 2017) or the appropriate policy and regulatory mix (Boswell et al. 2017) for immi-gration and mobility in the post-Brexit UK.[3]

Ending free movement?

The basic situation is easy to state but hard to elaborate with sufficient precision to cover all eventualities: leaving the EU means an end to the regime of 'free movement', which has fostered and protected mobility (by workers, the self-employed, service-providers, students, pensioners and others, including third-country national family members) within the EU for the last 60 years. But designing a revised legal regime for 'free movers' after Brexit is a task of immense complexity, given the intricacy of existing EU law in this field (e.g. for social security and pension issues). Resolving these scenarios brings into play governance structures at many different levels, including national and subnational law, EU law, the European Convention on Human Rights and Fundamental Freedoms, and potentially other sources of migrants' rights at the international level. Because of the large numbers of UK and EU27 citizens involved, reciprocity is the watchword, with an agreement at the point of withdrawal needed, in order to avoid negative impacts on individuals on both sides of the equation. As negotiations under Article 50 got underway, it became clear that all parties shared the view that free movement should be at the top of the agenda, even though agreement may be hard to reach.

By July 2017, the UK and the European Commission (leading in the negotiations on behalf of the EU and the EU27) had both put forward their outline positions on the situation of EU citizens in the context of withdrawal. There was a great deal of distance between the two starting positions, noted by the negotiators themselves, although this has gradually reduced over time as the UK has conceded on key points.[4] It has been widely noted that the original UK proposals would entail a significant degradation of rights for EU citizens compared with the status quo (Peers 2017; Reynolds 2017; Yeo 2017). For example, even EU citizens in the UK with the status of 'permanent resident', with documentation issued by the UK Home Office, would need to re-apply to the UK authorities in order to benefit from the new 'settled status'. If they failed to do so, they could find themselves in breach of UK immigration law, regardless of how long they had been resident in the UK, or under what conditions. This could potentially have very serious consequences if applied strictly, especially for vulnerable persons such as the elderly, those with disabilities, or persons suffering from ill health. It has also been noted that Brexit risks exacerbating the gender bias previously observed in free movement rules because EU law does not recognise caring as 'work' (O'Brien 2017). In addition, family reunion rights would be reduced (in line with the very restrictive income-based rules applicable to UK citizens and third-country nationals seeking family reunion) and those who left the UK for more than two years would lose their 'settled status' and would re-enter under whatever future regime applied to EU citizens (presumably as third-country nationals). The absence of an unconditional right of return (one of the classic citizenship rights) sharply differentiates the proposed 'settled status' from UK citizenship.

These are not trivial questions affecting just a few people. It is not an exaggeration to suggest that the loss of individual rights resulting from the UK's departure from the EU could be the most substantial loss of rights in Europe since the break-up of Yugoslavia in the 1990s, with the loss of the status of 'Yugoslav' citizen for millions of people. Just as with the break-up of Yugoslavia, which saw individuals in many of the successor states experience problems related to uncertain citizenship and immigration status (Shaw & Štiks 2012), so severing the bond of free movement law, which many have relied upon in order to build their lives, threatens to reduce life chances and life choices for millions now and in the future.

While none of the non-UK EU citizens resident in the UK ought to be at risk of statelessness as a result of the withdrawal of the UK, since they are by definition citizens of one (or more) of the EU27 Member States, the body of free movement law nonetheless offers substantial enhancements in the socioeconomic, political and civic domains. It offers outcomes that are well worth defending on both practical and philosophical grounds (de Witte 2016; Salomone 2017). Ironically, because of disenfranchisement effects in relation to national elections and referendums (most EU citizens resident in the UK and UK citizens resident long-term outside the UK could not vote), there were fewer opportunities for political voices to articulate the value of free movement during the EU referendum campaign (Shaw 2017). Simply to suggest that EU citizens resident in the UK should themselves become UK citizens misses the point: many cannot (for a variety of reasons); the process is very expensive; they may fail whatever probity or integration tests are applied; or they may not wish to risk losing their 'home' state citizenship. Finally, there is the sheer bureaucratic effort involved, with the UK not geared up to deal with millions of residence applications, never mind millions of new naturalisation applications. Ultimately, becoming a citizen in the formal sense (and the linkage thereby made between citizenship and immigration) is not the same thing as being a free mover. It is, however, clear from the famous 'citizens of nowhere' comment in her speech to the Conservative Party conference in October 2016, that the difficult situations in which those with fluid mobile residencies, complex multinational families and/or transnational work/study/life commitments do not inspire instinctive sympathy on the part of Prime Minister Theresa May.

It is also self-evident that the complexities of free movement law did not enter the minds of the vast majority of those who voted in the UK's referendum. Free movement had been constructed, in the minds of many, as one of the problems facing a UK struggling with austerity and stagnant wages, not one of the solutions (Shaw 2016a). One reaction has been to treat those exercising free movement rights as 'lucky' immigrants, not subject to the 'hostile environment' rules for third-country national immigrants, introduced by successive governments and substantially upgraded by Home Secretary Theresa May between 2010 and 2016. When that narrative is applied, it starts to look wrong that in some areas (e.g. family reunion) EU citizens do better than UK citizens. It has also been easy to blame EU citizens for shortages in public services, rather than budget restrictions imposed on providers. The notion of EU citizenship as a reciprocal bond founded on enforceable rights joining together citizens across the EU28 was completely lost within public discourse, not least because the Leave campaign was regularly punctuated by sweeping and unsubstantiated claims that EU citizens would have the same status after Brexit as before.[5]

Everything that has been done since June 2016 by the UK government has reinforced a sense of chaos and uncertainty for EU27 citizens, and for UK citizens resident in the EU27. There has been a very high rejection rate (reportedly up to 28 per cent) of applications for permanent residence documentation made by longstanding EU27 citizen residents (although the Home Office has claimed that this has not changed in recent years),[6] with many rejections referring to the notorious – and arguably both unnecessary and insurmountable – comprehensive sickness insurance requirement applicable to those not in employment (Davies 2017). Such rejections come with a letter from the Home Office stating that the unsuccessful applicant is not exercising treaty rights and should make arrangements to leave the UK. This spreads fear and despondency, even if such letters are not followed up on. Successful applications often entail costly consultations with lawyers. For months, there was no official government policy on what might come next, except for blandishments of a 'generous offer' in the making. Meanwhile the European Commission issued a set of principles agreed with the EU27 suggesting that EU/UK citizens (on both sides of the UK/EU27 divide) should enjoy the exact same rights they had enjoyed under free movement, even if that meant lifelong protection, complex arrangements for social security and pension aggregation, continuation of mutual recognition of qualifications, the right of return or onward mobility, and the maintenance of the juris-diction of the CJEU. The latter condition runs contrary to one of Prime Minister May's 'red lines' from her Lancaster House speech.[7] Absurdly, when the UK made its widely criticised 'offer' in June 2017, this was accompanied by calls from government politicians for the EU to recip-rocate the UK offer, something which was impossible since the EU paper had preceded the UK one by several weeks.

It is clear that the unravelling of the composite polity that is 'the UK in the EU' raises serious practical issues for those whom it affects directly (i.e. those who are already in the UK) – and also for those indir-ectly affected, including potential future movers as well as businesses and employers. There will be substantial opportunity costs for the UK economy in terms of losing access to a ready supply of labour coming from elsewhere within the Single Market under flexible conditions. But that point runs against another nostrum of Conservative Party policy, the commitment to reduce net immigration to below 100,000 per annum. Pursuing this policy is bound to push up prices for compa-nies and consumers and it is not clear that it will lead to higher levels of better remunerated employment for so-called 'native Britons' (Portes 2017a, 2017b).

These implications, plus the loss of personal freedoms, are perhaps just starting to gain traction with the wider UK public, with one survey indicating that 60 per cent of UK citizens, including 58 per cent of Leave voters, want to keep their EU citizenship even after Brexit.[8] It is worth setting this figure against the figures for EU citizens resident outside their Member State of citizenship, which sat at just 16 million in 2016 (against a population of over 500 million), and amounts to less than 4 per cent.[9] This is somewhat misleading, however, and a better under-standing of physical and virtual European mobilities emerges from the work of Salamońska and Recchi (2016), who assess the scale of the manifold cross-border practices of EU citizens and residents, across a number of dimensions including degree of permanence and frequency. They conclude that up to 20 per cent of the European population could be described as highly 'mobile' in this broader sense, but even this figure is still well short of those survey findings showing 'attachment' to EU citizenship. It is of course possible that the conflation of EU citizenship and free movement is starting to break down, so that the former is start-ing to be understood as a political value above and beyond the latter (e.g. giving the opportunity to participate democratically by voting in European Parliament elections). Or it could be a finding that correlates closely to another survey, which indicated that voters were more likely to say that any trade-off between the economy and immigration should be resolved in favour of policies promoting growth and trade, even if this meant more immigration or free movement.[10] The complexities – and unpalatable consequences – of unravelling free movement might just be a catalyst contributing to the collapse of the case for Brexit. Or perhaps this is just the early stirrings of 'euro-nostalgia' that will sweep across the UK in the years to come until memories fade. Brexit Britain truly is, as I have noted previously, an 'archipelago of contradictions' (Shaw 2016b).

Free movement and citizenship

The very idea that European citizenship as a legal status for UK citizens could somehow survive the separation of the UK from the EU brings us back to the core issue of what EU citizenship actually is, and how it relates both to free movement and to national citizenship (Mindus 2017; Schrauwen 2017). Exploring the relationship to national citizenship can lead us along well-trodden pathways, especially in terms of case law of the CJEU. EU citizenship is a creature of EU law, but it is based on access points controlled under national law. The *McCarthy* case suggested that those with dual citizenship of the host state and another Member State do not enjoy the protection of EU law,[11] although the pending *Lounes* case may well see a different approach taken by the CJEU in the case of a person naturalised *after* having enjoyed family life with a third-country national in the host state whilst only a citizen of another Member State, if the advisory opinion of the Advocate General is followed in the November 2017 judgement.[12] Furthermore, the CJEU has held that EU law requires the possibility of judicial review of decisions on deprivation of national citizenship, if this would have the effect of depriving an EU citizen of substantially all of the benefits of EU citizenship. However, this proposition was developed for a scenario where it was the actions of the EU citizen in question – in combination with national citizenship laws – which triggered the scenario in which he was deprived of the benefits of EU citizenship.[13] We do not yet know how the CJEU might approach the question of loss of EU citizenship because a Member State *withdraws* from the EU.

At first sight, it seems that if EU law no longer applies after secession/withdrawal of the UK, then EU citizenship must surely lapse. Absent any international agreement specifically preserving such a status or certain rights attaching to it (e.g. under Article 50), it seems obvious that a withdrawing state retains the power, under international law, to deprive its citizens of the status of EU citizen, and to render the legal effect of that status, for citizens of other continuing Member States, nugatory within its territory. In similar terms, other Member States have no obligation to treat UK citizens other than as third-country nationals on their territory. There is no parallel with the duties on states in circumstances of secession, as there is no risk that such an act could render affected persons stateless. They are still protected by national citizenship somewhere. There would be protection of non-citizen residents of the withdrawing state in relation to certain rights, such as family life, under international human rights law. The *Kuric* case of the European Court of Human Rights[14] (Vidmar 2014) appears to 'freeze' the rights of those who have regular residence in the host state and who do not accede to the citizenship of that state when it secedes. Although developed in the context of the secession of a former Yugoslav republic (Slovenia), the principles in this case can be applied to a UK withdrawal from the EU (Mindus 2017; Schrauwen 2017). This seems to be what the offer of 'settled status' is reflecting, although that status offers less than EU citizenship.

The general proposition must be that national citizenship status will be unaffected by Brexit. The only caveat upon that point comes from the *Tjebbes* case, pending before the CJEU, concerning legislation withdrawing Dutch citizenship from persons who are resident for more than 10 years in a third country and who have taken on that country's citizenship.[15] This case has obvious implications for the post-Brexit scenario, as the UK will be such a 'third country' after Brexit, so any intervention by the CJEU to suggest that Member States are not free to withdraw citizenship in such circumstances *because of EU citizenship* could be for the benefit of EU27 citizens resident in the UK.

For the future, we could speculate that further adjustments to national citizenship laws might be a desirable part of the solution to the upheaval brought about by Brexit, if a stronger parallel is drawn to the impact of secession from a state. Seceding parts of states must attend to issues of citizenship as a matter of urgency, as must states from which regions secede. But the UK, on withdrawal from the EU, is making no moves to facilitate citizenship access of resident non-citizens, despite the loss of their preferential 'free mover' status. On the contrary, it seems that this group must accommodate themselves to the UK's requirements, rather than the other way around, by applying for a form of 'settled status' that falls far short of both national citizenship and of the protections and freedoms previously offered by free movement. Initially, there was no sign of other Member States with restrictive approaches to dual citizenship, such as the Netherlands, Estonia or Austria, making adjustments to citizenship law to accommodate resident UK citizens or to offer wider access to dual citizenship to protect the interests of new or existing citizens. On the contrary, the prime minister of the Netherlands appeared to double down on his country's resistance to dual citizenship (Boffey 2017a; EUDO Citizenship 2015). However, perhaps in a harbinger of further changes to come, in October 2017 the new Dutch coalition adopted a more liberal approach to dual citizenship which was the existing policy of just one of the four coalition partners (the D66 Liberal Democrats party), offering assurances to Dutch citizens resident in the UK that they would be able to keep their Netherlands citizenship after naturalising in the UK (Boffey 2017b). The details of how this might work are not as yet known.

Despite, or perhaps because of, the absence of state action to remedy the situation, some European citizens – for whom it is possible and useful – are taking action to acquire new or additional citizenships as an insurance policy against the impending restriction of free movement. Quite substantial numbers of UK citizens are pursuing ancestry-based or family-relationship-based options in order to preserve or open up new options for mobility, in addition to the classic mode of acquisition by residence/naturalisation:[16] Irish citizenship has been heavily in demand reflecting the many millions of UK citizens who have at least one Irish-born grandparent; German citizenship is an option for those descended from persons deprived of their citizenship in Nazi Germany; Italian citizenship is accessible not only on the basis of descent, but also via a spouse. For those wealthy enough, there remains the option of purchasing citizenships and residencies in a number of Member States with minimal physical residence obligations (Džankic 2015).

Many EU citizens resident in the UK are pursuing the UK citizenship route despite the considerable expense and the numerous bureaucratic hurdles in place (e.g. the prior acquisition of the permanent residence documents that those same EU citizens are now being told will be valueless after Brexit).[17] The irony is that many are seeking UK citizenship not because they feel more integrated in the UK, but precisely because they face more hostility than ever before. A wave of xenophobia seems to have been unleashed by the UK's 'Brexit experience'.[18] But there are still many mixed-nationality families, as well as highly mobile persons and groups, who find that citizenship acquisition does not match up to the fluid flexible possibilities of free movement.

Conclusions

Free movement is not, and has never been, an unconditional 'right' with benefits attached, and it remains primarily linked to economic interests. It also has a 'dark' side in the form of the posting of workers by firms providing services on a transnational basis; the position of these workers is barely regulated under EU law, and they are therefore subject to the vagaries of national law alone (MacShane 2017). But what is interesting (and even ironic) about the post-Brexit period is that a clearer perspective on the value of free movement has now opened up. It is easier to argue how free movement for individuals has operated to obviate the restrictions of national citizenship and immigration regimes and to offer mobility options with low transaction costs over the lifecourse (for work, study, family or lifestyle reasons). This highlights the extent to which – in perception and practice, if not in law – EU citizenship has evolved into a form of transnational citizenship practice that complements the lacunae that arise where overlapping national citizenship and immigration regimes are all that is on offer (Mindus 2017).

For the EU, and indeed for the international community more generally, Brexit creates an unprecedented situation. It has given rise to equally unprecedented civic mobilisation around demands for the protection of acquired rights, including several European Citizens' Initiatives registered by the European Commission. Some have raised the possibility of EU citizenship becoming a freestanding status that can be acceded to other than through the nationality of the Member States, with UK citizens being offered the possibility of 'associate citizenship' (discussed in Schrauwen 2017), but at present such proposals remain utopian rather than practical in character. Eventually, unscrambling the eggs of free movement may demand some creative solutions going beyond the scope of the Article 50 agreement itself, including increased pressure on Member States to remove barriers to dual citizenship.[19] This seems appropriate in an increasingly global age.

18
The Emperor has no clothes

Brexit and the UK constitution

Piet Eeckhout

Introduction

In the nine months between the Brexit referendum and the triggering of Article 50, the principal development in the UK was not a search for what Brexit might mean – that search was cordoned off by the drawing of red lines, and was vacuously substituted with 'Brexit means Brexit'. The main development was a legal one: the *Miller* litigation, which decided the question of whether the Brexit referendum afforded sufficient authority for the UK government to notify the EU of the UK's intention to withdraw from the EU, or whether instead an Act of Parliament was required.[1] The litigation was conducted under conditions of unprecedented public attention, ranging far beyond the traditional echo chambers of lawyers and legal academics. For months the mainstream media focused on Gina Miller – now a celebrity – and her daring challenge to the government's plans. Concepts such as 'the royal prerogative' and the 'Sewel Convention', and cases like *De Keyser Royal Hotel*,[2] normally the preserve of sophisticated constitutional lawyers, became items of popular debate. In academia there was a veritable blogfest on what the litigation was about, and how it should be resolved.[3] This was the case of the century, and possibly of the last one too. The hearings before the Supreme Court were live-streamed in an unprecedented reality show, populated by star-studded barristers and a fearsomely erudite panel of Justices. The outcome was a set of judgments – one by the Divisional Court and one by the Supreme Court – which considered and analysed a range of constitutional instruments, across the UK's history, reaching back to Magna Charta and the Bill of Rights. Constitutional lawyers revelled in the judgments, and the litigation was seen as crowning an era which confirmed that the UK constitution was as thick as any other, even if unwritten.

This chapter challenges this conception. It argues that the Brexit saga reveals that UK constitutional law is threadbare, much more so than previously thought. The only constitutional principle that really stands, and indeed emasculates all others, is the principle that Parliament is sovereign. The constitutional version that this principle is said to confirm is called political constitutionalism, but its proponents seem oblivious to the idea that a true constitution – as its name suggests – *constitutes* politics as much as it is the product *of* politics. The chapter makes its claim in two parts. The first one looks at *Miller*, and what it revealed about the intensely political limits to UK constitutional law. The second focuses on the UK's external constitution: the principles governing international treaty-making and the treatment of foreign affairs. This chapter is no more than an attempt at an initial challege and the analysis is not a complete one, for there is much more that could be said about the defects of the UK constitution.

Miller and the limits of UK constitutional law

The claim this chapter makes appears to fly in the face of the intensive and extensive constitutional scrutiny of *Miller*. Both the Divisional Court and the Supreme Court focused on grand constitutional principles (though the former more so than the latter). The judgments were no less than a full judicial tour of the historical foundations of the division of powers between the legislature and the executive. It was on the basis of the lessons from that tour, and of an analysis of how EU exit would interfere with existing statutes, particularly the European Communities Act (ECA), that both courts concluded that legislation was required to trigger Article 50.

But consider the following assessment of *Miller*, focused on the positivist and doctrinal reading of UK constitutional law which the judgements offered, and on the approach towards devolution.

A positivist and doctrinal reading

This subsection looks at the unprecedented nature of the Brexit decision, and how the debate (judicial and academic) responded to this. The triggering of Article 50 is not just any international withdrawal notification. Article 50 itself speaks of a Member State's *decision* to withdraw, taken in accordance with its constitutional requirements. In virtually all other Member States such a decision would require a constitutional debate, about the country's approach towards European integration, and could also require constitutional amendment. Given the extent to which EU policies and laws penetrate the domestic sphere – and in many areas contribute to *constituting* the domestic public sphere – withdrawal is a wholly unprecedented decision, with massive political, economic, financial, legal and indeed constitutional consequences. One year into the Brexit process, this much one can say as an established fact. However, the *Miller* debate did not conceive of Brexit in this way. It focused immediately on judicial precedents regarding the royal prerogative, much of them pretty antiquated.[4] Complex doctrinal analyses were put forward to distinguish the various cases, and the different forms of royal prerogative and their relationships with legislative power (Craig 2016). The Brexit tiger, most of the legal community thought, had to be put back in the antiquated cage of positive, doctrinal law, and it was perfectly possible to contain it in that way. An astute analysis of past judicial statements was all that was needed.

This 'reading' of the UK constitution had its mirror image in the interpretation of the effect of the ECA. All that was required here was a proper characterisation of this Act of Parliament, with the aid of ingenious devices, such as the concept that the ECA is a mere 'conduit' (pipes and all) for EU law to flow into UK domestic law.[5] The ultimate crowning of this positivist reading, focused on form rather than substance, was (with great respect) the dissent by Lord Justice Reed. He considered that when Parliament adopted the ECA, shortly before the government ratified the EEC and other European Treaties, it was not prejudging the government's ultimate act of joining the EEC. Parliament did not decide to join; it merely made this possible.[6]

This positivist and doctrinal approach, focused on ancient precedent and textual construction, meant that there was hardly any debate on what the respective roles of the legislature and the executive ought to be in an age of globalisation and European integration. It was simply presumed that European integration is a branch of international relations, and that it was right for the executive to be in control, with a single proviso, namely, that it cannot use those executive powers (its 'royal prerogative') to make any changes to the law of the land. It is because of this approach that the question of whether the Article 50 notification is revocable became so significant. For Lord Pannick to make Gina Miller's case it was necessary to establish that the Article 50 bullet, once it left the notification arm, would irrevocably reach the target of the UK leaving the EU, and that Parliament would not be able to reverse course. For else the notification would not, in and of itself, change domestic law. The government, of course, agreed with the irrevocability thesis, clearly for political reasons. Both courts in *Miller* could base themselves on that consensus between the parties, and avoid an embarassing reference to the CJEU on the question of revocability – a question of interpretation of EU law, which can ultimately only be answered by that Court. In the meantime it is clear that most academic commentary argues that Article 50 *is* revocable (Eeckhout & Frantziou 2017, 711–14), but that does not mean that *Miller* was wrongly decided. Whatever precedent says about the scope of the royal prerogative, the decision to leave the EU is so far-reaching that it simply cannot be left to the executive.

The outcome of this positivist reading of the enormous constitutional questions which *Miller* raised is a decidedly narrow judgment. All the Supreme Court in the end established was that an Act of Parliament was needed to notify the EU of the UK's intention to withdraw. Nothing else was said about the process of withdrawal, or about Parliament's role in the Brexit negotiations, or indeed its role at the end of the process, when the withdrawal agreement (if there is one) will need to be ratified, and may need to be incorporated in UK domestic law. Parliament duly did what the government asked it to do, in an Act which is so short and exclusively focused on the Article 50 notification that there are still voices claiming that the UK has not yet decided to leave the EU, at least not in accordance with its constitutional requirements.[7]

Devolution

Antecedents and context are important here. For a couple of decades the UK has been embarking on a process of devolution of powers – in an asymmetrical manner – to Scotland, Wales and Northern Ireland. That process has reached its furthest extent in Scotland, culminating in the 2014 referendum on independence. Even if a majority voted against independence at the time, it is clear that Scotland regards itself as a country, rather than a mere region, with far-reaching powers. The political response to the referendum was to strengthen devolution.

The outside observer might therefore conclude that, in its own quirky constitutional way, the UK has become something of a federal state. But Brexit and *Miller* show that that is not the case. Notwithstanding the fact that withdrawal from the EU affects significant devolved powers (e.g. in agriculture, fisheries and the environment), the EU Referendum Act 2015 completely disregarded devolution by not requiring any specific majorities in the UK's constituent parts. A simple majority of voters across the UK were empowered to launch Brexit, as indeed they did, notwithstanding majorities for 'remain' in Scotland and Northern Ireland.[8] As a small excursus, it may be noted here that this disregard for devolution is but one manifestation of the constitutional failure to frame referendums. The EU Referendum Act regulated hardly anything at all – indeed, it was even silent on the referendum's very authority and legal force, thereby creating the juridical space for the *Miller* litigation.

Devolution became a significant component of that litigation. The debate focused mostly on the Sewel Convention. This is a constitutional convention according to which the UK Parliament will not normally legislate with regard to devolved matters without the consent of the affected devolved assembly. Such conventions are, as a rule, not embodied in legislation, even if they establish significant constitutional principles. However, the Sewel Convention is an exception in that it is incorporated in the Scotland Act 2016 (Section 2(8)).[9] The central issue of *Miller* was whether an Act of Parliament was required to trigger Article 50 and set the UK on the course of withdrawal. Clearly, such legislation 'affects' the powers devolved to e.g. the Scottish Parliament, as those powers extend to matters of EU law. But the Supreme Court rejected the relevance of the Sewel Convention, unanimously, on the simple basis that such conventions are not legally enforceable, and that it is not for judges to give legal rulings on their operation and scope, because those matters are determined within the political world.[10] The fact that the Sewel Convention was incorporated in the Scotland Act 2016 did not modify that assessment: the Supreme Court stated that it would have expected the UK Parliament 'to have used other words if it were seeking to convert a convention into a legal rule justiciable by the courts'.[11]

It is not the aim of this chapter to critique *Miller*, even if such a critique is called for. All this chapter seeks to do is to invite the reader to contemplate what *Miller* reveals about the UK constitution. The ECA has been called a constitutional statute, but all that is needed, constitutionally, to trigger its demise is a two-section act allowing the government to notify the UK's intention to withdraw. The Brexit process is tremendously complex and wide-ranging, and will fundamentally change the law of the UK, but there is no role for Parliament in the withdrawal negotiations which the constitution demands, other than that any changes to UK law will at the end of the day need to be approved by Parliament. Brexit is the outcome of a referendum, but there is no constitutional law framing such referendums, and Parliament can do as it likes with them. That is so even for referendums that affect devolved powers. There is a constitutional convention on the need to obtain the consent of the devolved assemblies, partially enshrined in legislation, but that convention has no force of law whatsoever.

The external constitution

The UK's approach towards the Brexit negotiations is characterised by a very traditional approach towards the conduct of 'foreign affairs', as opposed to domestic matters (Endicott 2016). Even if *Miller* decided that a statute was required to trigger Article 50, neither the Supreme Court nor Parliament went any further than the bare minimum such a statute had to contain. Neither of those constitutional actors determined any further role for Parliament in the Brexit negotiations. The UK government is adamant that it should completely control those negotiations, which are about the 'best deal' for Britain.

This traditional approach to the conduct of foreign affairs, which, paradoxically, leaves the royal prerogative unscathed, is based on the assumption that the executive is best placed to determine and implement external policies, and that Parliament's input is required only at the point of incorporating an international treaty in domestic law. However, the Brexit process, more than any other 'foreign' policy, shows how fundamentally outdated these constitutional concepts are.

As analysed in greater depth elsewhere, Brexit constitutes a massive interference with the vast body of individual rights conferred by EU law (Eeckhout & Frantziou 2017, 699–703). Most of those rights are concerned with cross-border matters: rights to live and work in the UK and in the EU27; rights to trade; rights to provide services, such as passporting in financial services or aviation; rights to have judgments enforced; rights to put products complying with EU regulations on the market and so on. Those rights are as much part of domestic law as they are rights involving 'foreign affairs'. Indeed this body of individual rights to cross-border activity would make no sense if the rights were not fully incorporated in the domestic laws of the EU Member States. One could even say that these rights *constitute* globalisation, in its European manifestation.

The process through which these rights have been defined and conferred – the process of making EU law – is one involving a range of constitutional actors. They principally include: Member State governments, which negotiate the EU founding treaties, but in this century with the aid of wider conventions;[12] those governments, in the Council, acting together with the Commission and the directly elected European Parliament for the purpose of enacting EU legislation; and the CJEU, which interprets and enforces the treaties and legislation, and ensures the coherence of EU law as a legal system. The claim is not that this is an ideal constitutional model, rather that it must be characterised as a legislative model – one in which a range of constitutional actors participate, which includes checks and balances, and published proposals which are debated and amended in open fora, under deliberative processes which are open to public participation. These legislative processes have in effect determined the bulk of the UK's foreign affairs, insofar as relations with other EU Member States are concerned, from 1973 onwards. In this respect, EU law has become the UK's external constitution.

The Brexit process, whose function it is to determine the future relations between the UK and the EU, is projected to be entirely different. The UK government will 'negotiate' a 'deal', and would have preferred to do that in conditions of secrecy, which the EU side have (fortunately) resisted. A traditional intergovernmental, rather than legislative, model. Few checks and balances, no deliberative processes in public fora, no formal public participation.

To illustrate the contrast, it may be useful to refer to the first negotiation 'offer' the UK government has made, at the time of writing, on the acquired rights of EU/UK citizens (HM Government 2017e). This proposal is intended to define the rights of around three million people, to work, to reside, to be reunified with family members, and to benefits and social security – rights which are clearly central to their lives. The UK government generated this offer in conditions of complete secrecy, without giving Parliament any opportunity to debate its terms, and it intends to conduct the subsequent negotiations in the same intergovernmental manner. It has emphasised that the resulting deal (if there is one) will come before Parliament in a take-it-or-leave-it vote, which in the leave-it version would mean that Parliament becomes responsible for there being no rights at all. The constitutional concept is that 3 million people can be stripped of a range of basic rights by mere executive action.

UK constitutional lawyers may retort that, whatever happens in the Brexit negotiations, at least some of the acquired rights will continue to be protected through the Human Rights Act (HRA), which incorporates the European Convention on Human Rights (ECHR). That is indeed the case, but even a quick glance at the HRA reveals further weaknesses of the UK's constitution. The UK courts cannot protect ECHR rights in the face of inconsistent primary legislation. Any treatment of acquired rights which Parliament would endorse and incorporate in domestic legislation could not be judicially overturned. Moreover, the HRA itself can be repealed at any time, and on the traditional understanding of the royal prerogative any UK government could decide to withdraw from the ECHR itself, without the need to involve Parliament.

Conclusions

For many years now UK constitutional lawyers have argued that the UK's unwritten constitution is thriving. One of the ways in which that constitution was said to be reinforced was through the presence of so-called constitutional statutes, with the ECA and the HRA as prime examples. However, the Brexit process reveals the extent to which these foundations of UK constitutional law are not as solid as they have at first seemed. A very short act allowing the government to notify under Article 50 is sufficient, so it seems, to emasculate the ECA. Of course that act followed a popular referendum, but that referendum, ill-defined as it was, is itself a manifestation of constitutional instability and shallowness. Brexit and the *Miller* litigation further confirm that core principles of the UK's devolution are not legally enforceable. Paradoxically, *Miller* seems to promote rather than halt the traditional approach towards the preeminence of the royal prerogative in foreign affairs. The government's position is that the Brexit negotiations, which are concerned, on one perspective, with a range of individual rights, do not require parliamentary involvement. That position is as yet unchallenged, by either the courts or Parliament itself.

Ultimately, the only principle that stands is that of parliamentary sovereignty. Any Parliament can always do as it likes, with any statute, at any time. Parliament can also choose to leave any 'foreign affairs' to the government, however much those affairs are intertwined with domestic ones, provided any negotiated changes to domestic law are ultimately incorporated by Parliament. Whether this is the best system for a twenty-first-century constitutional democracy which aspires to be 'global' is, however, an open question.

VI: Europe in the world

19
Britain against the world?

Foreign and security policy in the 'age of Brexit'

Amelia Hadfield

Introduction

Foreign policy is something of a paradox. Scholars are taught about the long-standing axioms of statehood, and schooled in the age-old verities of conflict and cooperation. Pragmatic policies, as Kissinger reminds us, 'must be based on some fixed principles in order to prevent tactical skill from dissipating into a random thrashing about' (Kissinger 1994, 98). Policymakers, however, operate on rather less fixed requirements of cost–benefit analysis and strategy construction, often requiring swift changes in the practice of statecraft.

While EU foreign policymaking has innovatively blurred distinctions between 'internal' and 'external' areas in scope, European foreign policy overall remains traditionally intergovernmental in practice. From the perspective of Brexit, this operates as both a benefit, and a problem. The benefit is obvious. Operating via state-to-state negotiations, the EU's Common Foreign and Security Policy (CFSP) and the Common Security and Defence Policy (CSDP) represent the least integrated areas of policy between the 28 EU Member States. The intergovernmental nature of the CFSP and CSDP allows the UK 'to preserve independence in its diplomacy while allowing for the coordination of policy where interests are held in common with other Member States' (Whitman 2016, 254). This suggests that in strategic terms there is less in the way of detailed unpicking of shared policies, legislation, budgets and resources between Britain and the EU, but rather a reorientation of Britain based on its preferred location within, alongside or beyond the EU on a case-by-base basis. Simple enough, but not wholly accurate. The problems come when looking in detail at what has constituted since 1993 the nature of Britain's involvement with the EU's emerging foreign and security policy structure. In brief these entail:

- the extensive nature of the CFSP in terms of sheer policy coverage (see Part 5, Treaty on the Functioning of the EU, which details the scope of the EU's cooperation with third countries);
- the multiple forms of interdependence that have evolved in implementing the CSDP;
- the increasingly *communitarian* and justiciable[1] nature of the commitments incumbent on all Member States flowing from the Area of Freedom, Security and Justice (AFSJ), covering external border controls, asylum, immigration and the prevention of crime, alongside specific tasks on border checks, asylum and immigration; judicial cooperation in civil matters; judicial cooperation in criminal matters; and police cooperation.

The following evaluates the risks and the opportunities to UK foreign and security policy on the basis of dissociating from, or remaining connected to, the EU in three key areas: the CFSP, CSDP and AFSJ. In each of these three areas, Britain has paradoxically exhibited both pioneering and reluctant attitudes, remaining defiantly autonomous in those areas touching on the retention of material forms of hard power (CSDP), while actively supporting European collaboration in others (Europol and Eurojust).

The potential change within these three areas rests upon two key key factors. First, the UK's ability to identify those foreign, security and defence requirements that would *benefit from continued cooperation* with the EU. Second, the ordering of those national preferences based on a hierarchy of strategic options identified between 2017–19 (and beyond) by UK decision-makers which supports both its traditional preferences and requirements of a post-Brexit status).

During the 2016 referendum campaign, foreign policy was largely sidelined in favour of trade access and business opportunities, as well as issues of migration, EU law and border control. The few foreign policy discussions that did surface merely itemised the UK's hard and soft power arsenals. Hard power for example focused on the UK's military hardware, defence industry size and nuclear capability, with soft power ranging from London's role as global financial hub to British diplomatic networks covering the UN Security Council, NATO, G8, the UK–US 'special relationship' and the Commonwealth. Such lists however represent merely one side of the British foreign policy structure, and are only made viable by the genuinely magnifying impact of the following two principles, which combine Britain's hard and soft power facets. First, UK membership of the EU has for 40 years been a substantive, and vital, element of its own national foreign and security policy. Second, while resistant to enhanced institutionalisation of some aspects of security and defence within the EU itself, the UK government itself has accepted that it is 'strongly in the UK's interests to work through the EU in a number of policy areas' based on the 'the extent to which EU external action correlates to UK national interests' (HM Government 2013).

Taken together, the problems are clear: in removing itself from both the *collective form* and the *collaborative content* of the CFSP, the CSDP and the AFSJ, Britain risks both a diminishment of its soft-power *diplomatic status*, and an attenuation of its hard-power security and defence capabilities across continental Europe in the short and quite possibly the long term. Equally however, the practical difficulties entailed in a wholesale removal from these three areas, which combine both intergovernmental and supranational decision-making, as well as the UK's uneven approach in collaborating on some aspects of EU foreign affairs whilst disengaging with others, may ultimately produce less uncoupling in foreign policy than in other areas. The hard/soft Brexit spectrum has complicated an easy understanding of Britain's preferred approach to leaving the EU. However, given the strategic imperatives of retaining both its hard and soft power attributes, including their European foundations, the government's initial message from the February 2017 White Paper will likely remain the priority, i.e. to 'continue to cooperate closely with our European partners on foreign affairs', recognising that in security terms, the UK is 'uniquely well placed to develop and sustain a mutually beneficial model of cooperation … from outside the Union' (HM Government 2017a, 61).

The Common Foreign and Security Policy (CFSP)

In terms of refashioning its foreign policy identity, the challenge is both essential and existential. Britain has already undergone a complete sea change in shifting from a post-imperial to a twentieth- and now twenty-first-century power. Decolonisation has further shrunk its geo-political footprint, and neither the Commonwealth nor the vagaries of its relationship with the US have yielded the opportunities promised in Churchill's three circles (which envisaged British leadership in Europe, the Commonwealth and the 'Anglosphere'). Austerity cost-cutting has forced the majority of shrinkages in twenty-first-century foreign and security policy. In terms of Brexit, however, if the emphasis is simultaneously upon cost efficiency and maintaining an effective British foreign policy presence, then decision-makers in London will need to explain – to national and European audiences alike – what genuinely constitutes the UK's ability to remain a 'networked' foreign policy actor both in and beyond the EU. Both the 2015 National Security Strategy and the Strategic Defence and Security Review relegated the role of the EU within the terrain of UK foreign policy. Yet networks are premised both upon connectivity with, and reach to, a range of partners, generally made easier via a larger bloc of coordinated actors drawing upon both financial and diplomatic tools to cultivate a range of third-party agreements. This is precisely what EU membership has produced for Britain. The combined clout derived from the EU's Single Market, trade agreements, development and economic partnerships, humanitarian assistance and wide-spread diplomatic engagement represents a wide and versatile range of foreign policy tools that could never be replicated by a single state. Taken together, the magnifying power of the EU undoubtedly boosts British connectivity with a range of EU and non-EU states, regions and institutions, which – overall – constitute a foreign policy 'plus'.

The benefits to retaining some form of partnership with the EU, whether as a quasi-integrated partner, mid-range associate, or aligned ally requires balancing Britain's interest in remaining an important player in Europe alongside post-referendum promises made by the British government to become a truly 'global' actor. However, the two are in no way mutually exclusive, indeed they are deeply connected, as far as mainland Europe, NATO and most international forms of governance are concerned. The British government itself conceded as much in the 2010–15 Review of the Balance of Competences, assessing that it is 'generally strongly in the UK's interests to work through the EU in foreign policy'. More broadly, the CFSP could offer a host of benefits to the UK, covering both general strategy and the day-to-day operations of European foreign, security, defence, development, humanitarian action and trade. These include for example continued CFSP influence via associate membership, consultative observership, or a case-by-case format in the European External Action Service (EEAS), Foreign Affairs Council (FAC), the Political and Security Committee (PSC) and related Working

Groups. The benefits of such a status would also present regional advantages to Britain in terms of presence and access, both *within* (e.g. in the Levant including Iraq, Lebanon and Turkey) and *beyond* (e.g. the Gulf, West and East Africa, Pakistan and Afghanistan, and Southeast Asia) the EU neighbourhood in tandem with current national strategies.

Equally, the opportunities afforded by disengagement from the EU can be categorised first according to the institutional and budgetary latitude of working outside formal EU structures, and second, on the basis of a redrafted global mandate. The first permits Britain to permanently sideline its involvement in areas like the European Neighbourhood Policy as a whole, or specific diplomatic approaches with the Ukraine, the Balkans and Turkey that have not been prioritised by the Foreign and Commonwealth Office (FCO). The second could spur Britain to improve its bilateral relationships with individual EU Member States while cultivating non-EU connections, allowing the UK to carve out its much-vaunted 'Global Britain' foreign policy, in parallel with, or consciously reoriented away from Europe (Chalmers 2017, 8). Whatever the specific EU+ format that emerges, 'it should not be too difficult to consider a number of informal mechanisms which would enable this cooperation to continue', ranging from formal participation to the agenda-based Gymnich format (Dijkstra 2016, 2).

The Common Security and Defence Policy (CSDP)

The UK's engagement with the CSDP is a tale of two attitudes. First, a pioneering commitment to the entire concept of autonomous European security in the 1998 St Malo Agreement. Second, the erosion of interest and commitment to subsequent initiatives, from leadership in military-oriented CSDP operations, including the role of Battlegroups and European Defence Agency (EDA).

The CSDP entailed for its members a novel series of security and defence objectives, tools and attitudes, all generally premised upon the prevention, management and resolution of conflict through the use of civilian and military resources. Known as the Petersberg Tasks, this challenging spectrum includes peacekeeping, monitoring disputed borders, maintaining ceasefires and enabling peace agreements, election monitoring, state-oriented capacity building, police and armed forces training and civil society support. Since 2003, this has been implemented in the form of a number of missions covering Africa, Asia, the Middle East, the Western Balkans, Eastern Europe and the Caucasus, most generally accredited as successful if low-level examples of bespoke European peace-keeping. Union-wide CSDP obligations to enhance the collective capabilities of EU Member States entail the coordination of military procurement and enhancing the interoperability of the joint military forces necessary to undertake the Petersberg Tasks. Measured against its own goals of defence spending, research and development and a fully functioning European Defence Agency, the EU's collective defence and security progress has proved less successful, with Britain having done little to assist this uninspiring trend.

As an EU member, the UK has remained distrustful of the entire concept of the CSDP, opposed to the coordination of military hardware or personnel, and a slim contributor to CSDP military ops, preferring capacity-building projects based on civilian missions. Further, the UK has not catalysed the voluntaristic method of hardware and personnel commitment, and opposed both the expansion of the European Defence Agency and the establishment of a permanent military EU operational headquarters. Instead, Britain prefers a balance of NATO multilateral frameworks and ex-EU bilateral defence relations (e.g. France, Germany and Poland). Arguably, the majority of UK security and defence decisions taken in the past decade 'have been made with no reference to military roles that might be undertaken by the UK through the EU' (Whitman 2016, 259).

It could of course be argued that, given the fall-off in UK commitment to the CSDP as a whole in recent years, there is far less to untangle in terms of decoupling the two sides, and that Britain's 'security' surplus combined with its defence punch will fall disproportionately heavily upon the EU. However, caution should be taken with this approach. First, the interdependent nature of defence, in terms of R&D, rationalised budgets, and geopolitical requirements of a restive Europe and volatile neighbourhood together suggest that Britain's role as a European defence provider, and a security underwriter will *increase*, not decrease. Second, the UK has had accredited successes in both military and civilian operations, and clearly views itself as a leader within, if not actually of, the CSDP.[2]

Third, these contributions are important, even impressive, and arguably permit the UK to claim to have 'helped increase stability in Europe' (van Ham 2017; HM Government 2017a, 63). They are also evidence of a trend that is likely to continue, with the UK participating as a non-EU Member State on an op-by-op basis, for example, via the 2011 established framework agreement on crisis management operations allowing US involvement. Recent non-EU involvement in EU Battlegroups on the basis of framework participation agreements by Norway, Turkey, Macedonia, Ukraine, Iceland and Serbia could therefore be easily complemented by the UK to boost interoperability and ensure strategic coverage (Tardy 2014).

Again, the choice to do so will simply echo current trends, with the UK balancing EU involvement alongside commitments to NATO, and against the context of its emerging post-Brexit foreign policy. The UK's voice has historically been uneven in this area, and its participation entirely driven by individuated rather than collective interests. Relative gains arising from European cooperation are an acknowledged plus, but their loss is not necessarily perceived as a minus; equally the multiplying effect used to explain the overall heft of the EU (if not its actual effectiveness) remains now – and post-2019 – fundamentally less important than the practical effects of the sheer capacity to implement policy *effectively*, and the prestige of doing so *credibly* in the eyes of European and international partners.

The Area of Freedom, Security and Justice (AFSJ)

An area of acknowledged UK leadership is the Area of Freedom, Security and Justice, which covers a host of areas within cross-border police and judicial cooperation. These are vital to the safety and security of both the UK and European states, and are likely to be prioritised in the post-2019 UK–EU Transitional Agreement. The requirement for cross-national security agreements also illustrate – as much as defence proper – the erosion of 'the benign security environment in Europe', and the increase of territorial, ideological, social and technology-based threats arising within Europe and its peripheries (Chalmers 2017, 2). The four areas set out in the 2017 White Paper include workers' rights, transport policy, science and research, and security, law enforcement and criminal justice (entitled 'cooperating in the fight against crime and terrorism'), with the latter strongly worded regarding the need 'to work more closely with our partners, including the EU and its Member States' (HM Government 2017a, 61). As with defence, the document lists examples detailing UK leadership of, and broader benefits from, collective efforts covering:

- Europol systems coordinating UK and EU police forces;
- participation in 13 of Europol's operational priority projects against organised crime;

- the use of the European Arrest Warrant to extradite 8,000 suspected criminals (2004–15);
- the benefits of the Schengen Information System II alert system;
- the EU Passenger Name Records rules;
- the European Criminal Records Information System (ECRIS) to enable criminal convictions.

Cooperation on such issues appears undeniably beneficial for both sides. The question is therefore not whether UK–EU security and criminal justice measures, as well as those concerning cyber security and anti-terrorism cooperation, should continue, but rather how, and on the basis of what institutional, legal and budgetary capacity. An operational membership of agencies including Europol and Eurojust, the maintenance of Joint Investigation Teams, as well as access to key databases like SIS II and ECRIS, and even the continued use of the EAW, could likely be negotiated without much difficulty (Bond et al. 2016). Equally, cooperation at the EU-level regarding anti-terrorism strategies, data-sharing and other issues is likely to be strongly supported by both sides, although the differing perspectives of Member States on data-sharing itself has yet to produce a clear 'European' position (Black et al. 2017).

More complex will be the daily challenges of border control, given the toxic nature of this issue before and after the referendum. Despite the rather blithe assertion in the 2017 White Paper that the UK will 'focus on operational and practical cross-border cooperation', no detail regarding the challenges of juxtaposed border control with France and Belgium has been forthcoming. Nor has clarity emerged regarding bilateral agreements for local police cooperation, e.g. between Kent and the Lille Prefecture, despite the pressing need for such settlements (Hadfield & Hammond 2016).

The UK's role outside the Schengen Area has produced a series of bilateral agreements covering border management relative to security, safety, transport and immigration. Most notable are the Canterbury Treaty (1986) regarding the operation of the Channel Tunnel (opened in 1994), the Sangatte Protocol establishing the principles of juxtaposed border controls, and the 2003 Le Touquet Treaty routinising pre-embarkation immigration checks between the UK, France and Belgium. At a minimum, effective bilateral relations between the UK and its proximate neighbours laying out the rights and obligations of either side pursuant to all forms of transport, transit and mobility must be swiftly established. More broadly, these agreements need to be framed against the emergent migration and asylum agenda of the EU, as well as seasonal and structural requirements for goods and passenger transport in key areas like Calais, Dunkerque, Dover, Folkestone and Portsmouth.

Conclusions

Timing is never easy. The EU's most recent attempt at redefining its regional and global foreign and security challenges was released within a day of the UK referendum. Article 50 itself fell within a fortnight of the 60th anniversary of the foundational Treaty of Rome, likewise the UK government's 2017 White Paper on Brexit and the European Commission's own White Paper on the Future of Europe. The latter made no mention at all of Brexit, conceding that 'for too many, the EU fell short of their expectations' while paraphrasing Jean Monnet by suggesting (possibly unhelpfully) that the 'Union has often been built on the back of crises and false starts' (European Commission 2017b, 6). Interestingly, each of the five scenarios which the 2017 White Paper outlines to move Europe forward provides some surface area for continued British involvement, from an emphatically reworked trade relationship, to framework agreements enabling a 27 + 1 approach to CFSP, CSDP and ASFJ, to enhanced cooperation on ringfenced policies with bespoke groups, to ex-EU bilateral relations. The UK may not be able to assist the EU in 'doing much more together', but it could dispose of its awkward reputation within the EU and become a more consistent partner from without.

20
Turning back the clock
The illusion of a global political role for Britain

Christopher Hill

It was almost inevitable that the Brexit decision of 2016 would lead British ministers to cast around for alternative points of reference for the country's general foreign policy orientation – even if the issue of diplomatic coordination with European partners was barely an issue in the referendum campaign. The government could hardly respond to the result by reaffirming Britain's geopolitical destiny as part of a European 'pole' in world politics. On the other hand the prospect of appearing to have no option but to become bag-carrier to the US also had little appeal. The election of President Trump made that even less attractive. Thus it was hardly surprising that Prime Minister Theresa May and her Cabinet started to talk increasingly of Britain's 'global' future. What this might mean in practice is by no means clear, and cannot be understood without reference to the historical background.

The historical background

Historians tend to date the start of Britain's decline as the world's leading power from the end of the nineteenth century, when economic difficulties and the emergence of Germany, Russia and the US as potential rivals began to expose the fault lines in the country's hegemonic position (Reynolds 2016, 131–42). Of course it took two world wars over the ensuing 70 years to sound the definitive death knell of British primacy, and another 20 before the empire came to an end, but by 1945 it had become clear to any independent observer that de Tocqueville's prediction from 1835, that Russia and America would dominate world politics, had come to pass (de Tocqueville 1839, 432–3).

It took British governments several decades before the practical meaning of this change was fully absorbed. Although Indian independence had to be conceded immediately, and the Mandate over Palestine was suddenly abandoned – with disastrous consequences – there was no question of embarking on full-scale decolonisation. Indeed when the young Elizabeth II came to the throne in 1952 on the death of her father, she spoke immediately of her responsibility 'to advance the happiness and prosperity of my peoples, spread as they are all the world over'. Even five years later, when the empire began to unravel, with most African colonies reaching independence by 1964, there was no presumption that Britain's geostrategic situation would change. It took the Vietnam War, the end of 'Confrontation' in Malaysia, and finally the economic crisis and devaluation of sterling in late 1967 to force withdrawal from the military bases 'east of Suez' and an associated rethinking of the country's world role (McCourt 2009).

For the next 15 years the principal concern of British foreign policy was to establish its European credentials. The UK joined the EEC in 1973, but it had already been participating informally in the new system of foreign policy coordination labelled European Political Cooperation. The combination of the Vietnam War and the decision by the Organization of the Petroleum Exporting Countries (OPEC) to use the oil weapon against the West seemed to make it imperative for Europeans to band together and to seek diplomatic rather than military solutions to the pressing problems of the Cold War and the Middle East. For Britain, however, it was thought imprudent to give up on the idea of the 'special relationship' with Washington, and so a balancing act had to be performed, on the basis of an optimistic belief in its ability to act as a political bridge between the two main pillars of the West.

The idea of British indispensability was turned on its head during the Falklands War of 1982, which was won with discrete military help from France and the US, together with European solidarity in imposing sanctions against Argentina (although Ireland and Italy broke ranks after a month). This was why Margaret Thatcher, in her memoirs, praised President Mitterrand, when on other issues she diverged sharply from him, especially over aspects of the European project (Thatcher 1993, 182–3). Still, it was on Thatcher's watch that the Single European Market was launched, and no serious debate took place about leaving the EC.

Significantly, however, Thatcher's successes, attracting more consensus abroad than at home, led her to revive the idea of Britain as a major independent power in the world – 'putting the Great back into Britain' – and to criticise the Foreign Office for its belief in the need for multilateral diplomacy, seen by her as mere defeatism.

The difficult interlude of John Major's governments between 1990–7 saw growing unrest among Conservatives, especially those dismayed by the coup which had forced out Thatcher. They focused increasingly on the perceived failings of the EU, as it had become, through the coincidence of the ambitious Maastricht Treaty of 1993 with Europe's inability to stop the savage wars which had broken out in former Yugoslavia (Hill 1993). The Conservative divisions, however, simply brought New Labour to power, and inaugurated a decade in which Tony Blair took forward Thatcher's ambitions for Britain to give a lead in international affairs, albeit with a different kind of spin.

Blair wanted to make Britain a force for good in the world, in line with the general trend towards 'good international citizenship' and the 'responsibility to protect'. Indeed, he and Foreign Secretary Robin Cook were both prominent in pushing that new agenda. There was, as so always in Britain, a sense of moral superiority about both the right and duty to take a central role in world politics – even if diminishing power meant that increasingly it had to take the form of 'thought leadership' and political entrepreneurship. At first it seemed that New Labour would be keen to use the EU as its platform, perhaps in conjunction with France, but that idea faded – first with the decision to stand apart from the new euro currency, and then with the fall-out from 9/11, which led Blair to see the UK–US alliance as the key bulwark against the forces of darkness. Steadily the distance from France and Germany increased, particularly through the traumatic divisions over the Iraq war of 2003 (MacShane 2015, 84–107). Growing Euroscepticism in Britain was encouraged more than assuaged by the referendum results in France and the Netherlands which killed off the idea of a European constitution. But it was the consequences of EU enlargement, working through unexpected ways, which really turned up the flame of popular antagonism.

Enlargement

Britain had long been a supporter of EU enlargement, as a onetime beneficiary itself, for largely strategic reasons. These took two forms.

First was the geopolitical concern to stabilise east-central Europe in the aftermath of communism, although there was also an enthusiasm (in principle) for Turkish accession, raising the questions of what kind of Europe the UK ultimately envisaged and of how far its borders should extend. The second reason was more devious, if hardly secret, as it amounted to the wish to stop integration in its tracks – the assumption being that the widening of the EU would inevitably make deepening much more difficult, if not impossible. It would also be likely to create more allies for Britain around the Council table, with many of the new members being fervently pro-US and pro-NATO – as well as, of course, most unwilling to envisage the disappearance of their newly regained national sovereignty. These assumptions proved to be largely correct, although their practical implication derived from a Faustian pact with Germany, which laboured under the illusion that it could promote widening and deepening in parallel. Another factor was the weakness of France, which was deeply sceptical about enlargement but lacked the political will and capacity to halt the UK–German project.

But enlargement proved to have negative externalities both for the EU and for Britain. It had not been widely foreseen how the accession of 12 new and predominantly poor countries would impact on social and economic life inside the existing Member States, given the principle of the free movement of labour enshrined in the Treaties. In particular, the British decision to allow free movement to occur from the first day of membership in 2004 (rather than to manage the flow of new arrivals through a transition period, as France and Germany did) led to nearly a million people coming to Britain over the following decade from the so-called A8 countries admitted to the EU in 2004 (Consterdine 2016). It led also to the image of the British economy as a kind of El Dorado for those living in European states with low wages and high unemployment rates – which soon came to include, once the financial crisis had started in 2007, not just the further new Member States Bulgaria, Romania, but also Italy, Spain and France. Unsurprisingly, this produced a backlash inside the UK against the sheer scale and pace of change, which had led even small country towns to face pressures on schools and housing, and inevitably weakened the bargaining position of workers over wages, in what was already becoming a 'gig economy'.[1] Although not the whole story of what happened in 2016, there can be little doubt that this combination of factors, replicated to differing degrees across the EU, had serious effects in terms of the rise of populism and Euroscepticism, which in Britain eventually led to the shock vote to leave the EU.

Between Europe and globalism

This sequence of events contains several ironies with respect to the ambivalence between a European and a global orientation in British society. For one thing the tensions arising over Afro-Caribbean and South Asian immigration from the late 1950s, which initially focused on the issue of colour, had by the turn of the millennium sufficiently subsided to give the impression that Britain had become a genuinely cosmopolitan country. Many Britons owned property in France and Spain, just as others maintained links with their roots in the diverse states of the Commonwealth. The 'little England' stereotype seemed increasingly out of date. Younger people enjoyed the freedom of movement offered by the EU, with stag nights in Prague and Tallinn booming and some starting to take advantage of the Erasmus network to spend a year in a continental university. It was, however, a warning sign that British universities were more populated by students and teaching staff from elsewhere in the EU than vice versa, while the boisterous British groups travelling abroad in search of cheap beer, sun and sangria tended to be noted for their parochialism, even xenophobia, more than any sense of cultural Europeanism.

This tendency was present in the narrow majority which voted for Brexit in June 2016. There were many strands to that coalition, but it does seem that education and age were significant factors in deciding preferences, with the older and less well educated tending to vote Leave, and the younger and better educated tending to vote Remain (although differential turnout was also a factor), an older generation seeming to be more resentful over the wave of immigration from the EU which had taken place since 2004. But many of all ages and levels of education were concerned about the associated loss of sovereignty, and remained unconvinced by the economic arguments made by the Remain side (Clarke et al. 2017, 146–174).

There are thus many who appear to favour the view of Britain regaining its independence through leaving the EU, and thus making its own way internationally. They might even believe the notion, trumpeted by the right-wing tabloids, that Britain is 'the greatest country in the world', and can regain its position as a great power. In this they find comfort in the government's embarrassing public relations campaign for exports and tourism simply labelled 'Great'. Even the reception desk to the Foreign and Commonwealth Office now greets its visitors with notices instructing them that the country is 'Great', in every possible way. Yet the prime minister and most of her colleagues, certainly including the senior reaches of the civil service, are fully aware that going it alone is wholly incompatible with the nature of the British economy, with the aspirations of British foreign policy, with its security and defence obligations, and with the transnational links of large numbers of its population. If the UK is now to place itself outside the network of EU institutions and close relationships, therefore, some alternative will have to be found.

For the reasons explained earlier, hugging the US even closer is not attractive either practically or politically. The relationship is hugely asymmetrical. For its part the Commonwealth is not the kind of organisation capable of becoming a major trading bloc or foreign policy unit, even assuming the UK has major interests in common with more than few of its members. All that remains, therefore, is the trope which has quickly come to dominate both the thinking of hard Brexiteers and of official discourse – that of a 'global Britain', creating a series of overlapping special relationships with key states and markets across the world, thus maximising its access, flexibility and influence while escaping the straitjacket of a supranational regional grouping, which in any case was beginning to display sclerotic characteristics. This idea, as it happens, is not so far removed from the 'bridge-builder' notion employed by Tony Blair and some of his predecessors, suggesting a unique role for the UK in connecting up the different regions and outlooks of the world. That in its turn was a version of Winston Churchill's post-1945 conception of Britain as being at the centre of three intersecting circles – Atlantic, European and imperial (Sanders & Houghton 2017). The difference now, of course, from both the Blairite and Churchill visions, is that Europe is pushed to the margins. If it has any place in conceptions of Britain's role, then it is only on the presumption that London will still enjoy close and influential relations with its ex-partners despite having snubbed the EU and damaged the prospects of the City remaining as Europe's key financial centre, particularly in relation to the highly profitable business of clearing euro-denominated securities.

Some practical implications

What are the practical implications of this latest iteration of resistance to the idea of Britain's regional destiny? They can be analysed at three levels: economic, politico-military and sociocultural.

It is at the economic level that most of the discussion has so far occurred, as the Brexiteers are anxious to show that the economy will not only not be damaged by leaving the EU, but will actually benefit from it.

This will apparently occur through freedom from regulatory constraints and from the burdens imposed by the Community budget and its common policies in trade, agriculture and fisheries. The UK will be able to conclude bilateral trade deals with more vibrant economies than those of the depressed European Single Market, and gradually diversify its economic life.

This may turn out to be a plausible scenario. But at best it will take a long time to realise, with considerable transition costs along the way. And the conceit that Britain will be the 'champion of free trade' runs into the considerable difficulty that the UK accounts for less than 4 per cent of the world's gross product, and is likely to be overtaken by emerging economies before long. Moreover, the bigger players like the USA, China and Japan are only qualified supporters of free trade, especially with the current wind blowing towards protectionism. In any case, tariffs on manufactured goods are already low with little scope for improvement. Given that the service sector, which accounts for around 75 per cent of the UK's GDP, is the most difficult area to open up, any drive for free competition led by the City of London is going to resemble a conductor without an orchestra. Indeed, Brexit has already convinced some financial houses to relocate staff into the eurozone.

On the politico-military front there is a prima facie case for seeing the UK as still having a global role. It is one of nine states in possession of nuclear weapons, and it has a sophisticated ICBM delivery system. It is a permanent member of the United Nations Security Council (UNSC), and a key player (if not the leader) in the Commonwealth, one of the few international organisations outside the UN with both developing and developed countries as members. This is the basis for the claim by Labour as well as Conservative politicians that Britain has special responsibilities for international order, beyond its particular national interests.

But closer scrutiny reveals a distinct thinness to these claims. The 'independent' deterrent is in practice very closely tied to US strategy and technology and is completely unusable when it comes to the global projection of power. In the Commonwealth the fact that most other Member States are the product of the British empire, with many negative memories of the experience, hobbles UK policy as much as it provides an advantage. As for the UNSC, Britain's position depends on a defence of the 1945 status quo which is seen as increasingly untenable by the majority within the General Assembly. A reconstitution of the UNSC to reflect contemporary conditions would be very unlikely to give either Britain or France the vetoes they currently enjoy. It is interesting, moreover, that while the government talks about 'a global Britain', that does not lead it to think of turning towards the universal institutions of the UN system to replace the regional EU network. Rather, the tendency is to go along with US scepticism towards the UN or at least to lack the enthusiasm and courage needed to revive it. A more honest version of globalism might have Britain taking a lead in the reform of the UNSC, perhaps by accepting the set of revolving semi-permanent memberships envisaged by Kofi Annan's High Level Panel in 2005, and by stressing the way the UN framework enables states to strike the balance between sovereign independence and the evident value of multilateral cooperation in so many fora.

Britain and France see themselves, with reason, as the only European states able to project military force outside their own region – as they have done over the last decade in Afghanistan, Libya and Syria. Yet none of these ventures has provided a successful template for future action. Indeed, in Britain, public opinion has turned decisively against putting troops on the ground even for humanitarian reasons. For their part the professional military have learned hard lessons through their relative failures in Basra in Iraq, and in Helmand province in Afghanistan. Their resources have been run down to the point where even small wars present serious dangers of overstretch. Given the continued determination to prioritise the defence of the Falkland Islands, the resources available for any British government to back up a forward foreign policy with serious military leverage are very limited. The idea of acting as a major power again in Africa, let alone the potential crisis zone of the east and south China seas, is simply implausible. Two new aircraft carriers are due to come into service in 2020 but it is by no means clear what foreign or defence policy they will be serving beyond that of adjunct to the US.

Thus in the politico-military field the idea of global Britain has little content. Emerging regional powers like Brazil, India and South Africa do not need to take the UK seriously into account when considering their own security, apart from the attractions of buying British arms. But what of the sociocultural dimension and Britain's famous 'soft power'? Are we capable of setting standards which others will wish to emulate, thus giving Britain a role of cultural, intellectual and political leadership? There is an obvious element of hubris here given the tendency to downplay the appeal of others, whether France, Germany and Italy in Europe or global success stories like China, Singapore and South Korea. Even President Putin has become a model for some, showing that not everyone wants, or even admires, what Britain has to offer. Yet the UK's higher education, legal and medical systems are still widely admired, while the health of its artistic, musical and literary scenes, assisted by the English language and Britain's heritage, means that the country has an unusually high global profile. This can to some extent be turned to economic and political advantage, but only indirectly and over the long term. It is hardly a substitute for being associated with the most successful regional organisation, market and zone of civility ever created, which, for all the EU's many faults, is seen in the rest of the world as a major point of reference – especially if a multipolar world system is ever to come about.

Britain has a population of 64 million with large minorities from India, Pakistan the Caribbean and a number of African countries. This multiculturalism gives it, by definition, many global linkages. Yet it also now has large minorities from many EU partner states, notably France, Italy, Poland, Romania and Spain. Whilst it is unlikely these people will be forced by Brexit to depart, they might start to drift away of their own accord, in which case labour market needs will probably seek cheap labour once again from Commonwealth sources. That would have implications for collective identity. It has always been revealing that the British media talk about 'Europe' as if it is a place apart, and it cannot be denied that a large part of the population does not feel European, lacking language skills and having tastes in food, music and film which look more towards the US, or towards Asia. So the idea of combining independence with a global rather than regional outlook may well continue to prove popular, especially if migration from Europe slows and that from other parts of the world picks up again.

Unfortunately, however, it does not follow that UK public policy will have much capacity to shape the international economy or the international political system. In fact, despite the Brexit decision the UK will be forced to find some way of working in partnership with the states of the European continent, albeit on worse terms than before. The government has implicitly recognised this fact, first with some strong statements about the importance of deepening the Franco-British defence relationship based on the Lancaster House Treaties of 2010, and then implicitly through its ham-fisted attempt to threaten the EU with the withdrawal of cooperation on security if a good exit deal is not on offer. Over recent years NATO and the EU have worked ever more closely together on security matters, a category which now routinely includes counter-terrorism, crime and migration – all of which cross over the domestic–foreign divide, and thus implicate questions of sovereignty. The UK cannot afford to disdain working closely with EU Member States on all this, for reasons of geographical contiguity and common values, as Theresa May acknowledged in November 2016 when she agreed to opt in to the scheme to share fingerprint and DNA data across the EU.

As for classical foreign policy, despite the derision of Brexiteers towards the idea of European harmonisation, Britain has actually been a leading player for 40-plus years in Europe's system of institutional coordination. It is a loose, often dysfunctional, but also indispensable system which accepts differences, but which also enables collective action on such issues as economic sanctions and the Iranian nuclear negotiations – not least because it can dispose of the EU's economic and human resources for political purposes. The prospect of London standing apart from this system, while the other Europeans confer on a wide range of key issues, from Ukraine to Algeria, from North Korea to Israeli settlements, and then (perhaps) associating itself post hoc, is neither plausible nor encouraging. In practice the UK will want to have a de facto seat at the European foreign ministers' table, as the US has managed to do discreetly over the years. But the US is Europe's indispensable ally and the world's only superpower. A state which has wilfully given up its privileged position in foreign policy consultations is not likely to be welcomed back to the centre of discussions. Ministers will therefore discover quite soon what its professional diplomats know already, that the notion of being able to opt in and out of European endeavours is an embarrassing mirage. The historical clock cannot be wound back.

21
A speculation on the future of Europe

John R. Gillingham

Speculation about the future is not necessarily to be sneered at. At times it can be useful and even necessary, if only to shed light on long-term historical trends often obscured by the crushing avalanche of daily news as reported by the media. Brexit is a case in point. Developing an understanding of its impact on Europe is no straight-forward matter. It will require explicating any number of complicated interrelationships that unfold across several planes. The domestic politics of Great Britain is only one of them. Another is, of course, the state of the EU. Finally, larger forces are in play: an emergent China and advanced new technologies are driving change forward at a breakneck pace. In addition, an erratic and untested American administration is in office.

The number of variables is daunting. The eventual consequences of the recent elections in Great Britain and France cannot be predicted. The actions and impacts of President Trump's foreign policy must still be subject to speculation. An even larger spectre hovers overhead: the possible creation – for better or worse – of a new international order to replace the American-designed system put into place after World War II.

Present uncertainty has given rise to both hopes and fears but also to public confusion as well as an inordinate amount of theorising about the future. It would be rash at this early date to project a scenario of events, let alone predict eventual outcomes. Surprises are in store. At the same time, long-run historical trends will likely in the end determine how Brexit changes both Europe and Britain's relationship to it.

An electoral shock

The first surprise of the summer of 2017 came with the mistaken decision of Prime Minister Theresa May to call for a snap election in order to strengthen Britain's hand in the then forthcoming Brexit negotiations. It cost the Tories their parliamentary majority. Since the Brexit talks are still barely under way, it is impossible at this point to gauge how much, and to what effect, the UK's bargaining position has been weakened. There will, however, be no turning back from the decision to leave. The British assertion of parliamentary sovereignty will stand, and laws crafted by the CJEU will be subordinate to law made in the UK.

None of the dire predictions of the former Remain campaign, which might have reversed the referendum results, has come to pass. Above all, the British economy has not tanked and shows no signs of doing so. If anything, it has done rather well. 'Buyers' remorse' has therefore not put in a significant appearance. Nor does the reproach made by the Remain party that Brexit will lead to isolation carry much conviction. The British government has not 'gone nativist' or turned its back on Europe but seeks a new accommodation with it which, God willing, will result in global trade liberalisation, promote innovation and, in the end, may even improve the prospects of a reformed EU. Nor should the election's outcome be understood as a rebuke to Tory policy towards Europe. The Brexit issue in fact barely figured in Labour's campaign, which emphasised domestic policy to the virtual exclusion of Britain's future relationship to the EU. The occasional remarks of party chief Jeremy Corbyn on the subject can charitably be characterised as confused.

In spite of Prime Minister May's recent setback, Britain's chances of withdrawing from the EU on suitable terms seem good, at least as viewed from the perspective of the domestic scene. She has effectively neutered UKIP. The Scottish Nationalists were crushed in the election, and the ineffective Labour opposition cannot possibly form a government. The real threat to May is resistance from hard-liners within her own party (Chaffin 2017).

The Trump factor

Britain's chances of success in the Brexit negotiations will hinge in no small measure on international events, and in particular on the actions of the brash and mercurial American President Donald Trump, whose administration is still emerging from an infantile, post-election phase of policymaking. Nonetheless, governance by Tweet is gradually giving way to business as usual, and egregious public outbursts are yielding to golf course diplomacy. Trump may actually be starting to act like a genuine Republican. This should not be unexpected. His cabinet and circle of advisors are dominated by the usual big boys: representatives of Wall Street, the Pentagon and corporate America – the latter now including the giants of Silicon Valley. Only one thing may be said with certainty about Trump's intentions: he is committed to a 'growth agenda' based on the 'supply-side' economics of his predecessor, Ronald Reagan. Its failure could bring down his administration. The main political task facing the bombastic president is to appease his core electoral constituency of less than well off white folk, by means of gesture and rhetoric, while adopting policies which, while arguably beneficial overall, are contrary to their specific interests.

Trump's foreign policies must be seen in light of this domestic priority. There is much less to their purported radicalism than meets the eye. Here one must tread carefully. The president's understanding of international affairs is limited – how limited is, at this point, anyone's guess. This unpleasant fact is surely alarming, but hardly unique in the history of the American presidency. Ronald Reagan's knowledge of the world beyond Hollywood was equally sketchy. As reality sets in, Trump will have little choice but to back away from the outrageous stances of his early presidency and revert to the path of traditional American foreign policymaking. This trend, already evident in instance after instance, still has a long way to go before one can speak confidently of a return to the norm. And what happens between now and then cannot, of course, be foreseen. Yet, Trump no longer bashes NATO, has done nothing recent of significance to restrict immigration, and has backed away from the proposed wall along the border with Mexico. NAFTA will furthermore not be trashed but cosmetically enhanced, the TPP (Trans-Pacific Partnership) can be revived by the stroke of a pen, and the trans-Atlantic counterpart, the TTIP (Transatlantic Trade and Investment Partnership), faces greater opposition from Europe than from the US, where it never has become a significant public issue.

The US president will also try to revise the terms of the commercial relationships between America and China and between America and the EU, the main sources of trade discrimination against the US. Washington's efforts to re-fashion such trade deals do not, however, herald a return to the evils of beggar-thy-neighbour, but do betoken a shift in the balance of power among those who indulge in unfair commercial policies. Events favour such an approach. World commerce is slated to increase substantially over the coming years (Thomas 2017). Export competitiveness will remain at a premium in economic policymaking – a truism that will repeatedly be reinforced by the president's economic advisors (Ross 2017a, 2017b).

Three considerations will increase the likelihood of Trump's future pursuit of trade liberalisation: a better understanding of global economic interdependence; an inkling that the world is on the brink of a new technological era; and a realisation that his growth agenda will require acceptance of, as well as accommodation to, these realities (*Financial Times* 2016b). The president is moreover being pushed in this direction by heavy lobbying of powerful conservative pressure groups like farmers and ranchers, manufacturing exporters, as well as the automobile and petroleum interests (Ross 2017c).

Trump's presidency can be counted upon to produce policies little different from those of his predecessor. Like it or not, the outspoken man in the White House must build upon a legacy of bipartisanship in foreign policy. Continuity should become the rule, unless, of course, a string of unwitting White House blunders topples the apple cart. The possibility cannot be ruled out that Trump's intemperate behaviour catalyses something heretofore absent at the EU: a sense of Euro-patriotism strong enough to unite an administrative and political entity that is both deeply demoralised and all but immobilised by institutional flaws as well as bad policymaking.

The EU faces Brexit

Such an outcome, though optimal from the European standpoint, would be improbable for any number of reasons. Democracy did not figure in Monnet's original scheme and since then has only entered EU politics as an afterthought. Official Brussels continues, as always, to mistrust and manipulate the public. It follows that the EU has never won its citizens' affections, not to say loyalty. Policy errors of the past 20 years have furthermore driven Europe into a decade of depression and internal strife. Neither the will nor the necessary means to turn around the grim prospects facing it are at hand, or are soon likely to be (Ross 2017c).

Even a severe critic of the EU must acknowledge its remarkable initial accomplishment – devising a diplomacy of reconciliation in post-World War II Europe. But its years of greatness belong to a distant past. The EU has gone out as a beacon of hope for Europe's future. The EU actually crossed a point of no return many years ago – with the collapse of the ill-considered constitutional project in 2004. The debacle put paid to the dreams that it could evolve into a political federation and that the Single Market would ever be more than partially completed (Gillingham 2006, 47–54). Unachievable by fiat, a policy trajectory leading to Europe's federal future would have required years of consensus-building anchored in a record of success. Such a thing is hard to detect.

The shoddy and self-serving constitutional document served up for the approval of the member states in 2004 was so byzantine and opaque that not even its official sponsors could make sense of it. The famous *Non* in the French constitutional referendum of that year, which doomed the federal project, thus could not have turned on the merits or demerits of a proposal that no one understood, but instead grew out of a campaign waged on an issue of only secondary importance in the document itself, which was, however, fundamental to the nation's voters: a deep-seated aversion to foreign competition for jobs. The rejection of the proposed constitution both killed the hope of a politically united Europe and undermined the credibility of the fourth supposedly inviolate fundamental principle of the EU – unrestricted labour mobility between Member States – which went up in flames (Gillingham 2016, 120–141).

The eurozone project was an attempt to circumvent the EU's mounting unpopularity by imposing an economic *fait accompli*. The idea underlying it was that a single currency would require and generate common economic policies, thereby eventually forcing the formation of a political union. This grand plan has failed so miserably as to call into question the existence of the EU itself. The one-size-fits-all straightjacket of the European Monetary Union (EMU) has plunged the continent into a decade of depression; cheated a generation of young people out of jobs and opportunities; impoverished southern Europe; driven a thick emotional wedge between creditor and debtor nations; stifled innovation across the community; weakened both public and private finance; restricted European policymaking essentially to crisis management; skewed the operation of EU institutions; and embittered the public from north to south and east to west (Gillingham 2016, 153–4).

If pro-EU-optimists, whose annual growth predictions have consistently been wrong for nearly a decade, are right this time, recovery from the protracted depression in Europe may have just begun, thanks albeit largely to the superior economic performance of the US and China. It will nevertheless be many years until European memories fade of chronic double-digit unemployment, catastrophic youth unemployment twice or more as high, and widespread underemployment. Only a thorough institutional re-configuration of the eurozone can restore healthy rates of growth. Yet the need for such far-reaching reform has never been accepted in official Brussels.

To the extent that one can speak of a European government, its locus is, however, no longer the official EU capital, but Frankfurt, the headquarters of the ECB (*Financial Times* 2017b, 2017c; *Wall Street Journal* 2017a). Its austerity policies remain in place and will not be jettisoned until German opposition to loosening monetary and fiscal policy is overcome. In the meantime, a still-fragile Europe facing re-invigorated challenges from American technology and Chinese dynamism cannot afford economic setbacks of any kind.

One nowadays rarely encounters the hoary defence often made on behalf of the EU as an optimal or essential policymaking mechanism. The very idea indeed seems ludicrous when crisis has become endemic, the institution's very survival is at stake, and policy planning is effectively on hold. In official Brussels, tough talk barely conceals a sense of panic. Hence the deep sigh of relief – akin to hysteria – with which Euro-elites greeted Emmanuel Macron's election as president of France.

Europhile pundits veritably leaped over one another to proclaim it a turning point in the EU's dismal recent history. It hardly qualifies for such a distinction. The ferociously ambitious photogenic 39-year-old won the election on an historically low turnout and with the support of only a minority of the French electorate. It is wishful thinking to interpret the French vote as a ringing endorsement of the European integration project and unrealistic to imagine that Macron will have a free hand in negotiating for a stronger and more centralised EU (*Financial Times* 2017d, 2017e, 2017f). He lacks the backing of a real political party. It is also by no means certain that his quasi-liberal reform agenda – lengthening the work week, raising the retirement age, and reducing the size of the bureaucracy – will fare any better in the chamber of representatives than similar attempts, which failed him as adviser to the cabinet of the deeply unpopular Francois Hollande. If so, the fate of his future government, and France's economy, may be no different from that of his predecessor (*Wall Street Journal* 2017b).

It would be a mistake to conclude that Macron seriously plans to open up the economy. A typical product of the elitist French educational system, he will, if given the chance, reinforce the power of the state in the economy. Nor have the differences between France and Germany on economic policy been better than papered over. More will be needed than photo-embraces and platitudinous expressions of goodwill to persuade the German voting public to assume the heavy burden of EMU debt. Macron could in fact go the way of the EU's previous White Knight, the dynamic and handsome former Italian Prime Minister Matteo Renzi, who, in the interests of economic reform, tried in vain to install a presidential model of government in Rome. The instability of the Italian political system, together with a stagnant economy and a financial community on the verge of bankruptcy, makes the country the prime candidate for the next existential threat to the EU. The need for a massive emergency bank bailout has long been obvious (*Wall Street Journal* 2017c). To provide it, the Italian state, in flagrant violation of EMU rules aimed at creating a single financial market, has stepped in with a massive injection of public money and may again be called upon to do so again. The need for such national intervention obviously makes a mockery of boasts that the euro will displace the dollar as the anchor of the international monetary system (*Wall Street Journal* 2017d).

There are few grounds for optimism given the present state of the EU. The refugee crisis and its ugly cousin, Islamic terrorism, are ongoing problems, which defy Europe-wide solutions. Obfuscation, secondly, has been the sole EU policy response to the festering diesel emissions scandal, which has also shred the credibility of the Parliament as people's advocate, and that of the Commission as honest broker in trade relations. Corruption also remains rife throughout much of the European community. Brussels' policymaking in the critical field of high-tech industry has recently shifted from one of mere harassment of American IT giants in the guise of anti-trust policy to a coordinated campaign of outright bashing – of imposing stupendous fines from which there is no judicial recourse. Hence, the more than two trillion dollars in their European earnings which, under more favourable conditions, could have been ploughed into investment, remain unspent (Gillingham 2016, 199–205). The evident anti-American bias and injustice of EU policy can, moreover, be counted upon to produce a powerful backlash in Washington as well as to drive Silicon Valley into an unsought, unwanted, and undesirable alliance with the Trump administration. It will move the USA one step closer to China and its European followers in adopting policies that rip up the seamless web of the internet and strengthen the power of the state vis-á-vis civil society,

Over the longer term, the EU's anti-US IT campaign will reduce American financial involvement in European high technology, raise costs, and cause the EU member states to lag still further behind in a crucial growth field. Europe will therefore remain a bystander to the most consequential economic breakthrough of the era. Such long-run perils pale, however, by comparison to an immediate threat, the single currency, which, unless abandoned, or at least re-configured, will condemn Europe to chronic low growth.

The present outbreak of Macron-mania in Europhile circles may provide a reprieve from the continent's ailments if, and until, a powerful new individual or institution can take over effective leadership of the EU. By general agreement such a development cannot arise from within the discredited Commission, but must somehow emerge from a consensus of the 27 post-Brexit Member States (*Financial Times* 2017g). Finding a common denominator of policymaking will be a tall order in a now bitterly divided European community. Nor it is by any means easy to imagine – given the dysfunctional Apparat of official Brussels – how such a person or party could make its influence felt through the badly malfunctioning governance machinery. The policy of building up EU institutions finds little support outside of Germany except among Euro-elites. The sole alternative to 'more Europe' remains the devolution of authority to the Member States, as long-championed by Britain, which would preserve a single market or trade area, while leaving the rest of the EU policy machinery up for grabs.

A British alternative?

Two important considerations favour London's Brexit negotiating position (Sinn 2017). Without Britain's net contribution, first of all, the EU will be poorer; bargaining for spoils will become that much more difficult, pressure for an increase in contributions that much greater, and the likelihood of budget shortfalls that much stronger. The absence of the UK will, moreover, eliminate the blocking position which, under current EU rules, the 'free trade faction' shares with that of the 'protectionist faction', thereby opening the door either to a bolt by the former, or divisive conflict between the two. The remaining free traders will, in any case, need a British ally whether outside or inside the EU. At the same time, London's advocacy of a reform like EFTA (European Free Trade Association) bristles with difficulties, not least of all because those countries taking an approach like Britain's – and insisting on the supremacy of national law – may need lengthy transition periods in which to dismantle the *acquis communautaire*, the corpus of directives and regulations that are the *ne plus ultra* of EU membership. No two of these national procedures will be quite the same and their relationships of the individual states to either a reformed EU or a successor organisation may vary from case to case.

For this reason Britain's exit negotiations must demonstrate that departure from the EU can be beneficial. One can only hope that Prime Minister May's constructive attitude is appreciated by her EU interlocutors. The latter will in any case face heavy pressure from national business and financial communities intent upon making Brexit as mutually painless as possible. Most important of all, Britain must provide practical assurance that departure from today's EU can bring prosperity and build national confidence because it is consistent with and can strengthen with most powerful international trends re-shaping today's world. The auguries are by no means inauspicious. The predictions of the Brexit naysayers have, up to now, been wildly off the mark. Theresa May's leadership may be shaken up – but no worse. Donald Trump is being gradually housebroken, and his antics may well prove to be 'disruptive' in the positive sense of the word as currently understood in business circles, which implies promoting innovation and growth. The world economy is, like Britain's, on an upswing, and growing at a substantially higher rate than Europe's – a performance gap that seems almost certain to increase (Open Europe 2017).

As a worldwide phenomenon, the influence of protectionism cannot be denied: globalisation in its many forms and guises may be thrown temporarily into reverse. As a long-term trend, however, it is unstoppable. There is at least a fighting chance that Brexit will lead to a new chapter in the opening of the world economy. If so, the power of a supranational but regional political and economic bloc like the EU can only weaken over time.

VII: Democracy and legitimacy

22
Whither the 27?

Michael Shackleton

Introduction

What effect will the prospective departure of the UK from the EU have on the remaining 27 Member States? Will it release them from the handicap that British exceptionalism imposed and enable them to pursue a clearer political agenda? Or will it reveal a continuing inability to overcome their heterogeneity in the face of a populist storm, with the potential for the whole structure to come crashing down? This chapter is not designed to give a direct answer to this dichotomy but rather invites the reader to consider the choices that the EU will face in the post-Brexit world. The 27 will not have the luxury, even if they had the desire, to stand still. Rather, it will be suggested that they will be obliged to enter into a renewed phase in which they seek to identify what it means to use the phrase 'we Europeans' and, in so doing, find fresh ways to create the sense that EU citizens are bound together as part of a common political project.

The chapter is organised around the three strategies that van Middelaar (2013) identifies as a means of lending credibility to the sense of the words 'we Europeans': a German strategy as the search for a common identity to create 'our people', a Roman strategy as the production of tangible benefits for people in the EU 'to our advantage', and a Greek (or perhaps better, Athenian) strategy as enabling European citizens to participate in the political process so that we make 'our own decisions' in determining the direction of the Union. All three of these strategies are visible throughout the history of the Union and none has enjoyed anything like undiluted success. Nevertheless, they offer criteria against which the progress of the Union can be measured in the years ahead.

From a British perspective, the further development of the three strategies may seem irrelevant: even before the referendum, in February 2016, David Cameron had persuaded the European Council to accept that the UK 'is not committed to further political integration' and that 'the references to ever closer union do not apply to the UK' (European Council 2016). However, it will be suggested here that no matter how far changes in the EU extend, they will only serve to underline the growing gap between the political discourse on the two sides of the Channel and the increasing difficulty and indeed unlikelihood of the UK's ever being able to rejoin the EU, should it wish to change its mind.

Identity politics

The search for a common European identity has been hugely problematic throughout the history of the EU. It is widely interpreted as a kind of nation-building that both conflicts with and challenges the interests of nation-states, who wish to guard the exclusivity of their links with their own citizens. The argument over the design of the euro notes and coins was a clear indicator of a determination to avoid any attempt at the creation of a historical narrative behind the establishment of the new currency (van Middelaar 2013, 238–44).

And yet it is an issue that keeps re-emerging and that has never been removed from the agenda. No other state has indicated its wish to follow Britain in removing the reference in the Treaty to 'ever closer union', whatever their reticence about elevating the status of European identity. Indeed, even after the Constitutional Treaty was rejected in 2005, 16 of the then 27 states expressly declared that the flag with a circle of 12 golden stars on a blue background, the anthem based on the 'Ode to Joy' from the Ninth Symphony by Beethoven, the motto 'United in Diversity', the euro as the currency of the EU, and Europe Day on 9 May, 'will for them continue as symbols to express the sense of community of the people in the EU and their allegiance to it' (Declaration 52, Lisbon Treaty). Such a declaration makes it impossible to return to a world where European citizens are not obliged to ask what it is that distinguishes them from others outside the Union. Invisibility is no longer an option, as opponents of the EU rightly recognise.

The nature of the debate evolves in the light of political developments. In recent times, there has been less talk of symbols of unity and more a sense of the EU as a beleaguered actor in an ever more dangerous external environment, in severe need of a reinforced sense of common purpose. Donald Tusk, as president of the European Council, wrote a remarkably frank letter to the 27 heads of state or government (excluding the UK) in advance of the Malta summit in February 2017. The letter illustrated this mood of future uncertainty well. He pointed to a new geopolitical situation in the world, starting with an assertive China, an aggressive Russian foreign policy and radical Islamist movements in the Middle East and Africa, going on to include the challenge posed by the new American president, stating that 'particularly the change in Washington puts the EU in a difficult situation, with the new administration seeming to put into question the last 70 years of American foreign policy' (European Council 2017b). He called for greater determination and solidarity as essential prerequisites for the EU to survive. As he put it, 'If we do not believe in ourselves, in the deeper purpose of integration, why should anyone else?'

The perceived need for unity in the face of external threat puts the rest of the EU in a very different place from the UK. One of the central planks of government policy in Britain has been to look for a new trade agreement with America as part of the post-Brexit settlement, without any wish to suggest publicly at least that there is any clash of values between the two countries. UK policy is that the country is perfectly able to act effectively on the world stage post-Brexit, whereas the discourse at EU level is that those outside will be, in the phrase of the Declaration prepared for the 60th anniversary of the signing of the Rome Treaty, 'sidelined by global dynamics'.

A central issue for the EU27 is the extent to which the rhetoric of the European Council filters down into the attitudes of the European public. Will European citizens be willing to share this notion of common values and to accept the kind of policies that might express that sense of community, not least by a reinforcement of the borders between the outside and inside of the EU? There is some limited evidence that attitudes towards the EU have become more positive since the UK referendum (Bertelsmann Foundation 2016), but it is much too soon to claim that we are witnessing the creation of a European public under the pressure of external threat. What we have is a yardstick against which to measure future developments.

Policy structure

What, then, of the 'tangible benefits' that the EU generates? There is much discussion in the UK about the loss of access to funding, for example, for research for universities, for structural support in poorer areas or for the agricultural sector. The question that these sectors ask is: will the UK government be ready to match that funding once the UK is outside the EU? From the perspective of the 27, however, the issue is quite different: it is how to deal with the loss of revenue arising from the UK's departure. It is estimated that the 'Brexit gap' in the budget could amount to around €10 billion (Notre Europe 2017). Whatever solution is found for this shortfall, it is almost certain to have an impact on the shape of EU policies designed to generate public goods.

At present the funding of EU policies is organised through a multi-annual financial framework (MFF), which covers the seven years from 2014 to 2020. With UK withdrawal due to take place in 2019, there is going to be a considerable argument about the extent of its financial commitments beyond that date. However, the 'divorce bill', as it is known, remains a short-term issue, even if it is certain to generate considerable political heat. The more long-term issue is how to respond to the loss of UK revenue in the next MFF for the years after 2020. As Notre Europe comments, 'if the EU wanted to keep its budget at the current level and use the money currently spent in the UK on other projects, the gap would amount to €17 billion per year or €119 billion over the course of an MFF'.

The options for the 27 are all very difficult, politically speaking. To keep spending at its present level would mean the Member States would have to increase their contributions. The biggest increases would fall on the four states (Netherlands, Sweden, Germany and Austria) who at present receive a reduction in their contribution to the UK rebate, negotiated at Fontainebleau over 30 years ago. To reduce spending so that no one's contribution increased would require a major overhaul of EU policies, as the cut would correspond to the equivalent of a 20 per cent reduction in the Common Agricultural Policy (CAP) or the entire EU research framework budget (Horizon 2020) plus the Fund for Asylum, Migration and Integration. Even a combination of increased contributions and policy cuts would fall unequally across the Member States and generate a major split between net payers and net recipients, which would be difficult to implement, since any agreement will require unanimous consent.

One way of addressing these difficulties is to look again at the whole way that the EU is financed. In January 2017, a High Level Group chaired by the former Italian prime minister, Mario Monti, presented a report which argued in favour of new forms of EU revenue designed to support specific EU policy objectives, such as targeted levies to fight climate change or to promote energy efficiency (High Level Group on

Own Resources 2017). The more cynical may dismiss such ideas as unlikely to survive the struggle of competing national interests, but the departure of the UK may be precisely the kind of shock that enables the EU to ask questions about its revenue that have been considered taboo for over 40 years.

However, even if the discussion remains concentrated on expenditure, a new balance will have to be found. Since the 1980s a fundamental trade-off within the EU budget has been between the development of the Single Market and support for economic and social cohesion through the structural funds. The creation of the Single Market was the product of a bargain whereby countries with weaker economies were willing to open up their markets in exchange for structural support. Hence it was accepted that, when the EU was enlarged in 2004 and 2007 to include the poorer states of Central and Eastern Europe, part of the deal would involve substantial cohesion funding. As a result, Poland is today the largest beneficiary of the structural funds, receiving over €9 billion a year.

Now we are witnessing the start of a different discussion about the balance between different policy priorities as expressed through the EU budget. The new emphasis on improving the security of European citizens rather than stressing the freedom of the market is changing the budgetary debate. Thus we see a link emerging between cohesion spending and solidarity in dealing with the refugee crisis and mass migration into the EU. Austria, for example, has warned that net payers will refuse to continue paying into cohesion funds if the Eastern Europeans take no refugees. Chancellor Kern has explicitly said: 'If countries continue to avoid resolving the issue of migration, or tax dumping at the expense of their neighbours, they will not be able to receive net payments of billions from Brussels … . Solidarity is not a one-way street' (Wintour 2017). In other words, the argument about the EU budget is moving on, reflecting the change in the policy agenda.

The difficulty for the EU as a whole remains the question of how to make the public goods it provides visible to its citizens. The revenue structure of the budget is completely opaque to the non-initiated, and the expenditure is as much the result of bartering between states as it is the product of public debate about priorities. Curiously, the UK leaving the EU will create an opportunity for the 27 to see how far they want to go in revising the way budgetary politics works. No longer will they have the excuse that their hands are tied by a country that has been obsessed by 'getting its money back' and unable to discuss the EU budget in terms of the provision of European public goods.

Political participation

One immediate effect of the UK's departure will be a reduction in the number of MEPs by 73. As the Treaty states that the European Parliament is composed of 751 members, the 27 will have to decide, on the basis of a proposal from the Parliament, whether to keep that figure and, if so, how to reallocate them. Redistribution amongst existing Member States is one possibility, as is the creation of a list for European candidates not linked to any national constituency but chosen by all European electors.

More important than the precise number of MEPs is the nature of the relationship between the Parliament and the electorate. The decline in participation in European elections (62 per cent in 1979, 43 per cent in 2014) has underlined the difficulty of making that relationship meaningful in the eyes of voters. Many ask why they should vote for a Parliament whose members they do not know, and whose impact they cannot see. Hence the constant efforts made to make Europeans feel the Parliament is 'our Parliament' or 'a channel for a European *vox populi*' (van Middelaar 2013, 283).

The 2019 European Parliament elections will offer another opportunity to assess the progress of these efforts because it will witness a repeat of the experiment that was tried for the first time in 2014. Before the last European elections, five of the European political parties (European People's Party, Party of European Socialists, European Liberals, Greens and European Left) put forward candidates for Commission president in advance, obliged those candidates to come forward with a political programme, and organised a set of debates between them. After the elections, the political groups in the Parliament indicated to the European Council that they would not accept as a Commission president nominee anyone who had not been a candidate in advance of the elections. Hence they invited the heads of state and government to propose as Commission President Jean Claude Juncker, candidate of the European People's Party which had won the most seats (though not the most votes) in the elections. The European Council reluctantly accepted this logic and proposed Juncker, despite the opposition of the British and Hungarian prime ministers, promising to review the nomination process before 2019.

As I have suggested elsewhere (Shackleton 2017), this was a transformative moment in the development of representative government at EU level. For the first time European elections were presented not simply as a way of selecting MEPs, but also as a means to link a parliamentary election with the holder of an executive office. As a result, the Commission president was seen as depending as much on having a majority in the European Parliament as having the support of the European Council, and indeed was obliged to establish a programme for five years which took explicit account of the wishes of the majority of political groups in the Parliament. 'One can now imagine a Commission that is not beyond democratic electoral reach and a European Parliament that can offer the possibility of policy change through executive renewal, a system where the 'rascals can be thrown out' (Shackleton 2017).

In Britain the overwhelming balance of political opinion was against this so-called *Spitzenkandidaten* (top candidate) experiment. It was regarded as a power grab by the European Parliament, one that would necessarily weaken the role of the European Council. None of the candidates for Commission president had the opportunity to campaign in the UK, not even those from the European socialist and liberal parties (Martin Schulz and Guy Verhofstadt) whose national parties had been involved in their selection. By contrast, whatever the reticence of national leaders in other countries, a majority were reluctant to deny the appropriateness of the logic behind the process: indeed, Angela Merkel was expressly challenged to accept that it was a more democratic way of selecting a Commission president (García & Priestley 2015, 160–3).

The absence of the UK from the 2019 elections makes it much more likely that the process for selecting a Commission president will be similar to that which prevailed in 2014. It may witness drama in the form of a stand-off between the institutions, but such drama may be precisely what the EU requires as it seeks to create a historical narrative and to make Europe a matter of direct public concern where voters can see the impact of their choices.

Conclusions

There can be no underestimating the continuing difficulty of developing the three strategies outlined above. Persuading national citizens to define themselves at least in part as Europeans, in accordance with the German strategy, is a task that requires overcoming widespread distrust of Brussels as well as the divergences of interest among Member States. Devising a trade-off between the policy priorities of the members of such a heterogeneous entity as the EU presents a major challenge for the Roman strategy. Giving EU citizens a more direct role in the choice of their leaders will require a reassessment at national as much as European level as to the scope of the Greek strategy. Nonetheless, as this chapter has sought to show, the 27 are condemned to continue their search for a common identity, to define and pursue European public goods, and to offer means for citizens to contribute to the political direction of the EU.

There can be no certainty as to the outcome, but at the very least we possess a set of common criteria against which success and failure can be measured. We will be able to observe the extent to which Europeans feel more aware of their common values, assess the popular success of a redefinition of the policy structure of the EU, and judge whether citizens feel more engaged by European elections in 2019 and thus more inclined to participate.

In Britain there will no doubt be a wish to dismiss such developments as illusory, to suggest that the divisions that they will no doubt provoke make a mockery of the notion of a common European destiny. The result of such a discourse will be to create an even wider gap between the 27 and the UK. Britain will be exempted from any need to identify what it means to use the phrase 'we Europeans', raising ever higher the barriers to rejoining at a future date. For the rest of the EU, however, the search for the meaning behind the phrase will continue.

23
Sustainable integration in a demoicratic polity

A new (or not so new) ambition for the EU after Brexit

Kalypso Nicolaïdis

Guardian of the long term: what future for the EU after Brexit?

The perennial question of the future of the EU has changed in tone and gravity since its 50th anniversary (Phinnemore & Warleigh-Lack 2009). While the multidimensional crisis besetting the Union since 2008 had already raised the stakes, with Brexit we have truly entered existential territory. If the EU is now demonstrably a polity that can shrink, who is to say that it cannot shrink to nothing? If vast pluralities across the continent echo the feelings of British nay-sayers, who is to say where this mood will take us next? Can we avoid tying to the mast a European public beguiled by the sirens of Brexit? How can European leaders signal that – Brexit or not – the European ship is still afloat? And how can European publics re-imagine their role in this endeavour?

The response from officialdom has been predictable; the classic three-pronged wheel of institutions, policies and structural 'solutions'. On institutions, magic bullets are shot around, such as an EMU parliament or more *Spitzenkandidaten*, as if these were the expressions of democracy citizens most cared about. On policies, leaders predictably promise 'concrete progress' – from control of migration and external borders to deeper cooperation in internal and external security or youth employment – but, judging on past record, these worthy goals are bound to be betrayed. And on structure, we hear about variable geometry, the hallmark of EU integration since Maastricht. But doing more with fewer countries is not only restating the obvious when it comes to EMU and Schengen, it also assumes that most citizens want to do more in the 'core' countries, while most citizens from the 'periphery' are happy to do less.

Here I argue that whatever the partial merits of these various recipes, unless European officials free themselves from the tyranny of dichotomies – where the agenda before us is solely framed as more vs less Europe – there is little chance of reconciling a majority of Europe's citizens with the project. Instead we need to talk about the common goals that require Europeans to continue to work together or separately at all levels of governance: We need to talk about substance. As Grabbe and Lehne (2017) argue, 'public debate about climate change, conflict resolution, and aging populations would bust the myth that societies can somehow return to a former golden age when national governments could solve problems by themselves'.

If in Europe and beyond we are plagued by short-termism – governments acting under emergency powers, markets wedded to short-term returns – what better way to justify anew the process of European integration than to proclaim loud and clear the EU's commitment to long-term goals irrespective of short-term expediency. I will argue that the EU is best placed to institutionalise the idea of sustainability, the idea that we must act together if we are going to survive as a species, and that a peace project such as ours can best justify short-term sacrifices for long-term goals.

Sustaining our polity as the guardian of the long term for its citizens, a means to an end, should be the new core motive for the European project committed to sustaining cooperation among states (Harari 2014). I have suggested that such a vision should be labelled 'sustainable integration' which is most fundamentally about turning the sustainability gestalt into a broader philosophy of transnational governance for the EU (Nicolaïdis 2010a, 2010b, 2010c). It is also an agenda that requires widening the conceptual toolbox of political science to social theory and anthropology to better apprehend the EU's social grounding. Sustainable integration is altogether a practice, an ethos and a state of mind. As a governing idea of integration it calls for pursuing fairer rather than faster or deeper integration, through processes that are politically acceptable across generations. I define sustainable integration in the EU as the *durable ability to sustain cooperation within the Union in spite of the heterogeneity of its population and of their national political arrangements*. In other words, sustainable integration calls for embracing the complexity of the task thanks to the simplicity of the vision (Innerarity 2014; Martinico 2017).

Paradoxically, such a long-term vision calls for eschewing the kind of teleology espoused by self-styled euro-federalists, who want to resolve once and for all the question of the nature of the EU as a polity bent on equating progress with ever more centralisation (Nicolaïdis 2010b). The infamous bicycle theory which commands us to choose between moving forward or falling makes no sense in a world where we need to move in all directions or sometimes stand still if we are to sustain our balance. Sustainable integration is about continuously maintaining the precious balance between the imperatives of cooperation and control, the cooperation whose benefit we seek, and the autonomy which we continue to crave as individuals and as groups (Nicolaïdis 2017). Better even, it calls for accommodating the different ways in which different national and local traditions are comfortable in striking this balance. Call this mindset *Brexit interruptus!*

In the wake of Brexit, sustainable integration could be seen as a truism: integration means staying together over time *by definition*. Except that it is not. Integration is only sustainable if it means staying together over time *by choice*. The idea that the peoples of Europe can exercise their right to leave democratically if they so wish is a truly good thing. Such a right of exit is what makes the EU a Union (whether you want to call it federal or not) rather than a federal State. Sustainable integration then starts with warding off disintegration, stating loud and clear to the world and to ourselves that the EU is here to stay, even if (and perhaps because) its peoples, like the UK, are free to go.

As a result, the key to sustainable integration is asking what kind of policies and institutional arrangements could make the exercise of exit less palatable. If we assume that such arrangements need to be adaptable in the face of internal and external shocks, and wholesale uncertainty, sustainable integration is about 'changing the way we change' within the EU. Such change needs to encompass goals and processes that take into account the differential impact of a world in transformation on various arrays of citizens, groups and countries *in the longer term*. Emergency decision-making can be necessary but it is never sufficient – even in the here and now.

This brings us back to the question of legitimacy. Activists and scholars agree that the EU is in dire need of more meaningful democracy but disagree on what this means exactly. No solution seems to avoid the Scylla of complexity without stumbling on the Charybdis of simplistic mimetism (reproducing state-like institutions at the EU level). I argue that focusing on sustainable integration allows us to chart a way through this aporia. First, by accepting that the EU is democratically challenged, in spite of all its mechanisms for representation, delegation and checks on power. Second, by turning this flaw into an asset: because it is a sum of governments which cannot be collectively impeached, the EU ought to be about democracy-with-foresight, partially shielded from the short-term ups and downs of electoral politics, yet solidly grounded on participatory networks and attuned to the overwhelming desire of the public to confront future threats for the sake of our children and grandchildren. To atone for its current shortcomings in collective accountability, the EU must become accountable to those who are not represented today.

A number of us have sought to theorise the novel kind of transnational democracy which the EU calls for under the label of *demoicracy*, which I define as 'a Union of peoples, defined both as citizens and states, who govern together but not as one' (Bellamy 2013, Chapter 24 in this volume; Cheneval et al. 2015; Lindseth 2014; Nicolaïdis 2004; 101; 2013). Accordingly, democratic sustainability is predicated on giving up the idea that European democracy can, and should, take the form of national democracy writ large. Instead, the EU needs to be gradually perfected as a demoicracy in the making – whose credo is based on the belief that since its inception, the EU has approximated (and at times subverted) a new political form predicated both on the autonomy of its peoples' governing arrangement and on their radical openness to each other.

Does demoicratic legitimacy represent an unstable equilibrium? An equilibrium *sociologically*, because it represents a third way between opposing forces – those who prefer to centralise the management of interdependence and those who prefer to minimise it; and an equilibrium *normatively*, in translating for a democratic era the Kantian requisite for 'perpetual peace' as a law-based arrangement between self-governing states. This equilibrium would be unstable if the opposing forces of federal messianism (typically EU officialdom and idealistic pro-European movements) and sovereignism (today expressed in new populist movements) pull the project apart. In this context, adopting the overarching goal of sustainable integration may help legitimise the novel demoicratic form that is the EU and ensure that it stays on a more stable path than competing alternatives.

In what follows I explore the implications of a commitment to sustainable integration in a demoicratic polity on the three fronts of institutions, policies and structure mentioned earlier.

Institutions: democracy of a different kind

While in the last decades too much political energy has been spent on discussing decision-making rules in the EU and the balance of power between its various institutions, the alternative is not simply to come back to a 'Europe of results'. To ask *what* a polity is about is to ask *who* is doing the asking and *how* action is pursued. Output legitimacy depends on input processes which set the ambition of collective action. And while it is a testimony to the staying power of EU institutions that they have hardly been reformed since the EU's inception, they have nevertheless permitted a dangerous drift away from the demoicrat's attachment to non-domination between demoi and individuals – big states overruling the preferences of smaller states, the rising coercive proclivities of the centre, the technocratic monopolisation of power, and the depolitisation of decision-making.

This means, first, that a shared commitment to fostering a sustainable integration culture could go a long way in reasserting shared leadership and ownership. The lasting power of EU institutions would be bolstered to the extent that they conduct affairs in systematically self-reflexive ways, even when emergency action is required (Caney 2016). EU actors could pool their different comparative advantages in systematically assessing short-term actions against long-term goals when bargaining over EU action. This could start by shaping bolder and more political versions of such current tools as the Strategic Environmental Assessment or Regulatory Impact Assessment, as well as methods involving foresight, horizon scanning, scenario development and visioning. In time, the trade-offs and predictions involved would be at the heart of public debate across the EU.

Second, sustainable integration requires a much deeper democratic *aggiornamento* bringing about 'social ownership' of long-term-oriented action. After all, the UN describes the sustainable development goals as 'an Agenda of the people, by the people and for the people'. In other words, for an agenda to be politically sustainable, *how* it is implemented is a prerequisite to *what* is pursued. Years of learning-by-doing have shown that such ambitious long-term goals need to be applied through empowerment rather than centralisation – in the spirit of the groundswell of 'bottom-up' climate action pledged under the COP21 fourth pillar (Hale 2016). If sustainable integration is best grounded in the decentralised enacting of transformative strategies by people individually, in groups or as national communities, then it must rely on the separate, if overlapping, democratic spaces that constitute the demoicratic polity. This is less about organised subsidiarity as a top-down criterion for refraining to act at the centre, and more about organic subsidiarity as a citizen-centred concept of EU democratic dynamics. Particularly so as to enrol young generations, the EU could do much to mirror patterns of technological innovation and harness networked forms of cooperation central to our virtual times, including notions of distributed intelligence and adaptive learning (Slaughter 2017). And we need to think about the impact of political 'neo-cleavages' and how the reassertion of place, localism and control will affect the sustainability agenda.

Policies: sustainability across the board

Sustainable integration privileges certain policy fields over others. It builds on our commitment to sustainability as a goal for our global environment, as well as for cities, security, welfare states, agriculture, landscapes, cultures or – in UN parlance – 'sustainable development goals' (SDGs). Crucially, the EU is now itself under the obligation to pursue the 17 SDGs spelled out in 2015 by the United Nations, building on lessons learned from the previous Millennium goals from which the developed world had been exempted.[1] The 'transition to sustainability' is about how all nations are (or should be) repositioning their economies, their societies and their collective purpose 'to maintain all life on Earth, peacefully, healthily, equitably and with sufficient wealth to ensure that all are content in their survival' (O'Riordan & Voisey 2013).

Two points need to be made on the relationship between the (political) idea of 'sustainable European integration' and this (substantive) 'transition to sustainability'. First, that the implementation of the SDGs require a profound change in mindset on the part of European institutions, governments and publics which can be best informed by a broader philosophy of sustainable integration. Second, that sustainable integration is a holistic conception which includes, but is not limited to, delivering policies classified under the UN-related sustainability goal. In other words, the latter is both conditioned on, and embedded within, the former.

Sustainability covers all aspects of living together but calls for emphasising the underlying features of society which make such togetherness easier, from equal rights and the rule of law to economically reasonable egalitarianism and the provision of equal opportunities. A sustainable society is one where economic growth is compatible with planetary limitations and distributed fairly among its citizens, the rapidly growing developing nations and the younger generation. In the words of Pope Francis, eminently citeable by atheists among us: 'Today ... we have to realize that a true ecological approach always becomes a social approach; it must integrate questions of justice in debates on the environment, so as to hear both the cry of the earth and the cry of the poor.'[2] There is of course a vast literature about the ways in which growth must gradually change in quality with the development of new concepts around green growth, natural capital, circular economy, ecosystem services or green bonds.[3] In this context global spatial sustainability must complement temporal sustainability with managed mobilities, whereby the deep principle of non-discrimination is made relevant to the challenge of global integration.[4] These debates must become mainstream across the political spectrum in Europe and beyond.

In an abstract sense, the policies advocated at EU level seem to chime with sustainability goals. But while the 2017 Rome declaration calls for a 'prosperous and sustainable Europe', the driving narrative occupies the defensive end of the sustainability spectrum. However, no matter how necessary, an emphasis on 'resilience' already assumes that sustainability strategies will fail, while a focus on 'protection' runs the risk of overreach by justifying a Europe with more powers, tools and resources (Nicolaïdis 2016). Instead, sustainability needs to start in the here and now. Finding a lasting solution to the well-known shortcomings of the single currency is a prerequisite for investment strategies that sustainability requires. While financial integration is desirable in the long term to share risks and spread resources across Europe, this does not mean that the EU needs to radically centralise its fiscal, regulatory and supervisory functions.

Ultimately, EU leaders need to seek the minimum integration necessary to sustain a common currency among national economies which will remain heterogenous for the foreseeable future, not only in terms of levels of development but in terms of social contracts and state–society relations (Begg et al. 2015; Nicolaïdis & Watson 2015). From a sustainable integration view point this means reconciling decentralised self-government and greater pooling of resources. On the one hand, European officialdom can no longer shy away from dealing with the main structural reason for EMU's failures, namely the tension between national ownership and the interdependence of European economies and societies. Governing at a distance is unsustainable when reforms and policies must be democratically sustainable in separate constituencies. Democratic sustainability requires informed debate on the part of national publics and genuine mutual recognition between their polities (Gatziou et al. 2016). On the other hand, resources can be better pooled – say if the EU as a whole leverages its capacity to borrow on capital markets – provided they are not managed at the centre. Sustainable growth requires public investment in research and development, schools, healthcare and social services, transport and infrastructure and most fundamentally a strategic approach to innovation in the EU (Madelin & Ringrose 2016).

Finally, Brexit and the populist wave accompanying it have brought home the fact that attention must be focused on the long-term consequences of openness for individual voters. A system in which states have given up control of crucial aspects of regulation (e.g. banking, food production, online markets) to international bureaucrats is not democratically sustainable. Rather than an exogenous force that is filtered through national cleavages, globalisation is a force that can radically change the political issue space as well as the institutional opportunities available to political actors – and the media have a crucial role to play in this story (Farrell & Newman 2017). Sustainable integration is about harnessing, but also taming, this force.

Structure: flexibility without fragmentation

Finally, much has been made of the idea that more 'variable geometry' would significantly help the EU survive its 'midlife crisis'.[5] Beyond the irony that ever closer union may require an ever smaller union, there is little doubt that the EU can survive only if it embraces the kind of flexibility required by the widely heterogeneous character of its economies, and widely diverse range of social, legal and political systems. This is not an original thought, especially when we note that asymmetric federalism – whereby the constituent units in the system relate to the whole through different degrees of autonomy and status – has historically been the rule rather than the exception.

But not all types of flexible arrangements necessarily serve sustainable integration. If the cooperative drive has largely been based on diffuse reciprocity and linkages across issues, sustainability implies that we learn to deal fairly with the externalities we create for each other over time, which in turn calls for more, not less, inclusiveness. Asymmetry of the wrong kind can also translate in a sense of powerlessness on the part of citizens who are under-represented at the centre (Bauböck 2002). Arguably, both versions of structural differentiation – a core 'federalised' Europe or permanent institutional structures for different groupings of states – could be harbingers of fragmentation and divergence between

Member States, not least as cleavages among states and actors in the EU crisscross possible groupings.

For the sake of sustainable integration we need to imagine overlapping agendas and differentiated approaches inside a single framework, rather than concentric circles or core–periphery dichotomies. The asymmetry produced by flexible integration should maintain the balance between the forces of fusion and fission that characterise the Union. Against structural approaches to differentiation, enhanced cooperation with flexible opt-in and opt-out clauses can be seen as a form of open-ended experimentation with cooperation whereby some actors can afford to be trail-blazers. This, of course, requires respecting the untouchable core of the EU through constitutional safeguards (Martinico 2017). It requires also that forms of 'enhanced cooperation' are open and transparent. Differentiation, moreover, needs to be principled, not *ad hoc*. Arrangements must be sensitive to local and national specificities and adjusted to conform to the precept of sustainable integration. For instance, the same norm of free movement of labour has a radically different impact in different states and their labour markets, which is why states require leeway in their interpretation. Similarly, a European refugee regime must balance Member States' shared commitment to free movement with the unequal distribution of absorption capacity within each of them.

What does this all mean for a country like the UK which claims to be leaving the EU, but not Europe? What the British saga over Europe has taught us is that if the EU as a whole does not sufficiently take account of the unequal impact of its principles and laws, if it does not offer differentiated and flexible approaches, then it is the Member States and their citizens who will take such differentiation in hand, unilaterally. And that, we have now learned, can mean walking out and shaking the whole edifice in the process. Brexit raises the interesting prospect that a kind of flexible integration that could not be worked out with an existing member might instead be devised for a third country.

Conclusions

The EU after Brexit needs to heed the British message: we must take what is good about the EU while guarding against its own propensity for overreach. We need to reshape a Europe that a majority of citizens in every EU Member State, including today's Britain, would want to be part of. It is not anti-European to read Brexit as a warning that political leaders must give up the kind of integration by stealth which has so damaged the integrity and popularity of the European project. British Leavers were generally not bigoted, racist or ignorant. But they are less educated and older than Remainers. Faced with what they perceived as the complacency of the London and Brussels elites, they were no longer ready to give the EU the benefit of the doubt.

In this chapter I have argued that only by making the pursuit of sustainable integration its *raison d'être* might the EU most credibly sign on for another 60-year stint. This means altering the way negotiated change occurs in the EU, reconnecting the project to its citizens' aspirations and recognising that inter-governmental deals need to be sustained by intersocietal and intergenerational bargains. It means that flexibility, differentiation and opt-outs need to exist in order to serve inclusiveness, because a mosaic EU is more appealing than pushing half of its states to the brink of exit, as has happened with the UK. Under these conditions, peace in Europe may not be perpetual – but it could outlast all of us.

24
Losing control

Brexit and the demoi-cratic disconnect

Richard Bellamy

Had the referendum on Britain's membership of the EU been decided on the economic case alone, then in all likelihood the UK would have voted to stay in. All the key economic actors, from the CBI to the City, urged a Remain vote. That view certainly underlay the government's strategy during the referendum, which stressed the economic risks and costs of leaving the EU. However, the debate ended up turning as much on politics as economics, and on that issue in particular the Remain campaign offered much weaker arguments, barely mentioning the political risks and costs of Brexit. In this regard, the Leave campaign's winning slogan was the claim that exiting the EU would allow the people of Britain to 'take back control' – at least indirectly, via their elected representatives in the government and Parliament (Cummings 2017b). The implication was that executive and legislative power over a range of important economic and social policies – not least those relating to immigration – had passed to EU institutions that were largely uncontrolled, or inadequately controlled, by British citizens, or indeed the citizens of any of the EU Member States. Leaving the EU would involve a repatriation of these competences to democratically accountable British administrators and politicians, re-enfranchising the British electorate in the process. Indeed, many Remainers had lent this argument a certain credibility through having contributed to four decades of criticism of the EU's democratic deficit. Stretching back at least to 1979 and the first elections to the European Parliament, the critiques of the democratic failings of the EU by Europhiles all too often paralleled those of Eurosceptics, and in some cases have been even harsher. The comparative failure of the Remain campaign to mount even a negative political case against leaving, let alone to give positive political (or, for that matter, economic) reasons for European integration, served simply to further legitimise the Leave campaign's democratic argument for Brexit.

In this brief chapter, I shall argue that the Leave campaign's political case was as misleading and misinformed as much of their economic case is being steadily revealed to be. From the alleged savings on payments into the EU budget and the assumption that a free trade agreement with the EU could be negotiated both swiftly and on advantageous terms to the City and UK producers, to the failure to take account of the inflationary repercussions of a fall in the pound and a consequent rise in interest rates, the economic claims of the proponents of Brexit have steadily unraveled (Bowler 2017). Nevertheless, a YouGov poll found 60 per cent of Brexit voters still believed the political gains of Brexit would justify any potential economic costs (Gillett 2017). However, the political costs are, if anything, even greater than the economic. Far from 'taking back control', leaving the EU involves the British electorate losing control over the global economic and social processes that shape so many key government policies. Yet, the EU fosters such control not by subsuming national democracies within a supranational democratic system, as many Europhiles assume – thereby giving rise to worries about both an EU and a domestic democratic deficit – but by offering a framework within which national democracies can collectively regulate such global processes in fair ways that show the relevant states and their peoples equal concern and respect. Outside such arrangements, states will inevitably be dominated by other states as well as by agents and agencies operating trans- or multinationally, such as financial institutions, companies and terrorist groups (Pettit 2010). None of these can be successfully controlled by any single state operating unilaterally. That has proved impossible even for the USA at the height of its hegemonic sway, even with the benefit of massive military might, a large domestic market and considerable natural resources. It certainly lies outside the capacity of a medium-sized economic and military power such as the UK, which is heavily dependent on international trade.

The basic problem can be formulated in terms of what Dani Rodrik has called 'the fundamental political trilemma of the world economy' (Rodrik 2011, xviii), namely, the impossibility of simultaneously achieving democracy, national self-determination and economic globalisation – one of these has to give (Rodrik 2011, xix, 200–205). As he explains, 'If we want to maintain and deepen democracy, we have to choose between the nation-state and international economic integration. And if we want to keep the nation-state and self-determination, we have to choose between deepening democracy and deepening globalization' (Rodrik 2011, xix, 200).

Given most (if not all) people regard national autarky as a non-starter, and unregulated free global markets unjust as well as likely to be inefficient and prone to failures, most subsequently conclude the only answer is to give up national self-determination and subsume national democracy and citizenship within some broader scheme for global democracy. Many federally minded Europeans adopt this line of thinking, regarding the development of supranational democracy at the EU level as the first stage in such a process (Habermas 2015). However, the concern with the EU's democratic deficit enters at this point, with Europhiles joining in an unholy alliance with Eurosceptics to argue that, in many core areas, decisional authority has passed upwards to Brussels without adequate democratic oversight. By and large, proposals for addressing this alleged deficit have turned on the practicality and justifiability of enhancing the powers of the European Parliament (EP) and electing the Commission, be it directly or indirectly, and invariably get linked to arguments for further political integration. Unsurprisingly, the main counter-arguments have mirrored this reasoning. They come from those opposing the justifiability of the integration process on democratic grounds. These critics regard the shift of political authority from national to European political structures as at best diluting the democratic influence of each individual voter, and at worst indefensibly undermining the self-determination of sovereign peoples. Such arguments suggest that the EU could never be democratically legitimate – indeed, that further empowering the EP or electing the Commission might deepen rather than lessen the democratic deficit.

These concerns are further buttressed by the fact that the EU has the promotion of economic globalisation largely hardwired into its constitutional structure (Isiksel 2016). Initially at least, the integration process was also deliberately pursued in non-democratic ways, in part to avoid potential resistance from the different demoi of the Member States (Müller 2011, 128, 142). Meanwhile, the rights that came to be associated with Union citizenship were largely tied to mobility and the exercise of the economic opportunities provided by the single market. As a result, they were largely exercised by less than 5 per cent of the EU population. Of course, the exception is the right to vote for the EP, but the exercise of this right has steadily fallen since its inception and has stood at below 50 per cent for decades, reaching a new low of 42.61 per cent in the 2014 election. It has been a far weaker venue for the exercise of citizen preferences than that offered by EU law to economic enterprises and social groups seeking to challenge laws and regulations that have been negotiated at the national level (Isiksel 2016, 143). The transfer of allegiance to the EU has been correspondingly shallow. So long as it was associated with the post-war period of peace and prosperity, it has enjoyed 'output' legitimacy and sustained a broad degree of 'banal' identification for the security and economic benefits with which it has been credited (McNamara 2015). But that has been sorely tested by the euro crisis and the more recent association of the EU in many countries with widespread austerity policies and the reduction of public spending, especially on social welfare. As Brexit indicated, those opposing the EU, who account for as much as a third of the electorate or more in many countries across the EU, are typically far more vocal and passionate than its supporters tend to be. Again, many pro-Europeans have seen the obvious response as being the adoption by the EU of more socially integrative policies – such as an EU-wide basic income (Van Parijs 2015) – that might support a transfer of democratic political authority to the EU level. Yet, such a move begs the question of whether EU citizens desire greater social integration in the first place. To many, such a move would be yet another top-down imposition, with a very real risk of further undermining the incomplete but nevertheless far superior social welfare systems existing at the national level, along with the democratic systems that facilitated their emergence (Streeck 2014).

How might we avoid this impasse? As Rodrik (2011) notes, an alternative response to the global 'trilemma' involves collaboration between democratic states to collectively regulate globalisation in 'smart' ways, as he believed Keynes's design of the Bretton Woods system achieved for the post-war period. From this perspective, the democratic legitimacy of the EU lies rather in it strengthening and legitimising the democratic systems of the Member States than offering an alternative to them. However, that cannot be achieved by treating the national self-determination of one state in isolation from that of other states – either morally or practically. The democratic decisions of almost all states affect, and are themselves affected by, the democratic decisions of other states, whether they are formally associated within a structure such as the EU or not. To the extent that democratically made decisions of one state undercut those of other states, or reduce the options available to them, while being in their turn partially determined by these other states, all states risk losing democratic legitimacy. Meanwhile, as I noted above, domestic democracy is further diminished by its inability to tackle problems that require cooperation between states, either because these problems are by their nature global in character – such as global warming – or because they involve transnational activities and processes among multinational organisations, be they financial movements, migration flows or terrorism. Therefore, a domestic democratic deficit exists from the very fact of democratic states being part of an interconnected world in which autarky no longer offers a plausible or desirable option (Bellamy 2013).

Meeting this challenge requires some regulation of the interactions between states and a mechanism for fostering cooperation among them. To achieve that purpose while still retaining meaningful forms of self-determination for the peoples of these states, we need to reconceive the purpose of supranational bodies. Instead of being superior and independent sources of democratic authority to their constituent states, we should see them as mechanisms that allow democratic communities to co-exist on mutually agreed and equitable terms. As such, these bodies have to remain subordinate to their constituent members as a delegated authority under their joint and equal control. The problem of democratic legitimacy thereby changes from being one of a democratic deficit at the supranational level to that of a democratic disconnect between the peoples of the constituent states and the inter- and multi-national decisions their domestic representatives make in their name, including the creation and control of supranational regulatory bodies (Bellamy & Weale 2015).

This proposal constitutes a 'demoi-cratic' solution to the democratic legitimacy issue, whereby, in Kalypso Nicolaïdis's phrase, the peoples of the EU 'govern together but not as one' (Nicolaïdis 2013, 351). On my account, they achieve this result through a form of 'republican inter-governmentalism' (Bellamy 2013), whereby decisions must conform to the normative logic of what Robert Putnam termed a 'two-level game' (Putnam 1988; Savage & Weale 2009). According to this argument, governments need both to agree amongst themselves on an equal basis at the international level, while at the same time securing the long-term democratic agreement of their citizens. As such, within their negotiations they must respect each other as the democratically authorised and accountable representatives of their respective peoples (Pettit 2010). Procedurally, that means ministers in the Council should be responsive to their respective national parliaments. Likewise, parties in the EP should be linked more strongly to their national parties, with national parliaments gaining a more direct and collaborative role in EU policy making, not simply through being the guardians of proportionality and subsidiarity, via the so-called 'yellow' and 'orange' cards, but also by being able to propose EU policies via a potential 'green' card (Kröger & Bellamy

2016). Substantively, it allows for a more differentiated system of integration – one in which, on democratic grounds, states may collaborate more or less than other states, depending on the greater or lesser stake they have in pursing collective policies at the EU level; opt out when collective policies infringe domestic constitutional and cultural norms; and insist common rules treat them as equals by taking into account relevant differences (Bellamy and Kröger 2017). Of course, all states have a moral obligation to participate in those collective policies necessary to secure such basic rights as are to be found in conventions such as the ECHR (Christiano 2016). Similarly, they have to guard against such clear collective harms as global environmental catastrophe and to assist what John Rawls called 'burdened societies' (Rawls 1999, 90, 106) – that is, societies so burdened by extreme poverty, a lack of natural resources and low human capital that basic rights cannot be secured and they lack the means to order themselves effectively in a democratic manner. Yet, the vast majority of the EU's competences operate beyond the morally obligatory. Here, it is appropriate to seek to protect the variety of capitalisms and related welfare systems of the Member States (Hall & Soskice 2001), while allowing cooperation to ensure greater efficiency and equity in their interrelations.

To a large degree, the EU already operates in this way (Bellamy 2013). After all, the EU prides itself on seeking to achieve 'Unity in Diversity'. Indeed, it derives much of its legitimacy from this fact, rendering many of the criticisms of its democratic deficit simply misplaced (Moravscik 2008). The intergovernmental processes of the EU and the forms of differentiated integration it produces can and should be regarded not as pragmatic compromises but as matters of principle, whereby the EU seeks to achieve equality of concern and respect among the peoples of Europe (Bellamy & Kröger 2017). Moreover, the free movement of persons among these peoples further legitimises the Union by ensuring no individual is dominated by such a system through having been born in one state rather than another (Bellamy 2015 and forthcoming, Chapter 5). It gives all citizens an equal opportunity to choose where to live and work without discrimination on the basis of nationality, while at the same time preserving the possibility for the different states of Europe to pursue and experiment with different social and economic arrangements. These opportunities and protections are denied to UK citizens through exiting the EU.

Against the Eurosceptic proponents of Brexit, I have argued that we can only exercise control through bodies such as the EU; against some Europhile proponents of political union, I have suggested that we achieve control through collaboration among European democracies, not by creating an EU-level democracy. Both these alternatives involve losing control. By leaving the EU, the British government and those who voted for this proposal have committed a moral and political wrong against themselves and others. They have placed themselves in a situation where they will inevitably be controlled and dominated by other states and organisations and can only respond by seeking, largely vainly, to control and dominate them in turn. The Leave campaign's favoured slogan had been 'go global' (Cummings 2017a). That represents a more accurate description of what they have achieved, contrary to the beliefs of many who supported them. In terms of Rodrik's trilemma, they have delivered a formal facade of national sovereignty, symbolised by certain immigration controls against the poor and powerless that disregard their moral obligations to assist those in dire need, combined with a total openness to global economic processes over which they will have little or no democratic control.

VIII: The idea of Europe

25
The heart of the matter

Emotional politics in the new Europe

Uta Staiger

> *We do not have too much intellect and too little soul, but too little intellect in matters of the soul.*
>
> (Robert Musil, *Helpless Europe*, 1922)

In most theories of contemporary democratic politics, reason looms large. For some, individual citizens determine their preferences by evaluating the probabilities, costs and benefits of available options, leading to choices which in their aggregation determine political decision-making. For others, individual citizens partake in fair and equitable discussions, carefully considering competing claims and viewpoints, in order to then agree upon the best course of action for the public good. Whether describing the decision itself, or the process that leads to it, reason is considered central to the very endeavour of politics. Indeed, the supremacy of reason has often been put down as a key stage in our progression toward human perfectibility: intellect is what allows us to rise above the animal nature in us; what grants us the maturity of thinking for – and by extension, fairly ruling – ourselves.

This tradition has left us with a two-fold dilemma. Not only do these analytical models disregard a fundamental element of human experience: emotions. They also hardly correspond to the political realities in Europe as we confront them today. Brexit may be the example *par excellence* – from the no-punches-pulled campaigning days to the acrimony fracturing the Cabinet, the hostilities traded on social media, or the deeply held convictions determining negotiations on either side – emotions have loomed large in every aspect of Brexit so far. And political emotionality is in evidence across Europe. This may be in formal electoral politics, such as with the populist surges in post-referendum French, Austrian, Dutch and German elections. Or it may be beyond, as with the anti-austerity movement of the young Spanish *indignados* ('the indignant ones') in 2011, their older, conservative German counterpart, the *Wutbürger* ('the angry citizen', Germany's Neologism of the Year 2010), or the interlocutors of Stéphane Hessel's 2010 bestseller *Indignez-vous!* (English title: Time for Outrage!). Politics these days seems anything but a process of measured preference formation.

To dismiss the role of the emotions in politics is thus to misconstrue the problem of contemporary politics twice over. This is not to hail them as an unalloyed good: unchecked emotions, certainly in some circumstances, can clearly be detrimental to politics. But in order to begin addressing the ramifications, we need a better understanding of how they are at work politically. For this, we can draw on a rich history of political thought, as well as an emerging set of research in political psychology, behaviour and theory. This brief chapter reflects upon three key roles played by emotions in European politics today: in decision-making, in mobilisation, and in political representation.

Emotions and decision-making

The epistemological and cognitive relevance of emotions, to begin with, is widely contested. Involving bodily sensations, perceptions, beliefs and desires, they may indeed be judgements, as the Stoics certainly held, about ourselves and our world – or at the very least contribute to them. But they are also considered fallible and unreliable, delivering potentially skewed assessments of reality. For Kant, the problem goes further, since it is a moral one. He makes an important distinction between the momentary flaring up of *Affekt*, an 'intoxicant' which impedes reflection but which 'can be slept off', and the slow-burning passion of *Leidenschaft*: an 'insanity which broods over an idea that is embedding itself deeper and deeper' (Kant 1789 [1996], 156–7). Both of these, Kant argued, corrupt reason, since they hamper our individual capacity to decide whether acts are right or wrong. Consequently, we tend to agree that in order to make fair judgements for the common good we need put aside our sentiments and ties – or at the very least, hide them behind a 'veil of ignorance' (Rawls 1971). In order to quarantine bias and ensure decision-making remains 'unsullied by irrationality' (Dworkin 2002, 365), it seemingly stands to reason that emotions need to be excised from democratic deliberation.

And yet, the empirical and normative supremacy of reason in deliberation has more recently been cast in doubt. Neuroscientists and political scientists alike now suggest that our ability to decide on a course of action is significantly impaired if we are unable to tap into our emotional resources (e.g. Damasio 1994; Marcus 2002). Practical reasoning, they posit, necessarily involves feelings. Normatively, too, emotions are increasingly held to have a distinct relationship to thought – whether as cognitive value judgements involving beliefs and desires, or as a *sui generis* form of rationality (e.g. Nussbaum 2001; de Sousa 1987). Emotions certainly provide us with additional elements on which we draw as we think and deliberate. They may work as intensifiers, drawing our attention to particular concepts and objects, or they may influence how we rank and prioritise them (Freeden 2013). In other words, emotions provide us with a sense of what matters, what is of *concern* to us as individuals. We ascribe value to one thing over another because we care more deeply about it.

Whether we like it or not, then, emotions seemingly have a place in individual decision-making. But how exactly? Recent, if pre-Brexit, research on national referendums and EU treaty changes offers some insights. Singling out two main emotions – anger and anxiety – Garry (2013) found that angry citizens were more likely driven by 'second-order' factors related to domestic politics and deep-seated political convictions, rather than by reflection on the precise proposition at stake. They were also more likely to support the 'risky' option. Anxious voters, by contrast, were more likely to seek out information, weigh up arguments and focus on the substantive issues at stake. They tended to be risk-averse, and opt for the status quo. This may be because anger and enthusiasm tend to be driven by long-standing convictions, political choices and life experiences which, 'even if wrongly attributed and misidentified, will recruit powerful habits' (Marcus 2002, 132). They emerge when we believe ourselves to have identified the cause of a threat and commit to redress it, stymying any further opportunities to gather and reflect on new information (Valentino et al. 2008). Anxiety and fear, by contrast, often disable customary behaviour (Marcus 2002). By making us less reliant on what we previously assumed, anxiety increases our tendency to look for new information, consider alternatives, reflect and learn. Kant's key distinction between a surge of *Affekt* temporarily clouding reflection and *Leidenschaft*'s deep-seated hold over a person springs to mind. It is strongly held and well-entrenched points of view that are particularly likely to shape moral or political judgement.

Making up one's mind about a key political issue is thus not an intellectual exercise only, but one determined to a significant extent by the way we feel about the implications and repercussions of the issue in question. And yet there are limits to this insight. By concentrating on the neuropsychological dimensions of decision-making, such research necessarily obviates both historical and contextual elements that might colour and generate emotions, as well as the collective, societal dimensions of decision-making. The key question – normatively and empirically – is how we ensure that deliberation reflects the concerns of all affected. David Hume (1741 [1987]) suggested that it is the *common concerns* – the things that matter to us as a society – that are the source of the standards, rules, principles and norms by which we live. And we arrive at these concerns (and by extension, the relevant norms) through what Hume called moral sentiments: reflective feelings which take in, communicate with and consider the viewpoints of others. There are thus at least two further aspects to consider if we are to take the role of emotions in politics seriously: first, how arguments are framed around common concerns in order to determine and generate public political action, and second, how the concerns of affected parties can, and should, be reflected in decision-making. I will consider both of these in turn.

Emotions, motivation and mobilisation

What is it that motivates us to take action, politically or otherwise? As the likes of Hume and Montesquieu have argued, reason by itself can neither prevent nor produce any action. While passions should not exclusively guide our actions, both considered them to be their primary source. This is of course not unparalleled. Take Aristotle who, regarding reason as supreme, also acknowledged that 'thought itself moves nothing' (NE V2 1139a, 32–3): it is one's desire to apply thought that produces action.[1] Or take Rousseau, who saluted those who 'do by inclination and passionate choice the things that men motivated by duty or interest never do quite well enough' (Rousseau 1782 [1985], 12). Or, for that matter, Emerson, who posited that 'nothing great was ever achieved without enthusiasm' – but nothing terrible either, as Michael Walzer drily noted (Walzer 2004, 118). Indeed, the lessons of history seem clear: the dangers of calling upon shared emotions as the basis of political action pervade, or should pervade, our very understanding of modern politics (Arendt 1951). Yet the appeal to a collective sense of emotion is precisely what drives the current politics of resentment.

We thus recognise with certain trepidation how Garry's suggestion – that actors who are confident that reasonable voters would agree with them may be incentivised to use campaigning devices that raise as much anxiety as possible in the minds of voters (2013, 25) – backfired in the 2016 referendum. Arguably, such a strategy could not compete with strongly held convictions, misidentified or not, which had created new communities of voters across the party-political spectrum. Whereas the Leave side banked on a rousing 'appeal to the gut, and the heart' (Hewitt 2016) in order to mobilise voters, the Remain campaign, oft-derided as 'Project Fear', never quite managed to convincingly commend the Union of which they advocated membership. UKIP leader Nigel Farage actively bolstered this view: 'People who've made up their minds on our side of the argument, it's almost like a conversion. Once you've decided, you believe it strongly ... and you're more likely to go out and vote', he argued in an interview. By contrast, Remainers 'might not be bothered to go down to the polling station and vote, because there's no passion' (Aitkenhead 2016). Analyses of voter turnout largely corroborate this account, showing higher turnout in the age group with the highest percentage of Leave voters. Indeed, Vasilopoulou (Vasilopoulou & Wagner 2017) has suggested that the adoption of positive strategies – the explicit recourse to enthusiasm for the European project – might have benefited the Remain campaign in both voter intention and voter turnout.

Normatively, however, this presents us with a conundrum. Can we really agree that outrage 'is more damaging than fear if we hope to foster an informed citizenry' (Valentino et al. 2008)? After all, the history of political thought and practice should make us rather wary of how political leaders use the public's fears – in both their affective and cognitive dimensions – in order to focus, (mis)construe and mobilise our judgements. Playing upon our own preconceptions, they all too often aim to provide explanations of the supposed causes of fear in order to elicit 'proper' responses to them (Robin 2004). By contrast, outrage and enthusiasm should not be all that easily dismissed. It may be true, in Hume's words, that the 'presumptuous boldness of character' of the enthusiast 'naturally begets the most extreme resolutions [and] produces the most cruel disorders in human society'. But enthusiasm is equally a 'friend' to civil liberty and 'naturally accompanied with a spirit of liberty' (Hume 1741 [1987], 77). Where would our civil rights be, had it not be for an infectious enthusiasm for change, a profound outrage against injustice? What else truly drives dissent – and the courage to speak up? This is the 'double truth', the 'inherent risk of politics as a purposeful activity', as Walzer put it (2004, 118). Like reason, emotions can be put to just, or to severely unjust, ends.

What is interesting in the case of recent political campaigns seeking a decisive break with the *status quo* is their ingenious use of mobilisation's heart and soul: credibility. It is not those who are most sincere who accumulate political capital, but those who perform sincerity most credibly. Suffice it to say that the leaders of traditional parties and career politicians, rightly or wrongly, tend not to be among them. But furthermore, by rounding on the credibility not only of 'the establishment' but that of 'the expert' (the 'voice of reason' *par excellence*), some of the referendum and electoral campaigns – Vote Leave prime among them – very effectively disarmed their counterparts' focus on anxiety by cutting out the very agents (politicians, civil servants, academics, industry representatives) on which they relied. Endlessly replicated by broadcasters and broadsheets, and spun ever further in the echo chambers of social media, personal conviction trumped analysis. In the Brexit referendum, what was meant to elicit anxiety was delegitimised, constructed as an attempt to belittle Britain – its identity, history and potential – and consequently turned into defiant pride. It is a feature that seems to empower a new radical critique on the fringes of the political spectrum: anger that is turned against deliberative practices and those who command them – and turned against the system of representative democracy as such.

Emotions and political representation

Speaking on BBC1's *Question Time* on 15 June 2016, one audience member summed up the discontent brooding among the electorate: 'I want my country back', he warned, 'we're all just so frustrated'. Condensed into the slogan 'Take back control', the advocates for a Leave vote skilfully channelled discontent with British political institutions *tout court* – institutions which are meant to structure our participation in the first place. In the UK, this played on the acute sense of disenfranchisement in a system where class divides are deep and regional disparities abundant, and whose first-past-the-post system effectively disregards all votes not cast for a constituency's winning candidate. The delegitimisation of established institutions is, however, a more general phenomenon. Take, for instance, the 2017 French presidential and German Federal elections, in which visceral campaigns from the far right – the Front National and

Alternative für Deutschland, respectively – successfully appealed to those disenchanted with 'mainstream' parties who had dominated government for decades, generating unprecedented levels of support.

Is it too far-fetched to link the resurgence of passionate convictions demonstrated by the success of these movements at least partially to the very suppression of passion in politics? In his counterintuitive reading of the eighteenth century, Alfred Hirschmann (1977 [2013]) influentially argued that many of the Enlightenment's philosophers encouraged the private pursuit of economic gain (by the commercial classes) precisely in order to curtail potentially disastrous passions (of the aristocratic elite), which all too often led to strife and war. His account suggests not only that personal interests can make for more rationally inflected political behaviour, but also has clear institutional implications. As Walzer (2004) noted, it is precisely through channelling interest that liberalism has adjusted itself to the passions. Seeking to exclude visceral conflict and affiliation, we understand our political institutions above all as facilitators and arbiters of private interests and competing conceptions of the good.

But of course, it is precisely the association between private interests and government that has raised the heat of the debate. Rather than a repository of rationality seeking to fairly administer the interests of citizens, state institutions have come under suspicion for collusion with powerful interests. As a triumphant Farage saw it in August 2016, Brexit was the victory of 'the little people': 'if the ordinary decent people are prepared to stand up and fight for what they believe in, we can overcome the big banks, we can overcome the multinationals', he argued (Jopson & Sevastopulo 2016). Liberal democracies may strive for adequate procedures, which ensure that citizens' concerns end up legitimately undergirding state action, including constitutional principles, fair procedures and norms of accountability, access or publicity. These, however, are constrained by other factors – in particular, socioeconomic inequalities – which prevent some groups from fully participating in political processes: from having their interests weighed, from shaping common concerns (Krause, 2008).

In this context, plebiscites have come to replace elections as the democratic mechanism of choice in the minds of many. Reducing the complexity of a wide-reaching question to a simple binary choice, in which every vote counts, a referendum presents itself as a purer, more legitimate form of democracy. By so doing, it fuels distrust in the very idea of representative parliamentary democracy – to which, paradoxically, British voters wanted to return 'control'. The problem here is one of trust, as central to good government as it is to social relationships. Ever since in the mid-seventeenth century John Locke described the close relationship between (a restricted circle of) citizens and their representatives, parliamentary democracy has been understood as a 'government of trust'; Burke spoke of Parliament as trustees representing, virtually, the whole of British society in a 'communion of interests' (Frevert 2013). While there are formal procedures to withdraw this trust, among the more dismal consequences of the referendum has been the sustained attack on anyone – member of parliament, Cabinet minister or judge – who, in discharging their role as public servant, has been deemed to betray 'the will of the people'.

Particular ire however has been reserved for the political and economic powers that now reside outside national borders, in particular for the EU institutions. Where the Leave campaign called for domesticating control, Marine Le Pen called for a 'revolution in proximity'. Indeed, the EU has consistently failed to bring the institutions 'closer to the citizen'. Its processes of negotiation and compromise seem remote, the rights it extends are noticeable above all to those who move across borders, its attempts at cultivating favourable public emotions appear inauthentic. Yet feeling that we – and our concerns – are well represented politically is essential for democratic politics to work. The yearning for self-government may be misguided in a thoroughly interdependent world; viscerally felt as it is, it still represents a fundamental challenge to our way of doing things.

To support legitimate government and the principle of redistribution, any society needs a minimum of 'sympathy' or 'fellow-feeling' between citizens, as Adam Smith readily recognised (Smith 1759 [1976]). Allowing us to engage with others – a 'habit of imagination' – emotions play an intrinsic part in sustaining political communities by establishing relationships on terms other than those of difference. Usually, these sentiments are managed at the level of the nation, which is prioritised as a defining, positively valorised framework that interprets the national community through both territorial boundaries and representative institutions. It is commonplace, if oversimplified, to contrast such 'hot' emotions of national identification with the 'cool', reflective ideal of transnational communities (Nash 2003). Just as we are unlikely to 'fall in love with a Common Market', as Jacques Delors once put it, there may be limits to our ability to invest affectively in a diverse community of 500 million. What current political movements teach us, if anything, is that too many feel the institutions do not represent them politically – that they lack the (ideal of) self-determination that characterises the nation.

The absence of a self-identifying *demos* has certainly troubled advocates of European integration. True, the recent crises of the EU, Brexit more than any other, have managed what decades of semi-permissive consensus have not: they have put the EU in the spotlight. Issue-based, rather than abstract, discussion has contributed to the mobilisation of interest groups and political parties alike across distinct national media spheres. People across the continent now 'talk Europe', if not always in an anticipated manner. Arguably, Eurosceptic movements have been able to tap into a pan-European anti-EU sentiment more successfully than their Europhile contemporaries (Usherwood & Startin 2012). But at the heart of this mobilisation is a fundamental discontent and anxiousness that takes aim at how democracies operate nationally and cooperate supranationally in order to address global processes and their repercussions. Misguided as the reasoning behind this anxiety might be, we need to address, rather than dismiss, its causes.

Conclusions

We live in interesting political times. In such times, the elusive ideal of rational deliberation untarnished by the messy, ungainly, and often pernicious influence of our passionate convictions holds great appeal. Yet banking on a form of reason that excludes all sentiment will offer an incomplete guide to Europe's political future. If we describe deliberation infused by heightened emotions as fundamentally flawed, we are only likely to fan cynicism. It might prove more useful if we acknowledge the fundamental role of these deeply held convictions that spill over into anger and enthusiasm. In other political times, raising doubts about the validity of a risky, if viscerally felt, course of action might have sustained the status quo. But in these times, cost–benefit calculations are unlikely to keep the EU – and national governments – in citizens' good books. Rather than playing to the gallery, public authorities need to invest in (re)gaining the trust of the electorate. After all, much of the resentment is not only issue-based but fanned by the fundamental feeling of not being heard: the emotional politics in Europe today is, at base, a judgement on the nature of liberal representative democracy itself, and the political norms on which it has developed.

26
Square peg, round hole
Why the EU can't fix identity politics

Turkuler Isiksel[1]

The 1990s witnessed a heated debate among political theorists regarding the extent to which social justice requires the fair distribution of resources versus the recognition of group differences (Barry 2001; Benhabib 2002; Fraser 1996; Kymlicka 1996; Levy 2000; Taylor 1994; Young 1990). While scholars advocating for a politics of recognition never underestimated the need for an equitable distribution of wealth, they pointed out that unjust social hierarchies do not always track socio-economic ones. Symbolic, cultural and identitarian dimensions of social value can also produce patterns of exclusion. Reducing social justice to the politics of wealth redistribution, they argued, made liberal political philosophy insensitive to racial, gendered, cultural and able-ist dimensions of privilege and privation.

Something of the dichotomy between redistribution and recognition is at play in the current debate over explaining support for populist movements and leaders across the West and beyond. While some observers maintain populism draws its energy from long-term post-industrial economic malaise that has been neglected by mainstream parties (Dreher 2016; Kitschelt 1995; Swank & Betz 2003), others point to anxiety over loss of cultural primacy on the part of formerly dominant groups (Betz 1994; Gibson 2002; Ignazi 2003; Inglehart & Norris 2016; Schain 1988). Still others regard these dynamics as inextricable: while contemporary populism typically (though not invariably) manifests itself as a form of identity politics (Mudde & Kaltwasser 2013), it reflects a misdirected backlash against insecurities perpetuated by the capitalist economic order. Still others take a wider lens, attributing the wave of populist success to a general erosion of public commitment to democratic values and procedures (Foa & Mounk 2016, 2017). The debate sparked by the British electorate's narrow decision to leave the EU illustrates the cleavage between identitarian and socioeconomic explanations in particular: while some view the Brexit vote as a flashpoint for anti-immigrant sentiment and, more broadly, as a bid to restore national sovereignty, others describe it as a manifestation of socioeconomic insecurities that establishment parties have failed to address.

Populist movements have also gained ground in such formerly steadfast members of the Union as France, the Netherlands, Germany, Austria and Poland. Many, though not all, of these movements incorporate anti-EU messages into their platforms. What could and should the EU's response be to the rising tide of populist politics? Are there steps the EU could take to allay the concerns that energise these movements? Or are such steps, particularly if they require giving greater powers to EU institutions, likely to add fuel to the fire? Clearly, the answer will depend on which accounts of populism's rise we find most compelling. Nonetheless, it is worth considering whether the EU is equally well-equipped (or ill-equipped) to respond to identitarian grievances as it is to socioeconomic ones.

At its origins, the European integration project was a response to identity politics. Supranational institutions represented an attempt to disarm and sublimate the national rivalries that had riven the continent. They were designed not only to order the relationships among member states on the basis of rules, to promote cooperation, reciprocity, and mutual trust, and generate a sense of shared interest, but also to reduce the appeal of nationalism for the masses by generating greater prosperity through cooperation. Economic interdependence would raise living standards, establish disincentives against autarky and jingoism and defuse the economic insecurity and privation that had fuelled extremist ideologies on the right and the left during the inter-war period. Writing in 1943 in Algiers as a member of the French Committee for National Liberation, Jean Monnet argued:[2]

> There will be no peace in Europe if states rebuild themselves on the basis of national sovereignty, which brings with it the politics of prestige and economic protectionism. If the countries of Europe protect themselves against one another again, the constitution of vast armies will again be necessary … European states are too

constrained [*étroits*] to guarantee their peoples the prosperity that modern conditions make possible and consequently necessary.

According to Monnet, politics and trade are interlocked in a feedback loop that can be vicious or virtuous: when states are goaded by nationalist sentiments into a 'politics of prestige', they jettison the benefits of foreign trade for protectionist policies that leave their citizens worse off and which can escalate into armed conflict. By contrast, free economic exchange is capable of easing the conflictual dispositions of the nationalist frame of mind. Accordingly, a supranational scheme that eliminated protectionism and attenuated states' ability to mobilise core industries of warfare would also mitigate the destructive potential of mass mobilisation (Müller 2011, 128). As Robert Schuman put it in his 9 May Declaration of 1950, integration would bring about a general 'fusion of interests' and 'a wider and deeper community between countries long opposed to one another by sanguinary divisions' (Schuman 1950). Inspired by inter-war plans to place the Ruhr and Lorraine heavy industries under multinational control (Diebold 1988), the initiative of a European Coal and Steel Community was symptomatic of this distrust of the nation state. The ECSC was hardly inspiring to ordinary citizens, but it was not meant to be. Monnet conceded that 'increased coal and steel production is not the basis of our civilization' (Monnet 1955). Rather, his incremental strategy of sovereign commitment was meant to marshal instrumentally rational calculations to keep nationalist passions in check. Furthermore, it supplied a workable framework of supranational governance whose legitimacy was based on technocratic competence. Although Monnet himself spurned the idea of market integration, the subsequently negotiated European Economic Community (EEC) repurposed the institutions he had designed. Most importantly, defining the immediate scope of integration in technocratic terms enabled the EEC to circumnavigate the jealously guarded shoals of national sovereignty on which more ambitious federalist projects such as the European Defense Community (EDC) and the European Political Community (EPC) had foundered.

Accordingly, supranationalism was precisely an attempt to resolve the conflicts generated by early twentieth-century nationalism by using the lure of technocracy. The Monnet/Schuman prescription was to wean European nations off the opioid of identity politics by offering technical and economic rewards. Meanwhile, Member States could jealously guard their sovereign prerogatives until the imperatives of the market led them seamlessly into a fully fledged political union. In sum, the European integration project represents a socioeconomic solution to the problem of identity politics.

The reason Monnet's gambit worked for as long as it did is because nobody in the two generations following World War II was in danger of forgetting that the economic project was ultimately about creating a peaceful and stable political order on a congested continent prone to radical political movements. The cost of his strategy, however, was to depoliticise supranational decision-making as far as possible. By substituting economic pay-offs for principled support for integration, it neglected the long-term need to generate sustained public engagement in the European project. Over time and with the expansion of supranational power, however, this strategy has become unsustainable. As supranational institutions have acquired greater decision-making authority from Member States, it is proving increasingly difficult to explain why those institutions must be so far attenuated from citizen control. Having been excluded from the decisions that drew them into an ever-closer union, European publics are contesting the arrogance of technocracy by supporting irreverent parties and movements. Meanwhile, because their legitimacy is predicated on little more than 'you're better off thanks to the EU', supranational institutions experience every crisis of competence, every economic slump, as an existential crisis.

Ironically, the crises of competence that the EU has experienced over the past decade threaten to undo some of the hallmark achievements of decades of European integration, not least the relationships of solidarity and mutual trust among Member States. The crisis that ensnared EMU for the better part of a decade starting in 2009 perfectly illustrates this problem. For starters, EMU failed the test of competence insofar as it amplified the effects of the global financial and sovereign debt crisis rather than cushioning them, impeded recovery and growth rather than promoting the same, and brought high unemployment and widespread privation to many Member States rather than raising living standards. Second, the rigid constraints it imposed on domestic fiscal policies not only deprived national legislatures of key levers of social policy, but also further attenuated democratic control of policymaking at the domestic level. This, in turn, has exacerbated voter disenchantment with the political process and fuelled support for anti-establishment parties.

Third and most important, the social and distributional consequences of monetary union have tapped into subterranean veins of the nationalist animus, reanimating grievances dormant since Europe's dark century of civil war. The euro crisis has opened up fault lines between creditor and debtor states, the former insisting on fiscal prudence, and the latter struggling to meet their repayment and structural reform obligations while providing basic social assistance to their citizens. Disagreements over culpability, crisis management, and institutional reform have frayed the social consensus required to keep the integration project going. In other words, the distributive conflict and sense of insecurity generated by the euro crisis has reactivated identitarian cleavages in Europe. If socioeconomic anxieties and identity politics are indeed mutually reinforcing, then the EU as it is currently configured exacerbates both.

Clearly, the EU has in significant respects failed to make good on its promise to mitigate the ravages of global casino capitalism, particularly insofar as its institutional configuration favours price stability and fiscal conservatism, emphasises monetary policy over public spending, and resists attempts to re-embed the market in a matrix of social protection.[3] The fiscal coordination that allows the EMU to function has steadily tightened, along with the disciplinary apparatus attached to it. Member states are required to coordinate their economic policy cycles and ensure the conformity of their economic priorities, budgetary choices and structural reforms with strict EU rules. The legislative and constitutional adjustments necessitated by the crisis have corralled Member States into a protracted austerity zone, forcing them to pare down public spending, and with it, the social protections they afford their citizens (Martinsen & Vollaard 2014; de la Porte & Natali 2014; OECD 2014). Rather than bolstering the capacity of Member States to protect their vulnerable domestic constituencies against the pressures of global economic interdependence, the EU has worked to exacerbate these pressures.

Part of the reason for this is that the EU lacks the fiscal capacity necessary to provide compensatory or redistributive programmes of its own. Although the Preamble of the EEC Treaty expressed the desire of signatory states to promote the 'improvement of the living and working conditions of their peoples' and 'ensure [the] harmonious development [of their economies] by reducing the differences existing between the various regions and the backwardness of the less favored regions', it did not create the institutional structure required to further these commitments (Maas 2005).[4] According to the post-war consensus on the 'compromise of embedded liberalism' (Giubboni 2006), multilateral institutions promoting trade and financial liberalisation would be counterbalanced by strong domestic institutions guaranteeing social cohesion and compensating those disadvantaged by international economic competition (Ruggie 1982, 379). In the classic formula coined by

Robert Gilpin, embedded liberalism meant 'Smith abroad' and 'Keynes at home' (Gilpin 1987, 355). In the European Economic Community, Member States retain the prerogative of providing the social protections necessary to cushion the impact of greater market competition. In the ensuing decades, integration in the social domain has been clipped by Member States' insistence on preserving their prerogatives over national welfare provision (Leibfried 2015). With limited power to issue binding rules, and lacking any significant redistributive capacity, the EU's role in this area has been limited to benchmarking objectives, articulating best practice, and comparatively assessing outcomes. As a consequence, 'the course of European integration from the 1950s onward has created a fundamental asymmetry between policies promoting market efficiencies and those promoting social protection and equality' (Scharpf 2002, 665). Although the 2009 Treaty of Lisbon enumerated the building of a 'competitive *social* market economy'[5] among the EU's aims, and listed justice and solidarity among its founding values,[6] it nevertheless preserved the domestic basis of welfare provision, thereby creating a 'disjunction ... between lofty Treaty proclamation[s] and lack of law-making instruments' (Dawson & de Witte 2012). Similarly, while it introduced means for the EU to 'encourage cooperation' between Member States on social policy, it left it up to Member States to design, implement and fund it.[7] Although the EU was subjected to a new general obligation to 'take into account requirements linked to the promotion of a high level of employment, the guarantee of adequate social protection, the fight against social exclusion', it was not given any new powers with which to carry out this mandate.[8] Instead, it was merely enjoined from stepping on Member States' toes as they walked a tightrope between the socio-economic needs of their citizens, on the one hand, and the imperatives of market liberalisation, on the other. Since the 1990s, a growing chorus of scholars has expressed concern that the singular emphasis on market integration and competitiveness is eroding the domestic social protections and delicate corporatist bargains that define the European social model (Menéndez 2009; Offe 2000, 2015; Scharpf 1997; Somek 2008; Streeck 2000). In sum, Social Europe has unquestionably made far less headway than Market Europe.

For some, these circumstances doom the European project. The EU's stark pro-market bias, the ever-tightening constraints around domestic public spending and social assistance, and the democratic attenuation of supranational decision-making have motivated some left-leaning observers to argue in favour of reverting to the national Eden of social democracy (Davidson 2016; Johnson 2017; Streeck 2014). In his influential

'Left Case for Brexit' published shortly before the June 2016 vote, British political philosopher Richard Tuck (2016) railed against the EU as 'a constitutional order tailor-made for the interests of global capitalism and managerial politics'. Tuck contends that the EU 'has consistently undermined standard left policies such as state aid to industries and nationalization'. The only way to regenerate social democracy, in his view, is to reclaim domestic parliamentary sovereignty. To bolster his point, Tuck recalls that Marx admired the House of Commons as the only political institution capable of introducing socialism by democratic means, without revolutionary confrontation.

If there was one thing Marx understood well, however, it was that capitalism is a global force that cannot effectively be countered on domestic terrain alone. This insight is more compelling than ever today, when the lives of individuals everywhere are increasingly subject to political, social and economic forces that elude the control of any one state. Although the world is carved up into nominally sovereign territorial units, the most formidable policy challenges are transnational. Global economic and financial shocks, forced population movements, transnational criminal networks, environmental degradation and climate change make national self-sufficiency an elusive aspiration. To be sure, transnational challenges do not come with obvious global (as opposed to local, national or regional) solutions. However, if we are to understand society as a 'cooperative venture for mutual advantage', then this venture no longer follows the contours of the sovereign, territorial state (Beitz 1999).[9] While it is not clear that supranational political units can easily re-enact the bonds of solidarity necessary for making social justice work (Miller 2000, 81–96), it is increasingly difficult for a political community on the scale of the nation state to effectively address the challenges that affect its citizens. Particularly from the viewpoint of economic production and consumption, the world already looks like a cosmopolis (Brooks 2005). The EU's promise today is that it is an institutional attempt, however modest, to catch up with that reality.

And the EU has been remarkably successful at resisting some of the deregulatory or disembedding pressures occasioned by global economic interdependence, even if it hardly gets the credit it deserves in this regard. For instance, it upholds stringent public health and consumer protection standards over the vociferous objections of its trading partners and against WTO rules. This means voters must either rethink their Euroscepticism or alter their preference for hormone-free beef. Similarly, many Member State citizens may find a new appreciation for the overbearing judges of the CJEU if they value the privacy of their personal data in the age of mass surveillance, Facebook and Google.[10] On each of these matters, the size of its Single Market lends the EU leverage over its trading partners and multinational corporations far beyond what Member States acting singly could command. These modest achievements suggest that the only effective way for states to 'take back control' in the face of the vicissitudes of economic globalisation is to work within the framework of supranational and international institutions. Furthermore, it is only through such arrangements that the benefits and burdens of global economic exchange can ultimately be shared in more equitable ways. While critics like Tuck and Streeck are correct to observe that the EU is far from being the optimal vehicle for a fairer socioeconomic order, it has a key advantage over better, more ambitious schemes: it exists. However difficult to achieve, redesigning or re-equipping an institutional framework that already exists is a likelier prospect than building one from scratch.

If we accept that identity politics can be defused by addressing economic and class-based insecurities, and that nation states are no longer capable of upholding generous social welfare provision given the vagaries of global casino capitalism, then the EU's supranational policy-making framework might not only be a remedy; it might be the *only* available remedy. The EU not only has the institutional apparatus for making and enforcing supranational policy, it also has substantial fiscal resources that go towards agricultural subsidies, cohesion funds and emergency financial assistance. To be sure, it needs a generous expansion of its powers in the domain of social policy, but this calls only for a *repurposing* of its existing institutional capacity and material resources, away from market-oriented goals towards socially oriented policies.

In this regard, Brexit may clear one pesky logjam. In making the left case for Brexit, Tuck neglects to note that the UK has consistently obstructed the development of a more muscular EU social policy and redistributive capacity. Britain's long-standing insistence on a free market model of European cooperation is an essential and long-standing reason why European integration has proceeded along precisely the neoliberal track Tuck laments (Müller 2016a; Streeck 2016b).[11] Insofar as there is a 'left case for Brexit', then, it is primarily that of removing the one hurdle among many that has kept the continental left from correcting the EU's free market bias.

Sadly, however, even if we accept that only a renewed emphasis on social welfare and fair redistribution could redeem the EU in the eyes of citizens, this does not mean that such changes will be popular or feasible. Hunger is not bread, as Jeremy Bentham quipped. In decades past, the project of redressing the EU's pro-market bias with a stronger social agenda would have needed to await an alignment of left-wing governments among an influential group of Member States. Alas, such an alignment may be a long time coming, and not only because the EU is larger and more diverse. The most important reason why a Social Europe remains more elusive than ever is the dwindling power of left parties in most Member States. In states like France, Germany, Britain and Denmark, populist movements have capitalised on working-class hostility to the EU and lured away some of the very constituencies that predictably buoyed the left-wing vote (Berman 2016; Rhodes 2013). As a result, the pendulum that used to swing between the left and right sides of the political spectrum now oscillates precariously between moderate and extreme right (Berman 2016, 73).

Moreover, insofar as the fiscal and sovereign debt crisis has strengthened Euroscepticism, understood as support for 'parties and movements actively calling for a reduction of EU competences, if not for a simple dismantlement of the institutions' (Nicoli 2017, 315), it has undermined the likelihood of any such major reorientation. Laudable though they are, the objectives of redressing the EU's lopsided reliance on market mechanisms and distributing the benefits and burdens of European integration more evenly require *greater* delegation of powers to the EU. Paradoxically, then, the very failures that warrant a leftward reorientation of the European project have made that reorientation less likely to succeed.

It ought to give us pause that the plan for refashioning the EU into a supranational social democracy is continuous with Monnet's strategy in one key respect. Both seek to diminish the purchase of identity politics by improving material standards of living. By the same token, both are vulnerable to the same problems of technocracy and democratic attenuation. Shifting the EU's priority from market regulation to social justice is politically difficult, but not unimaginable. But social justice is not the same thing as social democracy, and it is gratuitous to assume that, once created, a supranational welfare state would acquire the strong underpinnings of an engaged and invested citizenry. The optimistic expectation of European federalists in the 1990s was that a genuine constitutional re-founding would catalyse a vibrant European *demos* and meaningful democratic opinion- and will-formation at the supranational level (Habermas 1998, 161). If the failure of the EU's attempt to stage a constitutional moment showed anything, it was that democratic publics cannot be summoned by incantation. Similarly, the persistence of voter apathy towards European elections despite the amplified power of the European Parliament[12] suggests that it is futile to adopt a *Field of Dreams* approach ('if you build it, they will come') to animate new representative institutions with democratic life.

Furthermore, it is far from clear that identity politics can be understood as nothing more than misdirected socioeconomic anxiety. If the appeal of populism is irreducible to a crisis of the relations of production, and instead stems from worry over cultural displacement, then nothing short of the recognition of identitarian demands can satiate its constituencies. If the latter diagnosis is accurate, moreover, assuring greater economic security and a fairer distribution of wealth will do little to boost the EU's popularity. In fact, insofar as the EU fosters a conspicuous new cosmopolitan elite that speaks multiple languages and cashes in on foreign degrees, facilitates the movement of people and accelerates the intermingling of cultures, it exacerbates identitarian anxieties. The fact that the Brexit campaign successfully exploited the public conflation of intra-EU free movement and the admission of refugees originating in the Middle East and Africa to amplify its message illustrates this issue. The free movement of persons heightens the sense that European integration is a conspiracy to eliminate nation states and makes it less credible as an attempt to reinforce their efficacy and to patch up the 'leaky vessel' of national democracy (Bright & Geyer 2012; Milward 2000). Furthermore, if we take the demands expressed by today's populist movements at face value, the EU's cardinal sin is not that of standing in the way of social justice, but of eroding the cultural cohesion and solidarity of the national political unit. As political theorists cautioned in the 1990s, redistribution is not necessarily an appropriate response to the politics of recognition.

Take Estonia, a country of about 1.3m people that acceded to the EU in 2004. According to the 2011 Estonian census, 12.7 per cent of the Estonian population consists of first-generation immigrants, with an additional 12 per cent Estonian-born persons of at least partial immigrant background.[13] Individuals of Russian origin constitute a majority of these groups. By contrast, non-European migrants in Estonia add up to less than 2 per cent of the total population (Statistical Database of Estonia 2011).[14] For instance, the total number of Estonian residents hailing from an African country of origin counted in the 2011 census was a paltry 414,[15] while just 32 individuals were from Afghanistan or of Afghan heritage (Statistical Database of Estonia 2011).[16] Estonia's population growth has been negative for a long time: emigration outstripped immigration for 14 of the past 16 years (Statistical Database of Estonia 2011).[17] Despite its relative ethnic and racial homogeneity and isolation from worldwide refugee flows, however, 70 per cent of responses from Estonia mentioned immigration as one of the two most important issues facing the EU in the Autumn 2016 Eurobarometer survey (Eurobarometer 2016b). (The second most important issue, highlighted in 40 per cent of responses, was terrorism, despite the apparent lack of a significant terrorist threat against Estonia.)

Perhaps those surveyed were thinking of immigration as a challenge to the EU, rather than to their own country. After all, the 18 months preceding this survey had seen an EU-wide spike in asylum applications and bitter controversy among EU Member States over apportioning responsibility for processing them. While Estonians appeared disproportionately disquieted by terrorism compared with the EU28 average, they were joined by citizens of Member States such as the Czech Republic, Latvia and Cyprus in recording a heightened concern with this issue (Eurobarometer 2016b, 7). By contrast, only 20 per cent and 17 per cent respectively among the EU28 ranked 'the economic situation' and 'member state finances' as one of the top two issues facing the EU (Eurobarometer 2016b, 7). For their part, UK respondents were within a few percentage points of the EU28 average in terms of their priorities. When asked about the two most important challenges facing the EU, Brits ranked immigration first at 42 per cent, terrorism second at 26 per cent and economic situation third at 24 per cent (Eurobarometer 2016b, 7).[18]

Puzzlingly, however, when EU citizens were asked about the top two challenges facing their own country, economic concerns such as unemployment, housing, pensions and rising cost of living took centre stage (Eurobarometer 2016b, 11). Although immigration was the second most frequently mentioned item across all Member States at 26 per cent, the combined share of socioeconomic issues highlighted by respondents is 122 per cent.[19] And when asked which two most important issues they personally faced, most respondents cited the cost of living, pensions and financial security (Eurobarometer 2016b, 13). Here, too, Brits were representative, ranking rising prices, health and social welfare, their country's economic situation and pensions as the most important issues affecting their personal lives (Eurobarometer 2016b, 13).

These survey results suggest that when it comes to their own lives, a majority of EU citizens are most immediately worried about their living standards. As it happens, economic prosperity is also the EU's top priority, given that its core competences relate to trade, competition, market regulation and price stability. Puzzlingly, however, citizens associate the EU with a markedly different set of challenges – immigration and terrorism – which raise anxieties about the intrusion of disruptive, alien 'others' into their political communities. Apparently, Britons and Estonians and Cypriots and Czechs regard the EU less as a sphere of economic opportunity, personal mobility and geopolitical security, and more as an overcrowded boat floating precariously in terrorist-infested waters. It is no wonder, then, that significant constituencies in these countries want to distance themselves from a Union they associate with insecurity.

Of course, how far these distorted optics are due to the EU's own failures of competence and how far they should be attributed to wilful distortion by political actors for domestic political advantage remains a matter for debate. However, the EU itself is hardly in a position to mount an effective response to the misperceptions. The way that European integration has been packaged and sold over generations has encouraged popular estimation of its value solely in terms of euros and cents. Meanwhile, European societies are once more in the grip of the kind of identity politics that decades of carefully constructed economic relationships were supposed to obviate. If the EU is ill-equipped to meet this challenge, it is not so much because of its bias in favour of deregulation, as leftist critics contend, but because the only tools at its disposal for doing so are of an economic nature. For this reason, it is unclear whether an alternative, social democratic model of supranationalism would do much resolve the discontents of identity politics. In fact, since such a project would require vesting the EU with even greater power and fiscal capacity, it is likely to have the opposite effect, at least in the near term. Trying to defuse identity politics with redistributive politics at the supranational level could be like trying to fix an electrical failure with a monkey wrench. The likely outcome is electrocution, not illumination.

27
Fair Brexit for a just Europe

Philippe Van Parijs[1]

When discussing what a fair Brexit would be, one could quibble about such issues as whether the UK should pay for the full cost of the relocation of the EU agency that was meant to settle in London, or whether it should keep paying for the pensions of EU employees who were in service while it was a member, in what proportion, and for how long. But one should also have more than one eye on the bigger picture. Perhaps the quickest way of accessing this bigger picture is by having a close look at an article published in 1939 by Friedrich Hayek, one of the founding fathers of so-called neoliberalism, and by reflecting on the lessons Margaret Thatcher seems to have drawn from it, both while in power and afterwards. Against this background, it will be easier to focus on what matters most in the Brexit deal for the pursuit of social justice in Europe and beyond.

Hayek's trap

In his article, 'The Economic Conditions of Interstate Federalism', Hayek explains why he finds a multinational federation, much later exemplified by the EU, a wonderful idea. Essentially, this is because it combines two features. Firstly, there is the disabling function of the common market, i.e. the economic constraints on state-level policy that stem from the freedom of cross-border movement:

> 'If goods, men, and money can move freely over the interstate frontiers, it becomes clearly impossible to affect the prices of the different products through action by the individual state.
>
> (Hayek 1939, 258)

This disempowerment of national governments would not be limited to price fixing, moreover. As Hayek goes on to say:

> As has been shown by experience in existing federations, even such legislation as the restriction of child labor or of working hours becomes difficult to carry out for the individual state. ... Not only would the greater mobility between the states make it necessary to avoid all sorts of taxation which would drive capital or labor elsewhere, but there would also be considerable difficulties with many kinds of indirect taxation.
>
> (Hayek 1939, 260)

Alongside governments, all state-level economic organisations would be seriously weakened.

> Once frontiers cease to be closed and free movement is secured, all these national organizations, whether trade-unions, cartels, or professional associations, will lose their monopolistic position and thus, qua national organizations, their power to control the supply of their services or products.
>
> (Hayek 1939, 261)

Wonderful – for Hayek! But, one might ask, won't the diminished capacity to act at the national level simply be replaced by a new capacity to act at the newly created level of the federation? By no means – and this is the second feature that, combined with the first, accounts for Hayek's enthusiasm. For there are two serious obstacles to the creation of such a capacity. Firstly, for Hayek, economic differences are likely to be far more pronounced in a large entity than in a small one:

> Many forms of state interference, welcome in one stage of economic progress, are regarded in another as a great impediment. Even such legislation as the limitation of working hours or compulsory unemployment insurance, or the protection of amenities, will be viewed in a different light in poor and in rich regions and may in the former actually harm and rouse violent opposition from the kind of people who in the richer regions demand it and profit from it.
>
> (Hayek 1939, 263)

Secondly, and more seriously, a multinational federation lacks, according to Hayek, the common identity and associated disposition to solidarity that nation states can rely on.

> In the national state current ideologies make it comparatively easy to persuade the rest of the community that it is in their interest to protect 'their' iron industry or 'their' wheat production or whatever it be. ... The decisive consideration is that their sacrifice benefits compatriots whose position is familiar to them. Will the same motives operate in favor of other members of the Union? Is it likely that the French peasant will be willing to pay more for his fertilizer to help the British chemical industry? Will ... the clerk in the city of London be ready to pay more for his shoes or his bicycle to help ... Belgian workmen?
>
> (Hayek 1939, 262–3)

There is no doubt, for Hayek, as to the answer. Admittedly, he notes that

> [t]hese problems are, of course, not unfamiliar in national states as we know them. But they are made less difficult by the comparative homogeneity, the common convictions and ideals, and the whole common tradition of the people of a national state.
>
> (Hayek 1939, 264)

In particular, decisions are less difficult to accept if the government taking them is regarded as consisting of compatriots rather than as consisting mostly of foreigners.

> Although, in the national state, the submission to the will of a majority will be facilitated by the myth of nationality, it must be clear that people will be reluctant to submit to any interference in their daily affairs when the majority which directs the government is composed of people of different nationalities and different traditions. It is, after all, only common sense that the central government in a federation composed of many different people will have to be restricted in scope if it is to avoid meeting an increasing resistance on the part of the various groups which it includes.
>
> (Hayek 1939, 264–5)

The outcome of the combination of these two features – economic constraints on state government and political constraints on union government – should be clear enough.

> There seems to be little possible doubt that the scope for the regulation of economic life will be much narrower for the central government of a federation than for national states. And since, as we have seen, the power of the states which comprise the federation will be yet more limited, much of the interference with economic life to which we have become accustomed will be altogether impracticable under a federal organization.
>
> (Hayek 1939, 265)

Consequently, the creation of such a multinational federation is an essential, and indeed wonderful, tool for the realisation of Hayek's 'liberal program', which became known, much later, as 'neoliberalism'. Bluntly put: 'the creation of an effective international order of law [in the form of a multinational federation] is a necessary complement and the logical consummation of the [neo-]liberal program' (Hayek 1939, 269).

Thatcher's plot

If there is one person who understood Hayek's message perfectly, it was Margaret Thatcher. She campaigned for her country to confirm its membership of the European Economic Community in 1975. When in office between 1979 and 1990, she strongly supported both the further unification of the common market – particularly through the 1986 Single European Act – and later its further expansion, made possible by the collapse of the Iron Curtain in 1989. In accordance with Hayek's argument, the increased mobility created by the deepening of the common market further disempowered Member States, while the increased heterogeneity created by the post-1989 enlargements further undermined the potential for the federation to take over the regulatory and redistributive powers that Member States were increasingly unable to exercise. This is Hayek's trap: Member States disabled by their immersion in the Single Market, combined with a Union disabled by its heterogeneity. This is the trap we are in more than ever thanks to the 2004 and 2007 enlargements, and to the relentless defence of the 'four freedoms' by the European Commission and the CJEU.

How should we react? As lucidly explained by Hayek, if we exclude the possibility of resurrecting thick national borders, with the concomitant economic losses and uncertainties this would trigger, there is only one real option: We must build a genuine European polity to encompass the European Single Market, instead of letting each national polity struggle with constraints imposed by its immersion in this market and, beyond, in an increasingly globalised world market. In particular, we urgently need to build socioeconomic institutions that exercise at least part of the redistributive function on a higher scale. Such redistribution will foster the pursuit of justice both directly through Union-level transfers, which are better protected than national-level transfers against social and tax competition, and indirectly by protecting national-level redistribution against such competition and the 'race to the bottom' it induces.

I am leaving aside here the form this EU-wide redistribution could and should take (Van Parijs 2013, Van Parijs & Vanderborght 2017, Chapter 8). What is clear, however, is that its political achievability and sustainability require a further empowerment of the Union, which should be entitled both to tax its citizens and to redistribute income across borders to a less negligible extent than it does currently. The EU does not need to mimic the American federal state, but it needs to do more of what the latter does if it does not want to let its European social model degenerate – stuck as it is in Hayek's trap – into something far more pathetic than the American welfare state, so often the target of derision by European social democrats.

Such a move, urgently needed to get out of the trap, is of course exactly what Hayek's disciple Margaret Thatcher would have hated to see happening. In *Statecraft*, her 2002 book, she formulates a fiery plea against those who want to erect something like the United States of Europe:

> The parallel [with the United States] is both deeply flawed and deeply significant. It is flawed because the United States was based from its inception on a common language, culture and values — Europe has none of these things. It is also flawed because the United States was forged in the eighteenth century and transformed into a truly federal system in the nineteenth century through events, above all through the necessities and outcomes of war. By contrast, 'Europe' is the result of plans. It is, in fact, a classic utopian project, a monument to the vanity of intellectuals, a programme whose inevitable destiny is failure: only the scale of the final damage done is in doubt.
> (Thatcher 2002, 359)

In the aftermath of German foreign minister (and former student activist) Joschka Fischer's famous speech on the ultimate objective of European integration (Berlin, May 2000), she did not hesitate to get personal:

> It is no surprise to me that the strongest proponents of Euro-federalism today often first cut their political teeth in the infantile utopianism, tinged with revolutionary violence, of the late 1960s and the 1970s.
>
> (Thatcher 2002, 343)

As the realisation spreads that this is precisely what we need to get out of Hayek's trap, as pressure mounts to move in this direction, Thatcher's advice to Britain would be today to get out of the grip of this monster: after 'I want my money back', it is time for 'We want our country back'. However, the 'hard Brexit' demanded by many Brexiteers would not live up to the neoliberal ambition. Rather, to remain in accordance with Hayek's script, it is crucial that Britain should retain full access – and remain fully subjected – to the European market, which the UK and Margaret Thatcher herself can pride themselves in having helped deepen and enlarge. Keeping full access to the Single Market, while escaping from any attempt to do at Union level what the Single Market prevents Member States from doing, is the wonderful combination which an appropriate 'soft Brexit' would enable 'global Britain' to achieve. In this way, Britain, having regained its 'sovereignty' can quietly undermine, through tax and social competition, any serious attempt to pursue egalitarian justice in Europe, whether at national or Union level. In other words: 'Let us Brexit, but "softly", so as to keep our sabotage capacity intact.' This is what could be called, without too much fantasy, Thatcher's plot, the conspiracy aimed at saving Hayek's neoliberal programme from the threat of the 'classical utopian project' of a political, social and fiscal union.

Fair Brexit

Hayek himself, however, unwittingly advises us not to give up on this utopian project. Ten years after he wrote the article quoted earlier, in the aftermath of World War II, Hayek was in despair about the turn of events throughout Europe and North America. With the New Deal, the expansion of social security systems, nationalisation programmes and the spreading of socialist regimes in Eastern Europe from Estonia to Albania, 'statism' was gaining ground all over the world. In an article published in 1949 under the title 'The intellectuals and socialism', he urged his fellow liberals to erect precisely what Thatcher would have dismissed as 'a monument to the vanity of intellectuals'.

> If we are to avoid such a development, we must be able to offer a new liberal program which appeals to the imagination. We must make the building of a free society once more an intellectual adventure, a deed of courage. What we lack is a liberal Utopia, ... a true liberal radicalism which does not spare the susceptibilities of the mighty (including the trade unions), which is not too severely practical and which does not confine itself to what appears today as politically possible. ... The main lesson which the true liberal must learn from the success of the socialists is that it was their courage to be Utopian which gained them the support of the intellectuals and thereby an influence on public opinion which is daily making possible what only recently seemed utterly remote.
>
> (Hayek 1949, 194)

Thus, articulating a coherent utopian vision is not an idle pastime. It is what enables us to make possible what is currently impossible. Had Hayek not thought this to be the case, his neoliberalism would not be dominating the world a half-century later. If we do not wish to remain forever saddled with neoliberalism, or to leave the field open for nationalist and jihadist dystopias, we need to learn from what he said he himself learned from postwar socialists. What Europe needs today is bold utopian thinking, not least regarding the EU.

But if the utopian projects we need are to have any chance of being realised, they will have to be protected against the pressures of globalisation, including – throughout the tough Brexit negotiations – against aggressive tax and social competition from a potential pirate state across the Channel. There can be no serious hope for a fairer distribution of income between capital and labour, between those with skills highly valued by the market and the rest, without a sufficiently powerful supranational authority. For those of us in Europe, only the EU can give this hope any credibility. In the ultimate interest of the most vulnerable in the EU and in the UK alike, it is essential that the EU should refuse any deal that would give 'global Britain' the capacity to undermine any future European effort to better care for the losers of globalisation, of the Single Market and of the single currency. Access to the Single Market by outsiders must be subjected to any condition the EU may wish to impose on its Member States, especially as regards taxation and redistribution. Escaping the grip of Thatcher's plot would be well worth even the forgoing of *all* mutual benefits from trade.

Moreover, any reflection on the terms of a fair Brexit must pay due attention to the less material, but no less important, public goods on which the EU, by virtue of its sheer existence has produced and keeps reproducing, not least the taming of Germany's supremacy and the stabilisation of democracy in Southern and Eastern Europe. Like that of other members states with a GDP per capita above the EU average, much of the UK's net contribution to the EU budget can be viewed as a contribution to these public goods. Leaving the EU will not prevent the UK from benefiting from these public goods. Nor should it exempt it from contributing to their cost. How high this contribution should be, and what form it could take – including compensatory free riding, for example, on military protection – cannot possibly be determined in an uncontroversial fashion. But allowing any country that so wishes to free ride on the continuing investment made by the remaining Member States is doomed to shatter the whole enterprise, and in doing so to undermine the very existence of the public goods it produces.

A fair deal with the UK will not prevent it from playing an important role in Europe's future. On the contrary. Along with existing countries inside or outside the EU, Britain can be part of a thriving and mutually beneficial broader European partnership. But the deal with the countries that choose to remain peripheral must not enable them to free ride on the public goods produced by the core, nor to block what the core needs to do to protect the region's most vulnerable citizens, not least those among them who voted for Brexit.

Conclusion

28
Rethinking the futures of Europe

Uta Staiger and Benjamin Martill

Understanding Brexit outside of Britain

It has been the principal claim of this volume that neither the causes nor the consequences of Brexit can be adequately understood solely within the confines of the British state. This is not to say that elements of the Brexit vote were not idiosyncratic, that specific actors, institutions and discourses in the UK were irrelevant to the outcome, or that Brexit will not have profound consequences for British politics and society, or for the British economy. It is, rather, to say that any such assessment is incomplete insofar as it fails to acknowledge the context of European history and politics within which Britain's relations with the EU have been inextricably intertwined. Brexit is thus reflective of – and contributes to – broader issues and disagreements within Europe and the EU, including the 'democratic deficit', the tension between national sovereignty and supranational governance, and the persistent legitimacy crisis afflicting the Union.

And, just as Brexit has been shaped by developments in European politics over the decades, so too is Brexit of great significance for the future of Europe. Brexit will have important consequences across a broad range of European institutional arrangements, including the policy process, the relations between the community institutions and the balance of power within them, the forms of governance employed, the legal architecture of Europe, and the norms underpinning the ideal of Europe and the legitimacy of the EU. Brexit also presages major changes to Europe's foreign policy agenda – and governance – and to the Union's credibility and global clout, as well as to the crucial bilateral relationships that form the core of the EU. It is towards an understanding of these effects that the contributors to this volume have lent their considerable expertise and experience, asking as to the future of a Europe in which the UK is no longer a Member State of the EU.

Whilst the authors agree on the need to examine the effects of Brexit from a European perspective, they do not all see eye to eye on the principal challenges posed by Brexit, nor on the most appropriate conceptual lenses through which to understand the consequences of Brexit. How, then, to summarise the views of such a disparate group of scholars, representing a diversity of theoretical and disciplinary perspectives? We suggest here that the best way of drawing together the individual contributions in this volume is by focusing on the commonalities of their endeavour; namely, bringing a plurality of theoretical tools to bear on the consequences of Brexit for a troubled Union. Whilst there is no consensus on the precise effects of Brexit (and how these should be understood) the contributors all agree on two things: (1) that Brexit will have highly significant effects for the future of politics in Europe, and (2) that the critical juncture at which the continent finds itself requires careful, informed scholarly analysis of the options – and possible futures – of Europe and the EU.

By way of a conclusion, we draw several lessons from the contributions of this book, linked by their shared emphasis on the best means of understanding the futures of Europe after Brexit. We begin by defining Brexit as a 'wicked problem', before discussing how, when taken together, the contributions help us develop the tools to think through problems such as these. In doing so we make the case for an interdisciplinary approach to Brexit, for the value of theoretical and methodological eclecticism, and for the acknowledgement of contingency and the ontological commitments this entails. We then assess the present 'state of the Union', noting the critical juncture at which the EU presently finds itself, as well as the importance of political debate and creative thinking for setting the continent on the right path in the decades ahead.

Brexit as a 'wicked problem'

Originally defined in the 1970s' social policy literature, 'wicked problems' are characterised by having innumerable, complex causes, yet no precedent: each wicked problem is essentially unique. Difficult to define and delimit, wicked problems have no right or wrong answer, only a good or bad one – and solutions are generally a 'one-shot' operation (Rittel & Webber 1973). And, as if this were not enough, there is not just technical difficulty, but social complexity, to deal with: wicked problems tend to include many different stakeholders with radically different views, values and priorities. For all intents and purposes, and according to the criteria outlined above, Brexit is a classic 'wicked problem'.

Because of their complexity and the *sui generis* nature, 'wicked problems' do not lend themselves to comprehension using traditional problem-solving theories. In other words, Brexit, as with any problem of this kind, cannot be adequately understood or resolved from a single standpoint or disciplinary expertise. It needs addressing from a diversity of angles and methodologies. The very orientation toward complex problems tends to trigger research that is not limited to discipline-specific epistemologies, but strays across boundaries. Indeed, it is when the rules and boundaries of individual disciplines are transcended, or coalesce, that knowledge production itself is changed (Barry et al. 2008). This volume, even where individual contributions may remain entirely bound by disciplinary traditions, aspires to a form of interdisciplinarity that highlights divergences in approach and meaning-making. As chapters trace broader, perennial arguments in the social and political science, in history, or the law, the volume does not seek synthesis, but to keep incompatibilities in play. Beyond academic dialogue, however, it also aims to show the extent to which extra-academic, societal factors come into play. Part and parcel of the 'culture of accountability' (Nowotny 2003), which marks much interdisciplinary research, the volume's scope and format have been specifically designed to engage with wider public and policy audiences.

The worth of the academic toolbox to the study of Brexit lies, moreover, in its capacity to draw on a plurality of theoretical approaches. Theory, while context-specific, fosters abstract reflection. It allows us not only to elucidate specific policies, behaviours or outcomes, but to problematise these, and offer normative roadmaps. Crucially, theoretical approaches also help us uncover the assumptions upon which the various arguments already in the public domain are based: after all, 'the process of theorising is, to a very large extent, a mechanism for the generation and organisation of disagreement' (Rosamond 2000). Harking back to core theoretical controversies over the ontology of European integration – the nature of the beast – theory helps to highlight the multiplicity of potential scenarios available for the future(s) of Europe, and the methodologies by which these might be modelled. As such, theory also helps to contextualise Brexit both spatially and temporally, linking the present day to debates over politics more generally, and to other classes of events and processes. It also couches Brexit more firmly in the existing social science literature, affording students and scholars analytical leverage over Brexit as a phenomenon worthy of, and amenable to, academic study.

Moreover, the acknowledgement of contingency is core to the enterprise of understanding 'wicked problems'. Reflecting that things could have ended up differently represents both an important ontological claim and an important lesson in moderation. Making space for contingency in our analyses of Brexit requires attention to the three 'semantic pillars' of the concept (Schedler 2007). The first of these is the notion of indeterminacy – the real possibility that things could be, or could have been, otherwise. That the Brexit vote, and its consequences, could have turned out very differently must feature in our understanding of how the event will contribute to Europe's future. We must acknowledge, in other words, that there was nothing inevitable about the occurrence, or the consequences, of the decision. A second facet of contingency is that social phenomena may be conditional upon prior events and causes in ways that have not been anticipated, or as a consequence of unexpected factors, interactions, or causal chains. Brexit is no exception to this rule, to which the attention afforded novel areas of political study – regarding, for instance, social media and the 'losers' of globalisation – readily attests. And thirdly, it must be acknowledged that the consequences of contingent events cannot be predicted with certainty. The outcome, for Europe, of the Brexit vote will be in flux for some time, and will not be amenable to (easy) prediction.

All of these semantic parameters matter. After all, the future of Europe will depend, fundamentally, on contingencies in the years ahead. The actions of those representing Britain and the EU will matter more now than they will at other times, making careful scrutiny of policymakers on both sides of the channel ever more necessary. Events, too, may come to affect the final outcome of negotiations in ways that are difficult to predict. National elections, terrorist attacks, economic shocks or geopolitical crises may all come to exert an independent effect on the outcome of the negotiations. Theory, therefore, can only take us so far. It can help us map out scenarios and tease out underlying assumptions, but it will need constant refinement and careful attention to events as they unfold. Studying Brexit is like tracking a moving target.

The future of Europe

If the contributors to this volume agree on one, simple 'fact', it is that the EU is certainly in trouble. Indeed, the Union has been ailing for some time under the pressure of a multidimensional crisis which 'cuts to the core of EU itself' (Dinan et al. 2017). Be it the migration and refugee crisis, the structural problems afflicting the eurozone, long-standing concerns about governance and institutions, the rise of illiberalism in the East, or the rift between Germany's economic vision and Greece's economic needs – the credibility and legitimacy of EU institutions have taken a severe hit. Geopolitically, moreover, the EU finds itself in a difficult situation; threatened by a resurgent Russia on its Eastern borders and in its 'neighbourhood', spurned by Trump's isolationist posturing vis-à-vis the transatlantic relationship, and lacking the coherence of alternative rising power centres – like China – in the emerging multipolar order (Anheier & Falkner 2017; Cox 2017). The vote for the UK to leave the Union contributes a further item to this litany of problems. As Brexit takes centre stage, these structural crises may be pushed to the margins of public perception, but their challenge will continue to need addressing.

To conclude on something of a positive note, nothing enlivens conversation quite like a crisis, and the moment of salience experienced by the question of Europe's future must not be wasted. The Brexit vote has spurred conversation across the continent about the purpose of the EU and the appropriate place of Britain in Europe. The referendum has placed core issues of European integration at the heart of domestic debates in the UK and in other Member States across the Union (not to mention in Brussels). Choice is back on the table. Proposals from the European Commission have varied from 'doing less more efficiently' to 'doing much more together', among other options (although it is evident which of these the Commission would prefer) (European Commission 2017b). Important questions, moreover, are being asked about what it means to be democratic in an age of globalisation, how economies should be structured so they work efficiently for all, how the future relationship between Britain and Europe should be construed, how we define ourselves as citizens of Europe and of our own countries, and how Europe can articulate its values within the changing global environment. This re-politicisation of the European project, and the opening up of public debate on the question of Europe's future, represent positive developments for European politics, wherever one lies on key ideological fault lines.

The outcome of the Brexit negotiations may not (indeed, probably cannot) please everyone, but British and European democracy will be healthier, *ceteris paribus*, if the citizens of Europe engage in greater levels of political deliberation and understanding. Brexit, in this sense, has acted as a wake-up call to decision-makers and the public to face the reality of Europe's problems and to undertake serious action to identify solutions, given the enormity of the stakes. There is no reason to think, moreover, that the UK cannot be a part of this discussion. After all, the recognition that Europe is in crisis is 'apolitical' in the broadest sense. Discussion of Europe's problems is not to take a position on the Leave/Remain debate, nor is it to identify oneself as a Eurosceptic or a Europhile. Indeed, Theresa May acknowledged as much in her Florence speech of 22 September 2017 when she noted that the 'success of the EU is profoundly in our [the UK's] national interest and that of the wider world', and referred to the 'vibrant debate going on about the shape of the EU's institutions and the direction of the Union in the years ahead' (May 2017b).

Europe, and the EU, thus find themselves at a 'critical juncture' (Sus 2017, 115); one hastened, for sure, by Brexit, but also reflecting broader social, institutional and geopolitical challenges facing the continent. And yet, it is this very sense of crisis that galvanises both citizens and elites alike, and offers the possibility of meaningful reform at the European level aimed at improving the lives of European citizens. In this new and complicated political environment, carefully articulated ideas about Europe's problems, and their potential solutions, are more relevant than ever before, since agency matters more than ever at times of crisis and upheaval. The contributions in this volume have all taken seriously the question of where Europe's future lies after Brexit. In offering cogent analyses of crucial actors, institutions, relationships and issues, they help us to rethink the future of the European project and contribute to vital debates taking place across the continent.

Notes

Introduction

1. First found in the Preamble to the 1957 Treaty establishing the European Economic Community (Treaty of Rome), as the aspiration to create 'the foundations for an ever closer union of the peoples of Europe'. A cornerstone of then Prime Minister David Cameron's renegotiation deal of the UK's EU membership was to exempt the UK from this commitment.
2. As the exercise is so vast, the government plans to 'correct the statute book where necessary' without full parliamentary scrutiny, using what are known, after the Statute of Proclamations 1539, as Henry VIII clauses.
3. *R (Miller)* v *Secretary of State for Exiting the EU* [2017] UKSC 5.
4. On 3 May 2017, the European Commission adopted and published its recommendation to open the Article 50 negotiations with the UK, based on the European Council guidelines of 29 April 2017. On 22 May 2017, the Council adopted the Commission's recommendation. The negotiations will also be conducted with due regard to the European Parliament's resolution of 5 April 2017.

Chapter 3

1. All quotes in the text are to Cummings (2017c) unless stated otherwise.

Chapter 4

1. This phrase appeared in the Preamble to the Treaty of Rome establishing the European Economic Community in 1957, where the six original signatories to the Treaties (France, Germany, Italy, Belgium, the Netherlands and Luxembourg) – see also Note 1 in the introduction.
2. Protocol no. 32 to the Treaty on EU and the Treaty on the Functioning of the EU on the Acquisition of Property in Denmark.
3. Protocol no. 35 to the Treaty on EU and the Treaty on the Functioning of the EU on Article 40.3.3 of the Constitution of Ireland.
4. *R (Miller)* v *Secretary of State for Exiting the EU*, judgment of the High Court of 3 November 2016 (available at: https://www.judiciary.gov.uk/judgments/r-miller-v-secretary-of-state-for-exiting-the-european-union/). The judgment of the Supreme Court on appeal was given on 24 January 2017. See the headline of the *Daily Mail*, 3 November 2016, 'Enemies of the People: Fury over "Out of Touch" Judges who Have "Declared War on Democracy" by Defying 17.4m Brexit Voters and who Could Trigger Constitutional Crisis'.

Chapter 8

1. This chapter is based on a lecture delivered at the School of Public Policy at UCL on 17 November 2016 and initially published (in French) in the *Revue trimestrielle de droit europeen* (see van Middelaar 2016).
2. Michael Gove, the former Secretary of State for Justice, famously said: 'the people in this country have had enough of experts'.
3. Commission proposal of 8 March 2016 to revise the 1996 Directive on Posted Workers.
4. On 14 September 2016, the European Parliament and the Council approved Regulation EU 2016/1624 on the European border and coast guard, for which a political agreement between the institutions had been found early July, just a few days later than the deadline set by the EU heads of state or government at their December 2015 meeting (European Council Conclusions, 17–18 December 2015, point 8).

Chapter 11

1. In the December 1993 Downing Street Declaration, UK Prime Minister John Major and his Irish counterpart, Albert Reynolds, affirmed the right of the people of Ireland to self-determination but also that Northern Ireland would only become part of the Republic if a majority of its people supported such a change. This provided an important foundation for the subsequent Good Friday Agreement.
2. Interview, Irish Embassy in London, October 2015.
3. These can be summarised as: (i) remaining in the Single Market; (ii) establishing a bespoke Customs Union with the EU; or (iii) negotiating a deep and comprehensive free trade agreement (Hayward 2017b).
4. It is significant in this regard that at its summit in April 2017, the European Council agreed that if a united Ireland emerged at some point in the future, Northern Ireland would automatically become part of the EU.

Chapter 12

1. *Official Journal of the EU*, 2010/718/EU.
2. TNA, FCO 33/4669, Statement Motzfeldt, 2 October 1981.
3. Historical Archives of the EU (HAEU), Florence, CM2/1963, 885, Letter Ben Bella to Hallstein, 24 December 1962.
4. HAEU, CM2/1963, 885, EEC, Council, G, Rat, Note, secret, 25 June 1963.
5. The National Archives at Kew, FCO, 33/4670, Hatford, British Embassy Copenhagen, to Spreckley, FCO, 6 November 1981.
6. HAEU, CM2/1972, 1709, EC, Council, Relations with Algeria, 30 January 1968.
7. See, e.g., 'Grønland udskyder selvstændighed', in *Information*, 22 April 2015.

Chapter 13

1. Various experts quoted in Schelkle and Lokdam (2016, 13–14).
2. According to Tony Halmos, quoted in Schelkle and Lokdam (2016, 13).
3. At the end of 2015, banks in the euro area had almost €28 trillion assets while US banks had a bit more than €14 trillion, so about half of that. Both are surpassed by Chinese banks, however, with over €28 trillion or about €500 billion more than the euro area (Schoenmaker and Véron 2016, 12).

4. Rahman (2015) is a useful source on CCPs.
5. Source: *Select Statistics* blog based on HMRC data (available at: https://select-statistics.co.uk/blog/uks-major-trading-partners/).
6. An effective exchange rate is a summary measure of a country's exchange rate vis-à-vis all main trading partners by weighting the bilateral exchange rates with each by their export or trade shares.
7. Ring-fencing means that a national supervisor does not allow a resident bank to provide liquidity to headquarters or a subsidiary in another Member State threatened with capital flight. Italian banks have accused the German supervisor BaFin of practising this protectionist policy and the latter defended it as a protective measure (Arnold 2014).

Chapter 14

1. There are echoes of this in the writings of Robert Tombs and in the arguments made by 'Historians for Britain'. See Tombs (2008) and, for example, Abulafia (2015).
2. This has been a central feature of Marine Le Pen's 2017 French presidential campaign. It is at the core of many academic studies, such as Kriesi et al. (2012).
3. The importance of changes in state–society relations for the dynamics of EU integration is being captured in recent innovations in EU integration theories. See for instance the work of Hooghe and Marks 2008; Bickerton et al. 2015; and Leuffen et al. 2012.
4. Of all the advanced economies, only Greece has had lower real-wage growth than the UK since 2008 (Giles 2017).
5. It is worth noting that this was already challenged by the Syriza government when it tried to politicise the Eurogroup discussions. This attempt – particularly by Varoufakis – was entirely at odds with the etiquette of the Eurogroup and showed how unused its members were to principled political disagreements between national government representatives. Indeed, it showed that when such disagreements occur the Eurogroup is simply not fit for purpose.

Chapter 16

1. HC Deb (10 October 2016) c55.

Chapter 17

1. This is a deliberate oversimplification. These are the largest affected groups, but there are others who may find that their accrued rights may be at risk, such as those who have previously been resident in another Member State, have now moved (on, or back) and may want to return to the first host state.
2. The position of Labour leader Jeremy Corbyn has been a matter of extensive conjecture, but in July 2017 he used harsh language which indicated strong hostility to the particular model offered by free movement: e.g. 'Jeremy Corbyn: "Wholesale" EU Immigration has Destroyed Conditions for British Workers', *New Statesman*, 23 July 2017 (available at: http://www.newstatesman.com/politics/staggers/2017/07/jeremy-corbyn-wholesale-eu-immigration-has-destroyed-conditions-british).
3. Only in July 2017 was the Migration Advisory Committee commissioned to study existing practices in relation to the free movement of labour as well as the future needs of the UK economy in relation to migration: Home Secretary Amber Rudd's commissioning letter to the chair of the Migration Advisory Committee, 27 July 2017 (available at: https://www.gov.uk/government/publications/commissioning-letter-to-the-migration-advisory-committee).

4. *Joint Technical Note on the Comparison of EU-UK Positions on Citizens' Rights*. Department for Exiting the EU, 20 July 2017 (available at: https://www.gov.uk/government/publications/joint-technical-note-on-the-comparison-of-eu-uk-positions-on-citizens-rights).

5. See for example the statement signed by Michael Gove, Gisela Stuart and Priti Patel on immigration policy, 1 June 2016 (available at: http://www.voteleavetakecontrol.org/restoring_public_trust_in_immigration_policy_a_points_based_non_discriminatory_immigration_system.html).

6. The original claim stems from work done by the Liberal Democrats and published in a *Guardian* report in February 2017 (available at: https://www.theguardian.com/uk-news/2017/feb/27/rejections-eu-citizens-seeking-uk-residency). This was further amplified in a *Financial Times* article highly critical of the permanent residence application process: 'EU Citizens Face 85-page "Nightmare" Brexit Britain Form', 1 March 2017 (available at: https://www.ft.com/content/2119a554-fce6-11e6-96f8-3700c5664d30) to which the Home Office issued a set of 'clarifications' (available at: https://homeofficemedia.blog.gov.uk/2017/03/02/financial-times-article-on-the-permanent-residency-application-process/).

7. 'The Government's Negotiating Objectives for Exiting the EU: PM Speech', 17 January 2017 (available at: https://www.gov.uk/government/speeches/the-governments-negotiating-objectives-for-exiting-the-eu-pm-speech).

8. 'Poll Finds that 60% of Britons Want to Keep their EU Citizenship.' *Observer*, 1 July 2017 (available at: https://www.theguardian.com/politics/2017/jul/01/poll-european-eu-rights-brexit).

9. Available at: http://ec.europa.eu/eurostat/statistics-explained/index.php/Migration_and_migrant_population_statistics (data extracted March 2017).

10. 'Attitudes to Brexit: Everything we Know so Far.' *YouGov*, 29 March 2017 (available at: https://yougov.co.uk/news/2017/03/29/attitudes-brexit-everything-we-know-so-far/).

11. Case C-434/09 *McCarthy* v *SSHD* ECLI:EU:C:2011:277.

12. Case C-165/16 *Lounes* v *SSHD Opinion of AG Bot*, 30 May 2017, judgment pending.

13. Case C-135/08 *Rottmann* v *Freistaat Bayern* ECLI:EU:C:2010:104.

14. *Kuric and Others* v *Slovenia*, No 26828/06, [2013] 56 EHRR 20.

15. Case C-221/17 *Tjebbes* v *Minister van Buitenlandse Zaken*; for details see 'The Council of State of the Netherlands Sends a Preliminary Ruling Request to the CJEU.' *EUDO Citizenship Blog*, 20 April 2017 (available at: http://eudo-citizenship.eu/news/citizenship-news/1811-the-council-of-state-of-the-netherlands-sends-a-preliminary-ruling-request-to-the-cjeu).

16. 'The Surge in Britons Seeking a Second Passport.' *FT Brexit Briefing*, 21 July 2017 (available at: https://www.ft.com/content/9a38e93a-6e11-11e7-b9c7-15af748b60d0). This matter has also reached the attention of the press in France: 'Brexit: hausse de 254 % du nombre de Britanniques demandant la nationalité française en 2016', *Le Monde*, 19 June 2016 (available at: http://www.lemonde.fr/referendum-sur-le-brexit/article/2017/06/19/hausse-de-254-du-nombre-de-britanniques-demandant-la-nationalite-francaise-en-2016_5147585_4872498.html).

17. For a regularly updated review of naturalisation trends and concepts in the UK, see Migration Observatory Briefing, *Naturalisation as a British Citizen: Concepts and Trends*, 18 July 2017 (available at: http://www.migrationobservatory.ox.ac.uk/resources/briefings/naturalisation-as-a-british-citizen-concepts-and-trends/).

18. See House of Lords EU Committee, *Brexit: Acquired Rights*, 10th Report of Session 2016–17, HL Paper 82.

19. 'Dutch Nationals Taking UK Citizenship "Will Lose Netherlands Passports".' *Guardian*, 17 July 2017 (available at: https://www.theguardian.com/politics/2017/jul/17/dutch-nationals-brexit-uk-citizenship-lose-netherlands-passports-mark-rutte). For details on loss of citizenship by acquisition of foreign citizenship, see EUDO Citizenship Modes of Loss database (available at: http://eudo-citizenship.eu/databases/modes-of-loss).

Chapter 18

1. *R (Miller)* v *Secretary of State for Exiting the EU* [2016] EWHC 2768 (Admin); *R (on the application of Miller and another) (Respondents)* v *Secretary of State for Exiting the EU (Appellant)* [2017] UKSC 5.

2. *Attorney General* v *De Keyser's Royal Hotel Ltd* [1920] AC 508.

3. See in particular the *UK Constitutional Law* blog (available at: https://ukconstitutionallaw. org/blog/).
4. That was so even in the seminal blog post by King et al. (2016).
5. *Miller* Supreme Court, para 65.
6. *Miller* Supreme Court, paras 179–197.
7. EU (Notification of Withdrawal) Act 2017.
8. Note that in Scotland 62 per cent voted 'Remain' – the clearest majority, either way, in any UK region.
9. 'But it is recognised that the Parliament of the UK will not normally legislate with regard to devolved matters without the consent of the Scottish Parliament.'
10. *Miller* Supreme Court, para 146.
11. *Miller* Supreme Court, para 148.
12. Art 48 TEU.

Chapter 19

1. The Area of Freedom, Security and Justice is both communitarian in terms of its decision-making via the use of qualified majority voting, and justiciable in law on the basis of Article 3(2) TEU (available at: http://www.europarl.europa.eu/atyourservice/en/displayFtu. html?ftuId=FTU_5.12.1.html).
2. The 2017 White Paper makes explicit 'priority missions [that] have had some notable successes', including ALTHEA in Bosnia (2004), ATALANTA in the Horn of Africa (2008–ongoing), Rule of Law in Kosovo, Policing in Afghanistan, Assistance in Ukraine (2014) to the most recent, SOPHIA in the Mediterranean, as well as further civilian support in Georgia, Libya, Palestine and Somalia.

Chapter 20

1. There are disputes over the issue of the effect of immigration on wage levels. Jonathan Wadsworth concluded in 2015 that 'there is little evidence of a strong correlation between changes in wages of the UK-born (either all or just the less skilled) and changes in local area immigrant share over this period' (Wadsworth 2015, 9). But this does not address the question of the structural power, or lack of it, of labour in relation to seeking a better deal from employers in the context of high employment. It is also clear that employers are precisely employing migrant labour because they cannot get local people to work at the low wages offered. In any case Wadsworth acknowledges that public perceptions of the effects of migration on jobs and wages are very different from the evidence he is presenting.

Chapter 23

1. In addition to the 17 goals, there are 169 targets and 230 global indicators. 'Sustainable development' was put on the UN agenda in 1987 by the Brundtland report.
2. GOD, A.C.O., 2015. Encyclical letter Laudato Si' of the Holy Father Francis on Care for Our Common Home.
3. Starting of course with the Club of Rome's 1972 'Limits to Growth' report.
4. I thank Adrian Favell for pointing this out to me.
5. The old idea was bottled anew by the Commission in the run-up to Rome, pitted against the straw-scenarios of 'muddling through', focusing on the Single Market or federalising further. For an overview see: http://www.praguesummit.eu/docs/sustainable-european-integration:-eu-for-the-21st-century-223.pdf.

Chapter 25

1. The reference to Aristotle's work is represented as a 'Bekker number', allowing reference to any translation of the *Nicomachean Ethics*.

Chapter 26

1. This chapter is an attempt to further develop ideas presented in Chapter 5 of my book (Isiksel 2016) in light of Britain's decision to leave the EU ('Brexit').
2. Jean Monnet, *Note de Réflexion de 5 août 1943* (available at: http://www.cvce.eu/obj/ note_de_reflexion_de_jean_monnet_alger_5_aout_1943-fr-b61a8924-57bf-4890-9e4b-73bf4d882549.html).
3. The metaphor of embedding is borrowed from Polanyi (1944 [2001]), who characterises the dynamics of modern capitalist society as a 'double movement' whereby market forces strain against regulatory measures by which the state seeks to contain its deleterious effects on society.
4. This passage rephrases the ECSC Treaty's preambular pledge to 'raise the standard of living' by expanding productivity.
5. Art. 3(3) TEU. Emphasis added.
6. Art. 2 TEU.
7. Art. 153(1) and (2).
8. Art. 9 TFEU.
9. Charles Beitz was the first to argue (with qualifications) that Rawls' conception of society as a cooperative venture for mutual advantage must be global in scope.
10. For instance, the Court of Justice invalidated the Data Retention Directive of 2006 for disproportionate interference with the rights to privacy and data protection enshrined in the EU's Charter of Fundamental Rights. Joined Cases C-293 & 594/12, *Digital Rights Ireland Ltd and Seitlinger and others*, ECLI:EU:C:2014:238, 8 April 2014. Similarly, it held that the 1995 Data Protection Directive entailed a 'right to be forgotten': in this case, an entitlement to the removal of personal data from search engines. Case C-131/12 *Google Spain SL, Google Inc. v Agencia Española de Protección de Datos (AEPD), and Mario Costeja González*, ECLI:EU:C:2014:317, 13 May 2014.
11. Although Streeck maintains that 'the neoliberal revolution, led by the US and the UK, has forever closed [the] window' for building a supranational welfare state.
12. Turnout in European Parliament elections has declined from 62 per cent in 1979 (the first year of direct elections) to >43 per cent in the 2014 elections, even though the powers of the EP have been enlarged in successive treaty changes over the same period (available at: http://www.europarl.europa.eu/elections2014-results/en/turnout.html).
13. 'Population and Housing Census 2011.' *Statistics Estonia News Release*, No. 80, 21 June 2013 (available at: http://www.stat.ee/dokumendid/70026).
14. This number was obtained by calculating the total number of persons originating in European and EU states other than Estonia, and subtracting it from the general population of Estonian residents.
15. The category used in the database search was 'PC0521: POPULATION, 31 DECEMBER 2011 by Sex, Place of residence, Parents' country of birth / Region, Country of birth and Ethnic nationality'. Search query included persons of foreign and Estonian birth whose parents' country of birth was one of the countries listed in the region of Africa.
16. Search query included persons of foreign and Estonian birth whose parents' country of birth was Afghanistan.
17. Based on data between 2000–16. 'The Population of Estonia Increased Last Year', *Statistics Estonia News Release*, No. 8, 16 January 2017 (available at https://www.stat.ee/news-release-2017-008).
18. Interestingly, in the May 2016 Eurobarometer survey conducted just six months earlier, more UK survey responses flagged immigration (at 51 per cent), alongside 38 per cent for terrorism (Eurobarometer 2016a). The steep drop in UK respondents reporting worry over immigration

and terrorism relative to the EU28 suggests that the British electorate's decision to leave the EU in the intervening period may have assuaged some of the UK public's anxiety over these issues.

19. Because the survey allows each respondent to give more than one response (respondents may choose *up to two* top issues from a list), the total percentage share of issues adds up to 190 per cent across the EU28 in the Autumn 2016 survey.

Chapter 27

1. Part of this contribution is a slightly revised version of 'Thatcher's Plot – And How to Defeat It' (*Social Europe*, 29 November 2016), itself consisting largely of the final part of 'Just Europe', the Max Weber lecture delivered at the European University Institute (Florence) on 16 November 2016.

Bibliography

All URLs were live at 2 November 2017.

Abulafia, David. 2015. 'Britain: Apart from or a Part of Europe?' *History Today*, 11 May (available at: http://www.historytoday.com/david-abulafia/britain-apart-or-part-europe).

Adler-Nissen, Rebecca. 2015a. 'Through the EU's Front and Back Doors: The Selective Danish and Norwegian Approaches in the Area of Freedom, Security and Justice.' In *The Nordic Countries and the European Union*, edited by Caroline Howard Grøn, Peter Nedergaard & Anders Wivel, 188–205. Abingdon: Routledge.

Adler-Nissen, Rebecca. 2015b. *Opting Out of the European Union: Diplomacy, Sovereignty and European Integration*. Cambridge: Cambridge University Press.

Aitkenhead, Decca. 2016. 'The Guardian Saturday Interview: Nigel Farage.' *Guardian*, 20 May (available at: https://www.theguardian.com/politics/2016/may/20/nigel-farage-ukip-eu-referendum-interview-vote-leave-brief-every-day).

Amón, Rubén. 2016. 'Brexit ¡Gibraltar español!' *El País*, 24 June.

Anheier, Helmut & Falkner, Robert. 2017. 'Europe Challenged: An Introduction to the Special Issue.' *Global Policy* 8(4): 5–8.

Arendt, Hannah. 1951. *The Origins of Totalitarianism*. New York: Schocken Books.

Armstrong, Kenneth A. 2017. *Brexit Time: Leaving the EU – Why, How and When?* Cambridge: Cambridge University Press.

Arnold, Martin. 2014. 'ING Chief Hits out at German Financial Regulator BaFin.' *Financial Times*, 6 August (available at: https://www.ft.com/content/909ad0a0-1d83-11e4-8f0c-00144feabdc0).

Asthana, Anushka & Mason, Rowena. 2016. 'UK Must Leave European Convention on Human Rights, says Theresa May.' *Guardian*, 25 April (available at: https://www.theguardian.com/politics/2016/apr/25/uk-must-leave-european-convention-on-human-rights-theresa-may-eu-referendum).

Baccaro, Lucio & Pontusson, Jonas. 2016. 'Rethinking Comparative Political Economy: The Growth Model Perspective.' *Politics and Society* 44(2): 175–207.

Bagehot, Walter. 1867 [1963]. *The English Constitution edited with an introduction by R.H.S. Crossman*. London: Fontana/Collins.

Baker, George, Gibbons, Robert & Murphy, Kevin J. 2002. 'Relational Contracts and the Theory of the Firm.' *Quarterly Journal of Economics* 117(1): 39–84.

Barnard, Catherine. 2008. 'The "Opt-Out" for the UK and Poland from the Charter of Fundamental Rights: Triumph of Rhetoric over Reality?' In *The Lisbon Treaty: EU Constitutionalism without a Constitutional Treaty*, edited by Stefan Griller and Jacques Ziller, 257–283. New York: Springer.

Barr, Nicholas. 2015. *The Economics of the Welfare State*. 5th edition. Oxford and New York: Oxford University Press.

Barry, Andrew, Born, Georgina & Weszkalnys, Gisa. 2008. 'Logics of Interdisciplinarity.' *Economy and Society* 37(1): 20–49.

Barry, Brian. 2001. *Culture and Equality: An Egalitarian Critique of Multiculturalism*. Cambridge, MA: Harvard University Press.

Bates, Ed. 2017. 'Is the UK Going to Withdraw from the ECHR? What about the Human Rights Act?' *UK Strasbourg Spotlight Blog* (available at: https://ukstrasbourgspotlight.wordpress.com/2017/03/10/is-the-uk-going-to-withdraw-from-the-echr-what-about-the-human-rights-act/).

Bauböck, Rainier. 2002. 'United in Misunderstanding? Asymmetry in Multinational Federations.' ICE Working Paper Series, No. 26.

BBC News. 2014. 'Austerity Creating "More Unequal NI society".' 15 January (available at: http://www.bbc.co.uk/news/uk-northern-ireland-25737952).

BBC News. 2016. 'EU Vote: Where the Cabinet and other MPs stand.' 22 June (available at: http://www.bbc.co.uk/news/uk-politics-eu-referendum-35616946).

BBC News. 2017. 'Prison Suicides Rise to Record Levels in England and Wales.' (available at: http://www.bbc.co.uk/news/uk-38756409).

BBC Radio Four. 2017. 'Breakfast with the Disruptors.' Series 1. Property. 22 May (available at: http://www.bbc.co.uk/programmes/b08s8gt5).

Begg, Iain, Bongardt, Annette, Nicolaïdis, Kalypso & Torres, Francisco. 2015. 'EMU and Sustainable Integration.' *Journal of European Integration* 37(7): 803–16.

Beitz, Charles. 1999. *Political Theory and International Relations.* Revised edition. Princeton, NJ: Princeton University Press.

Bell, Christine. 2016. 'Brexit, Northern Ireland and British-Irish Relations.' *European Futures,* 26 March (available at: http://www.europeanfutures.ed.ac.uk/article-3093).

Bell, Duncan. 2017. 'The Anglosphere: New Enthusiasm for an Old Dream.' *Prospect Magazine,* 19 January.

Bellamy, Richard & Kröger, Sandra. 2017. 'The Demoi-cratic Justifiability of Differentiated Integration in a Heterogeneous EU.' *Journal of European Integration* 39(5): 625–39.

Bellamy, Richard & Weale, Albert. 2015. 'Political Legitimacy and European Monetary Union: Contracts, Constitutionalism and the Normative Logic of Two-Level Games.' *Journal of European Public Policy* 22(2): 257–74.

Bellamy, Richard. Forthcoming. *A Republic of European States: Cosmopolitanism, Statism and Republican Intergovernmentalism in the EU.* Cambridge: Cambridge University Press.

Bellamy, Richard. 2013. '"An Ever Closer Union Among the Peoples of Europe": Republican Intergovernmentalism and Demoicratic Representation within the EU.' *Journal of European Integration* 35(5): 419–516.

Bellamy, Richard. 2015. 'A Duty Free Europe? What's Wrong with Kochenov's Account of EU Citizenship Rights.' *European Law Review* 21(4): 558–65.

Ben Bella, Ahmed. 1963. *Discours du Président Ben Bella du 28.9 au 12.12.1962.* Algiers: Ministry of Information.

Benhabib, Seyla. 2002. *Claims of Culture: Equality and Diversity in the Global Era.* Princeton, NJ: Princeton University Press.

Berman, Sheri. 2016. 'The Lost Left.' *Journal of Democracy* 27(4): 69–76.

Bernanke, Ben. 2016. 'Ending "Too Big to Fail": What's the Right Approach?' *Brookings Institution Blog,* 13 May (available at: https://www.brookings.edu/blog/ben-bernanke/2016/05/13/ending-too-big-to-fail-whats-the-right-approach/).

Bertelsmann Foundation. 2016. 'November 2016 Survey' (available at: https://www.bertelsmann-stiftung.de/en/topics/aktuelle-meldungen/2016/november/brexit-boosts-eu-survey-results/).

Betz, Hans-Georg. 1994. *Radical Rightwing Populism in Western Europe.* New York: St. Martin's Press.

Bickerton, Chris. 2012. *European Integration: From Nation-States to Member States.* Oxford: Oxford University Press.

Bickerton, Chris. 2017a. 'Nation-State to Member State: Trajectories of State Transformation and Re-Composition in Europe.' In *Reconfiguring European States in Crisis,* edited by Desmond King and Patrick Le Galès. Oxford: Oxford University Press.

Bickerton, Chris. 2017b. 'Europe in Revolt.' *Prospect,* January.

Bickerton, Chris. 2017c. 'Angela Merkel is no Neoliberal Fanatic.' *New Statesman,* May.

Bickerton, Chris, Hodson, Dermot, & Puetter, Uwe. 2015. 'The New Intergovernmentalism: European Integration in the Post-Maastricht Era.' *Journal of Common Market Studies* 53(4): 703–22.

Black, James, Hall, Alexandra, Cox, Kate, Kepe, Marta & Silfversten, Erik. 2017. *Defence and Security after Brexit: Understanding the Possible Implications of the UK's Decision to Leave the EU.* RAND Corporation.

Blockmans, Steven & Weiss, Stefani. 2016. 'Estrangement Day: The Implications of Brexit for the EU.' Centre for European Policy Studies (CEPS) Commentary, 27 June.

Boffey, Daniel. 2015. 'Half of all Teachers Threaten to Quit as Morale Crashes.' *Observer*, 4 October (available at: https://www.theguardian.com/education/2015/oct/04/half-of-teachers-consider-leaving-profession-shock-poll).

Boffey, Daniel. 2017a. 'Dutch Nationals taking UK Citizenship "will Lose Netherlands Passports".' *Guardian*, 17 July (available at: https://www.theguardian.com/politics/2017/jul/17/dutch-nationals-brexit-uk-citizenship-lose-netherlands-passports-mark-rutte).

Boffey, Daniel. 2017b. 'Dutch Nationals Living in Britain will be Allowed Dual Citizenship.' *Guardian*, 10 October (available at https://www.theguardian.com/world/2017/oct/10/dutch-nationals-living-britain-allowed-dual-citizenship-brexit).

Bond, Ian, Besch, Sophia, Gostyńska-Jakubowska, Agata, Korteweg, Rem, Mortera-Martinez, Camino & Tilford, Simon. 2016. 'Europe after Brexit: Unleashed or Undone?' *Centre for European Reform* (available at: http://www.cer.eu/publications/archive/policy-brief/2016/europe-after-brexit-unleashed-or-undone).

Borio, Claudio. 2014. 'The International Monetary and Financial System: Its Achilles Heel and What to do About It.' BIS Working Papers, No. 456. Basel: BIS.

Bossuat, Gerard. 2006. *Faire l'Europe sans défaire la France. 60 ans de politique d'unité européenne des gouvernements et des présidents de la République française (1943–2003)*. Brussels: Peter Lang.

Boswell, Christina, Kyambi, Sarah & Smellie, Saskia. 2017. 'Scottish Immigration Policy After Brexit: Evaluating Options for a Differentiated Approach.' Working Paper, School of Social and Political Science, University of Edinburgh (available at: https://www.scer.scot/database/ident-2735).

Boukala, Salomi, & Dimitrakopoulou, Dimitra. 2016. 'The Politics of Fear vs. the Politics of Hope: Analysing the 2015 Greek Election and Referendum Campaigns.' *Critical Discourse Studies* 14(1): 39–55.

Bowler, Tim. 2017. 'How has the Economy Fared since the Brexit Vote?' (available at: http://www.bbc.com/news/business-36956418).

Brennan, Geoffrey & Buchanan, James M. 1980. *The Power to Tax: Analytical Foundations for a Fiscal Constitution*. Cambridge: Cambridge University Press.

Bright, Charles & Geyer, Michael. 2002. 'Where in the World Is America?: The History of the United States in the Global Age.' In *Rethinking America in a Global Age*, edited by Thomas Bender. Berkeley, CA: University of California Press.

British Election Study. 2016. 'Brexit Britain: British Election Study Insights from the post-EU Referendum wave of the BES Internet Panel.' British Election Study Report, 6 October (available at: http://www.britishelectionstudy.com/bes-resources/brexit-britain-british-election-study-insights-from-the-post-eu-referendum-wave-of-the-bes-internet-panel/#.Wc5tWVtSyHt).

Brooks, Stephen G. 2005. *Producing Security: Multinational Corporations, Globalization, and the Changing Calculus of Conflict*. Ithaca: Princeton University Press.

Burke, Edward. 2017. 'Brexit's Threat to Northern Ireland.' *The World Today*, August and September (available at: https://www.chathamhouse.org/publications/twt/brexit-s- threat-northern-ireland).

Campbell, John. 2004. *Margaret Thatcher Volume Two: The Iron Lady*. London: Pimlico PB.

Campos, Nauro F. & Coricelli, Fabrizio. 2015. 'Why did Britain Join the EU? A New Insight from Economic History.' *Mostly Economics Blog*, 3 February (available at: http://voxeu.org/article/britain-s-eu-membership-new-insight-economic-history).

Caney, Simon. 2016. 'Political Institutions for the Future: A Fivefold Package.' In *Institutions for Future Generations*, edited by Axel Gosseries and Iñigo González Ricoy, Oxford: Oxford University Press.

Carrera, Sergio, Guild, Elspeth & Luk, Ngo Chun. 2016. 'What does Brexit Mean for the EU's Area of Freedom, Security and Justice?' Brussels: Centre for European Policy Studies (available at: https://www.ceps.eu/publications/what-does-brexit-mean-eu's-area-freedom-security-and-justice).

Carter, William Horsfall. 1966. *Speaking European: The Anglo-continental Cleavage*, London: George Allen & Unwin.

Chaffin, Joshua. 2017. 'How Theresa May Won the hearts of Britain's Brexiters.' *Financial Times*, 21 April (available at: https://www.ft.com/content/d927eb6c-267e-11e7-8691-d5f7e0cd0a16).

Chalmers, Malcolm. 2017. 'UK Foreign and Security Policy after Brexit.' London: Royal United Services Institute (available at: https://rusi.org/publication/briefing-papers/uk-foreign-and-security-policy-after-brexit)

Cheneval, Francis, Lavenex, Sandra & Schimmelfennig, Frank. 2015. 'Demoicracy in the European Union: Principles, Institutions, Policies.' *Journal of European Public Policy* 22(1): 1–18.

Christensen, Clayton, M., Raynor, Michael E. & McDonald, Rory. 2015. 'What Is Disruptive Innovation?' *Harvard Business Review*, December (available at: https://hbr.org/2015/12/what-is-disruptive-innovation).

Christiano, Thomas. 2016. 'Replies to David Alvarez, David Lefkowitz, and Michael Blake.' *Law, Ethics and Politics* 4: 221–36.

Cini, Michelle & Pérez-Solórzano, Nieves. 2016. 'How Much of a Threat does the "Brexit" Referendum Pose for the European Union.' *Oxford University Press Blog*, 17 April (available at: https://blog.oup.com/2016/04/brexit-european-union-threat/).

Clarke, Harold D., Goodwin, Matthew & Whiteley, Paul. eds. 2017. *Brexit: Why Britain Voted to Leave the European Union*. Cambridge: Cambridge University Press.

Clift, Ben & Woll, Cornelia. 2012. 'Economic Patriotism: Reinventing Control over Open Markets.' *Journal of European Public Policy* 19(3): 307–23.

Cole, Alistair. 2012. 'The Fast Presidency? Nicolas Sarkozy and the Institutions of the Fifth Republic.' *Contemporary French and Francophone Studies* 16(3): 311–21.

Consterdine, Erica. 2016. 'The Huge Political Cost of Blair's Decision to Allow Eastern European Migrants Unfettered Access to Britain.' *The Conversation*, 16 November (available at: https://theconversation.com/the-huge-political-cost-of-blairs-decision-to-allow-eastern-european-migrants-unfettered-access-to-britain-66077).

Consterdine, Erica. 2017. 'What Britain's Post-Brexit Immigration Policy Could Look Like.' *The Conversation*, 30 March (available at: http://theconversation.com/what-britains-post-brexit-immigration-policy-could-look-like-74488).

Cooper, Charlie & Marks, Simon. 2017. 'Progress, but no Solution to Ireland's Brexit Problem.' *Politico*, 16 August (available at: http://www.politico.eu/article/progress-but-no-solution-to-irelands-brexit-problem/).

Copsey, Nathaniel & Haughton, Tim. 2014. 'Farewell Britannia? "Issue Capture" and the Politics of David Cameron's 2013 EU Referendum Pledge.' *Journal of Common Market Studies* 52(S1): 74–89.

Council Implementing Decision. 2017a. 'Council Implementing Decision (EU) 2017/290 of 17 February 2017 amending Decision 2009/935/JHA as Regards the List of Third States and Organisations with which Europol Shall Conclude Agreements.' *Official Journal of the European Union*, L 42/17, 18 February, 17–18.

Council Implementing Decision. 2017b. 'Council Implementing Decision 7281/1/17 REV 1 of 28 April 2017 Approving the Conclusion by the European Police Office (Europol) of the Agreement on Operational and Strategic Cooperation between the Kingdom of Denmark and Europol' (available at: http://data.consilium.europa.eu/doc/document/ST-7281-2017-REV-1/en/pdf).

Coveney, Simon & Naselli, Jason. 2017. 'Facing Brexit: Ireland, Northern Ireland and the EU.' Chatham House Expert Comment, 20 July (available at: https://www.chathamhouse.org/expert/comment/facing-brexit-ireland-northern-ireland-and-eu).

Cox, Michael. 2017. 'Europe – Still between the Superpowers.' *Global Policy* 8(4): 9–17.

Coyne, E. (2017) 'People in Britain not Bothered about Border.' *The Times*, 12 August (available at https://www.thetimes.co.uk/article/people-in-britain-not-bothered-about-border-qfdb3v8zt?shareToken=83ce8c36c5b581e274b099ac9ec47c2c).

Craig, Robert. 2016. 'Casting Aside Clanking Medieval Chains: Prerogative, Statute and Article 50 after the EU Referendum.' *Modern Law Review* 79(6): 1019–89.

Crouch, Colin. 2005. *Capitalist Diversity and Change: Recombinant Governance and Institutional Entrepreneurs*. Oxford: Oxford University Press.

Crouch, Colin. 2009. 'Privatized Keynesianism: An Unacknowledged Policy Regime.' *British Journal of Politics and International Relations* 11(3): 382–99.

Crump, Larry. 2006. 'Multiparty Negotiation: What Is It?' *ADR Bulletin* 8(7): 1–10.

Cummings, Dominic. 2013. *Some Thoughts on Education and Political Priorities* (available at: https://dominiccummings.files.wordpress.com/2013/11/20130825-some-thoughts-on-education-and-political-priorities-version-2-final.pdf).

Cummings, Dominic. 2017a. 'On the Referendum #21: Branching Histories of the 2016 Referendum and "the Frogs before the Storm"' (available at: https://dominiccummings.wordpress.com/2017/01/09/on-the-referendum-21-branching-histories-of-the-2016-referendum-and-the-frogs-before-the-storm-2/).

Cummings, Dominic. 2017b. 'On the Referendum #23, a Year after Victory' (available at: https://dominiccummings.com/2017/06/23/on-the-referendum-23-a-year-after-victory-a-change-of-perspective-is-worth-80-iq-points-how-to-capture-the-heavens/).

Cummings, Dominic. 2017c. 'How the Brexit Referendum was Won.' *The Spectator*, 9 January (available at: https://blogs.spectator.co.uk/2017/01/dominic-cummings-brexit-referendum-won/).

Damasio, António. 1994. *Descartes' Error: Emotion, Reason, and the Human Brain.* London: Random House.

Davidson, Neil. 2016. 'The Socialist Case for Leave.' *The Jacobin*, June 22.

Davies, Gareth. 2017. 'The UK and Sickness Insurance for Mobile Citizens: An Inequitable Mess for Brexit Negotiators to Address.' *European Law Blog*, 17 March (available at: http://europeanlawblog.eu/2017/03/17/the-uk-and-sickness-insurance-for-mobile-citizens-an-inequitable-mess-for-brexit-negotiators-to-address/).

Dawson, Mark & de Witte, Bruno. 2012. 'The EU Legal Framework of Social Inclusion and Social Protection: Between the Lisbon Strategy and the Lisbon Treaty.' In *Social Inclusion and Social Protection in the EU: Interactions Between Law and Policy*, edited by Bea Cantillon, Herwig Verschueren and Paula Ploscar. Cambridge: Intersentia.

de la Porte, Caroline & Natali, David. 2014. 'Altered Europeanisation of Pension Reform in the Context of the Great Recession: Denmark and Italy Compared.' *West European Politics* 37(4): 732–49.

de Sousa, Ronald. 1987. *The Rationality of Emotions.* Cambridge, MA: MIT Press.

de Tocqueville, Alexis. 1839. *Democracy in America, Volume One.* New York: George Adlard.

de Witte, Floris, Bauböck, Rainer & Shaw, Jo. 2016. 'Freedom of Movement under Attack: Is it Worth Defending as the Core of EU citizenship?' EUDO Forum, RSCAS Working Paper 2016/69 (available at: http://cadmus.eui.eu/handle/1814/44567).

Dehousse, Renaud & Tacea, Angela. 2012. 'The French 2012 Presidential Election: A Europeanised Contest.' Paris: Les Cahiers européens de Sciences Po, No. 2/2012.

Department for Exiting the European Union. 2017. 'Legislating for the United Kingdom's Withdrawal from the European Union.' March 2017. Cm 9446.

Diebold, William. 1988. 'A Personal Note.' In *Die Anfänge des Schuman-Plans 1950/51*, edited by Klaus Schwabe. Baden-Baden: Nomos Verlagsgesellschaft.

Dijkstra, Hylke. 2016. 'UK and EU Foreign Policy Cooperation after Brexit.' *RUSI Newsbrief* 36(5): 1–3 (available at: https://rusi.org/sites/default/files/dijkstra_newsbrief_sept_vol.36_no.5.pdf).

Dinan, Desmond, Nugent, Neill & Paterson, William. E. eds. 2017. *The EU in Crisis.* London: Palgrave Macmillan.

Dixon, Ruth & Hood, Christopher. 2015. *A Government That Worked Better and Cost Less? Evaluating Three Decades of Reform and Change in UK Central Government.* Oxford: Oxford University Press.

Doherty, Brian, Temple Lang, John, McCrudden, Christopher, McGowan, Lee, Phinnemore, David & Schiek, Dagmar. 2017. 'Northern Ireland and "Brexit": The European Economic Area Option.' Queen's University Belfast Law Research Paper No. 2933715, March.

Dombret, Andreas. 2017. 'The Possible Impact of Brexit on the Financial Landscape.' Speech delivered at 'zeb', 24 February (available at: http://www.bis.org/review/r170228a.htm).

Dorussen, Han & Kyriaki Nanou. 2006. 'European Integration, Intergovernmental Bargaining, and Convergence of Party Programmes.' *European Union Politics* 7(2): 235–56.

Douglas-Scott, Sionaidh. 2015. 'A UK Exit from the EU: The End of the United Kingdom or a New Constitutional Dawn?' *Cambridge Journal of International and Comparative Law*. Oxford Legal Studies Research Paper No. 25.

Drake, Helen & Reynolds, Chris. 2017. 'Sixty Years On: France and Europe from the Treaty of Rome to the 2017 Elections' *Modern and Contemporary France* 25(2): 111–16.

Drake, Helen. 2013. 'Everywhere and Nowhere: Europe and the World in the French 2012 Elections.' *Parliamentary Affairs* 66(1): 124–41.

Dreher, Rod. 2016. 'Trump: Tribune of Poor White People.' Interview with J.D. Vance, *The American Conservative*, July 22.

Duff, Andrew. 2016. 'The Case for A New Association Agreement.' *The UK in A Changing Europe* (available at: http://ukandeu.ac.uk/the-case-for-a-new-association-agreement/).

Duff, Andrew. 2017. 'How Europe sees Brexit.' European Policy Centre Discussion Paper, 24 January.

Dunleavy, Patrick. 1991. *Democracy, Bureaucracy and Public Choice.* London: Harvester Wheatsheaf.

Dworkin, Ronald. 2002. *Sovereign Virtue: The Theory and Practice of Equality.* Cambridge, MA: Harvard University Press.

Džankic, Jelena. 2015. 'Investment-based Citizenship and Residence Programmes in the EU.' EUDO Citizenship, RSCAS Working Paper 2015/08.

Economic and Social Research Institute. 2015. 'Scoping the Possible Economic Implications of Brexit on Ireland.' Research Series No. 48, November (available at: http://www.esri.ie/pubs/RS48.pdf).

Economist. 2003. 'That F-Word.' 7 February (available at: http://www.economist.com/node/1574753).

Economist. 2016. 'Explaining the Brexit Vote.' *The Economist*, July 14 (available at: http://www.economist.com/news/britain/21702228-areas-lots-migrants-voted-mainly-remain-or-did-they-explaining-brexit-vote).

Economist Intelligence Unit. 2011. 'Democracy Index 2011: Democracy under Stress' (available at: http://www.eiu.com/Handlers/WhitepaperHandler.ashx?fi=Democracy_Index_2011_Updated. pdf&mode=wp& campaignid=DemocracyIndex2011).

Eeckhout, Piet & Frantziou, Eleni. 2017. 'Brexit and Art 50 TEU: A Constitutionalist Reading.' *Common Market Law Review* 54: 711–14.

Endicott, Timothy. 2016. 'Parliament and the Prerogative: From the Case of Proclamations to Miller.' Judicial Power Project, 1 December (available at http://judicialpowerproject.org.uk/wp-content/uploads/2016/12/Endicott-2016-Parliament-and-the-Prerogative.pdf).

EUDO Citizenship. 2015. 'Global Database on Modes of Loss of Citizenship.' San Domenico di Fiesole: European University Institute (available at: http://eudo-citizenship.eu/databases/modes-of-loss).

Eurobarometer. 2016a. 'Public Opinion in the EU: First Results, No. 85.' Directorate General for Communication, European Commission, Spring.

Eurobarometer. 2016b. 'First Results. Standard Eurobarometer Survey, No. 86.' Directorate General for Communication, European Commission, Autumn.

Eurobarometer. 2017. 'A deux ans des élections européennes de 2019: Eurobaromètre spécial du parlement européen.' 28 April (available at: http://www.europarl.europa.eu/thinktank/fr/document.html?reference=EPRS_STU(2017)599336).

European Commission. 2014. 'Northern Ireland in Europe: Report of the European Commission's Northern Ireland Task Force 2007–2014.' October (available at: http://ec.europa.eu/regional_policy/sources/activity/ireland/report2014.pdf).

European Commission. 2016. 'Regional Policy – Northern Ireland Task Force.' 21 March (available at: http://ec.europa.eu/regional_policy/en/policy/themes/northern-ireland-peace-programme/).

European Commission. 2017a. 'Regional Policy.' 17 August (available at: http://ec.europa.eu/regional_policy/index.cfm/en/).

European Commission. 2017b. *White Paper on the Future of Europe: Reflections and Scenarios for the EU27 by 2025*, 1 March. Brussels.

European Commission. 2017c. 'Directives for the Negotiation of an Agreement with the United Kingdom of Great Britain and Northern Ireland Setting out the Arrangements for its Withdrawal from the European Union' (available at: https://ec.europa.eu/info/sites/info/files/annex-recommendation-uk-eu-negotiations_3-may-2017_en.pdf).

European Council. 2016. 'Conclusions of the European Council of 18 and 19 February 2016.' Annex 1, Section C, Sovereignty.

European Council. 2017a. 'European Council (Art. 50) Guidelines following the United Kingdom's Notification under Article 50 TEU.' Press Release 220/17, 29 April (available at: http://www.consilium.europa.eu/en/press/press-releases/2017/04/29-euco-brexit-guidelines/).

European Council. 2017b. 'United we Stand, Divided we Fall.' Letter by President Donald Tusk to the 27 heads of state or government on the future of the EU before the Malta summit, Press Release, 35/17, 31 January.

European Parliament. 2016. 'The UK Rebate on the EU Budget: An Explanation of the Abatement and other Correction Mechanisms.' Brussels: European Parliament (available at: http://www.europarl.europa.eu/RegData/etudes/BRIE/2016/577973/EPRS_BRI(2016)577973_EN.pdf).

European Parliament. 2017a. 'European Parliament Resolution of 5 April 2017 on Negotiations With the United Kingdom Following its Notification that it Intends to Withdraw From the European Union.' 2017/2593, Brussels: European Parliament.

European Parliament. 2017b. 'Northern Ireland PEACE Programme' (available at: http://www.europarl.europa.eu/atyourservice/en/displayFtu.html?ftuId=FTU_5.1.9.html).

European Parliament. 2017c. 'Committee on Civil Liberties, Justice and Home Affairs – meeting 24/01/2017' (available at: http://www.europarl.europa.eu/news/en/press-room/20170118IPR58664/committee-on-civil-liberties-justice-and-home-affairs-meeting-24-01-2017-am).

European Union Committee. 2016. 'Brexit: Future UK–EU Security and Police Cooperation.' London: Authority of the House of Lords (available at: https://www.publications.parliament.uk/pa/ld201617/ldselect/ldeucom/77/77.pdf).

Europol. 2017. 'Agreement on Operational and Strategic Cooperation between the Kingdom of Denmark and the European Police Office.' Signed 29 April 2017 (available at: https://www.europol.europa.eu/publications-documents/agreement-operational-and-strategic-cooperation-between-kingdom-of-denmark-and-europol).

Falkner, Gerda. 1996. 'The Maastricht Protocol on Social Policy: On Theory and Practice.' *Journal of European Social Policy* 6(1): 1–16.

Farage, Nigel. 2014. 'I'd Rather be Poorer with Fewer Migrants.' *Daily Telegraph*, 7 January (available at: http://www.telegraph.co.uk/news/uknews/immigration/10555158/Id-rather-be-poorer-with-fewer-migrants-Farage-says.html).

Farrell, Henry & Newman, Abraham. 2017. 'BREXIT, Voice and Loyalty: Rethinking Electoral Politics in an Age of Interdependence.' *Review of International Political Economy* 24(2): 1–16.

Fenton, Siobhan. 2017. 'Power-sharing Collapses in Northern Ireland, After Sinn Fein Refuse to Return to Stormont Executive.' *Independent*, 16 January (available at: http://www.independent.co.uk/news/uk/politics/northern-ireland-power-sharing-latest-collapse-end-sinn-fein-refuse-stormont-dup-martin-mcguinness-a7529111.html).

Ferrera, Maurizio. 2017. 'The Stein Rokkan Lecture 2016. Mission Impossible? Reconciling Economic and Social Europe after the Euro.' *European Journal of Political Research* 56(1): 3–22.

Financial Times. 2016a. 'Support for EU Rises, Survey Shows, 20 November' (available at: https://www.ft.com/content/9cfdad52-ada7-11e6-9cb3-bb8207902122).

Financial Times. 2016b. 'Elon Musk and Travis Kalanick Sign on as Trump Advisers.' *Financial Times*, 14 December.

Financial Times. 2017a. 'After Brexit: The UK will Need to Renegotiate at least 759 Treaties.' 30 May.

Financial Times. 2017b. 'ECB Criticised for Overstepping Mandate in Eurozone Crisis.' 30 March.

Financial Times. 2017c. 'Schulz Sticks to Germany's Austerity recipe for EU.' 10 April.

Financial Times. 2017d. 'Martin Schulz and Emmanuel Macron Could Save Europe.' 27 March.

Financial Times. 2017e. 'What Emmanual Macron Means for Brexit.' 25 April.

Financial Times. 2017f. 'Macron Poll Success Buoys Markets but Assembly Vote also Crucial.' 24 April.

Financial Times. 2017g. 'Germany's Schäuble Moves Away from Federalist EU Vision.' 23 March.

Flanagan, Charles. 2015. 'British-Irish Relations: Implications of a Possible Brexit.' Speech delivered at Chatham House, 7 September (available at: https://www.chathamhouse.org/sites/files/chathamhouse/field/field_document/08092015BritishIrish.pdf).

Flinders, Matthew. 2008. *Walking Without Order: Delegated Governance and the British State.* Oxford: Oxford University Press.

Foa, Roberto Stefan & Mounk, Yascha. 2016. 'The Danger of Deconsolidation: The Democratic Disconnect.' *Journal of Democracy* 27(3): 5–17.

Foa, Roberto Stefan & Mounk, Yascha. 2017. 'The Signs of Deconsolidation.' *Journal of Democracy* 28(1): 5–15.

Ford, Mark & Goodwin, Matthew J. 2014. *Revolt on the Right: Explaining Support for the Radical Right in Britain.* Abingdon: Routledge.

Fox, Liam. 2016. 'Free Trade Speech.' 29 September (available at: https://www.gov.uk/government/speeches/liam-foxs-free-trade-speech).

France Diplomatie. 2017. 'Entretien exclusif. Emmanuel Macron: "L'Europe est une nécessité absolue.' 13 July (available at: http://www.diplomatie.gouv.fr/fr/dossiers-pays/allemagne/evenements/article/entretien-exclusif-emmanuel-macron-l-europe-est-une-necessite-absolue-13-07-17#).

Franklin, Mark, Marsh, Michael & McLaren, Lauren. 1994. 'Uncorking the Bottle: Popular Opposition to European Unification in the Wake of Maastricht.' *Journal of Common Market Studies* 32(4): 101–17.

Fraser, Nancy. 1996. *Justice Interruptus: Critical Reflections on the 'Postsocialist' Condition.* London: Routledge.

Freeden, Michael. 2013. 'Editorial: Emotions, Ideology and Politics.' *Journal of Political Ideologies* 18(1): 1–10.

Frevert, Ute. 2013. *Vertrauensfragen: Eine Obsession der Moderne.* Munich: C. H. Beck Verlag.

García, Nereo Peñalver & Priestley, Julian. 2015. *The Making of a European President.* London: Palgrave Macmillan.

Garry, John. 2013. 'Emotions and Voting in EU Referendums.' *European Union Politics* 15(2): 235–254.

Garulund Nøhr, Karoline. 2016. 'Vælgerbedrag? Her er Dansk Folkepartis Europol-garantier. Politiken.' 30 September (available at: http://politiken.dk/indland/politik/art5637783/V%C3%A6lgerbedrag-Her-er-Dansk-Folkepartis-Europol-garantier).

Gathmann, Florian & Wittrock, Phillip. 2017. 'Lasting Questions from Hamburg: Was the G20 Summit really worth it?' *Der Spiegel*, 8 July.

Gatziou, Kira, Nicolaïdis, Kalypso & Sternberg, Claudia. 2016. *Mutual Recognition Lost: The Greco-German Affair in the Euro-Crisis.* Oxford: Palgrave-Macmillan, Pivot.

Geddes, Andrew. 2016. *Britain and the European Union.* Basingstoke: Palgrave Macmillan.

George, Stephen. 1998. *An Awkward Partner: Britain in the European Community.* 2nd edition. Oxford: Oxford University Press.

Gibson, Rachel K. 2002. *The Growth of Anti-Immigrant Parties in Western Europe.* Lewiston, NY: Edwin Mellen Press.

Giles, Chris. 2017. 'Britain's Misplaced Sense of Economic Superiority.' *Financial Times*, 27 April (available at: https://www.ft.com/content/4b61aa54-2a96-11e7-bc4b-5528796fe35c).

Gillett, Francesca. 2017. 'Six in 10 Brexit Voters say Economic Damage is 'Price Worth Paying' for Quitting EU.' *Evening Standard*, 1 August (available at: https://www.standard.co.uk/news/uk/six-in-10-brexit-voters-say-economic-damage-is-price-worth-paying-for-quitting-eu-a3601476.html).

Gillingham, John. 2006. *Design for a New Europe.* New York: Cambridge University Press.

Gillingham, John. 2016. *The EU: An Obituary.* London: Verso.

Gilmore, Andrew. (2015) 'European Views on the UK's Renegotiation: Ireland, Portugal, Austria and Croatia.' LSE *European Politics and Policy Blog*, 21 October (available at: http://blogs.lse.ac.uk/europpblog/2015/10/21/european-views-on-the-uks-renegotiation-ireland-portugal-austria-and-croatia/#One).

Gilpin, Robert. 1987. *The Political Economy of International Relations.* Princeton University Press.

Giubboni, Stefano. 2006. *Social Rights and Market Freedom in the European Constitution: A Labour Law Perspective.* Cambridge: Cambridge University Press.

Giuliani, Jean-Dominique. 2017. *Pour quelques étoiles de plus … Quelle politique européenne pour la France?* Paris: Lignes de repères.

Glencross, Andrew. 2016. *Why the UK Voted for Brexit: David Cameron's Great Miscalculation.* Basingstoke: Palgrave Macmillan.

Goodwin, Matthew & Heath, Oliver. 2016. 'The 2016 Referendum, Brexit and the Left Behind: An Aggregate-level Analysis of the Result.' *Political Quarterly* 87(3): 323–32.

Goodwin, Matthew & Heath, Oliver. 2016. 'Brexit Vote Explained: Poverty, Low Skills, and Lack of Opportunities.' Joseph Rowntree Foundation (available at: https://www.jrf.org.uk/report/brexit-vote-explained-poverty-low-skills-and-lack-opportunities).

Grabbe, Heather & Lehne, Stefan. 2017. 'The Closing of the European Mind – and How to Reopen It.' *Carnegie Europe* (available at: http://carnegieeurope.eu/2017/03/17/closing-of-european-mind-and-how-to-reopen-it-pub-68317).

Green, David Allen. 2017. '"In Some Possible Branches of the Future Leaving will be an Error" – an Exchange about Brexit with Dominic Cummings.' *Jack of Kent Blog* (available at: http://jackofkent.com/2017/07/in-some-possible-branches-of-the-future-leaving-will-be-an-error-an-exchange-about-brexit-with-dominic-cummings/).

Guardian. 2016. 'David Cameron: Brexit Vote Part of "Movement of Unhappiness".' 9 December.

Habermas, Jurgen. 1998. *The Inclusion of the Other: Studies in Political Theory*, edited by Ciaran P. Cronin and Pablo de Grieff. Cambridge, MA: MIT Press.

Habermas, Jurgen. 2015. 'Democracy in Europe: Why the Development of the EU into a Transnational Democracy is Necessary and How it is Possible.' *European Law Journal* 21(4): 546–57.

Hadfield, Amelia & Hammond, Mark. 2016. 'Kent and Medway: Making a Success of Brexit.' Centre for European Studies, Canterbury Christ Church University, December.

Hale, Thomas. 2016. '"All Hands on Deck": The Paris Agreement and Nonstate Climate Action.' *Global Environmental Politics* 16(3): 12–22.

Hall, Peter A. & Soskice, David W. eds. 2001. *Varieties of Capitalism: The Institutional Foundations of Capitalism*. Oxford: Oxford University Press.

Hanretty, Chris. 2016. 'Revised Estimates of Leave Vote Share in Westminster Constituencies' (available at: https://medium.com/@chrishanretty/revised-estimates-of-leave-vote-share-in-westminster-constituencies-c4612f06319d#.ckhtkhwez).

Harari, Yuval Noah. 2014. *Sapiens: A Brief History of Humankind*. London: Harvill Secker.

Hart, Oliver, Schleifer, Andrei & Vishny, Robert W. 1997. 'The Proper Scope of Government: Theory and an Application to Prisons.' *The Quarterly Journal of Economics* 112(4): 1127–61.

Hayek, Friedrich. 1939. 'The Economic Conditions of Interstate Federalism.' *The New Commonwealth Quarterly*, 2. Reprinted in Friedrich Hayek. 2012. *Individualism and Economic Order*, 255–72. London: Routledge.

Hayek, Friedrich. 1949. 'The Intellectuals and Socialism.' *University of Chicago Law Review* 16(3). Reprinted in Friedrich Hayek. 1967. *Studies in Philosophy, Politics and Economics*, 178–94. London: Routledge.

Hayward, Katy. 2017a. 'How Does the Lack of Agreement in Northern Ireland Bode for Brexit?' *The UK in a Changing Europe*, 2 August (available at: http://ukandeu.ac.uk/how-does-the-lack-of-agreement-in-northern-ireland-bode-for-brexit/).

Hayward, Katy. 2017b. 'The UK Needs to Come up with Flexible and Imaginative Solutions for the Irish border.' *LSE Brexit Blog*, 9 August (available at: http://blogs.lse.ac.uk/brexit/2017/08/09/the-uk-needs-to-come-up-with-flexible-and-imaginative-solutions-for-the-irish-border/).

Hewitt, Gavin. 2016. 'EU Referendum: Don't Discount Raw Emotion.' BBC News, 14 April (available at: http://www.bbc.co.uk/news/uk-politics-eu-referendum-36029874).

High Level Group on Own Resources. 2017. 'Future Financing of the EU, Final Report and Recommendation Submitted by Mario Monti, Chair of the Group, to the Presidents of the European Parliament, of the Council of the Union and of the European Commission' (available at: http://ec.europa.eu/budget/mff/hlgor/index_6n.cfm).

Hill, Christopher. 1993. 'The Capability-Expectations Gap, or Conceptualising – Europe's International Role.' *Journal of Common Market Studies* 31(3): 305–28.

Hirschmann, Alfred. 1977. [2013]. *The Passions and the Interests: Political Arguments for Capitalism before Its Triumph*. Princeton, Princeton University Press.

Hix, Simon. 1997. *The Political System of the European Union*. Basingstoke: Palgrave Macmillan.

Hix, Simon & Hagemann, Sara. 2015. 'Does the UK Win or Lose in the Council of Ministers?' *LSE European Politics and Policy Blog*, 2 November (available at: http://blogs.lse.ac.uk/europp-blog/2015/11/02/does-the-uk-win-or-lose-in-the-council-of-ministers/).

Hix, Simon & Benedetto, Giacomo. 2017. Dataset: *The Rise and Fall of Social Democrats, 1918–2017*. LSE/Royal Holloway College.

Hix, Simon & Follesdal, Andreas. 2006. 'Why There is a Democratic Deficit in the EU: A Response to Majone and Moravcsik.' *Journal of Common Market Studies* 44(3): 533–62.

HM Government. 1998. 'The Belfast Agreement.' April (available at: https://www.gov.uk/government/publications/the-belfast-agreement).

HM Government. 2013. 'Review of the Balance of Competences between the United Kingdom and the European Union. Foreign Policy.' Crown Copyright, Her Majesty's Stationery Office, November, London (available at: https://www.gov.uk/government/consultations/foreign-policy-report-review-of-the-balance-of-competences).

HM Government. 2014a. 'Review of the Balance of Competences between the United Kingdom and the European Union. Agriculture.' Crown Copyright, Her Majesty's Stationery Office, July, London (available at: https://www.gov.uk/government/consultations/agriculture-report-review-of-the-balance-of-competences).

HM Government. 2014b. 'Review of the Balance of Competences between the United Kingdom and the European Union. Cohesion.' Crown Copyright, Her Majesty's Stationery Office, July, London (available at: https://www.gov.uk/government/consultations/review-of-uk-and-eu-balance-of-competences-call-for-evidence-on-cohesion-policy).

HM Government. 2014c. 'Review of the Balance of Competences between the United Kingdom and the European Union. Single Market – Financial Services and the Free Movement of Capital.' Crown Copyright, Her Majesty's Stationery Office, July, London (available at: https://www.gov.uk/government/consultations/balance-of-competences-review-single-market-financial-services-and-the-free-movement-of-capital).

HM Government. 2017a. 'The United Kingdom's Exit From and New Partnership with the European Union.' Cm9417, Crown Copyright, Her Majesty's Stationery Office, February, London.

HM Government. 2017b. 'Prime Minister's Letter to Donald Tusk Triggering Article 50.' 29 March (available at: https://www.gov.uk/government/publications/prime-ministers-letter-to-donald-tusk-triggering-article-50).

HM Government. 2017c. 'Future Customs Arrangements: A Future Partnership paper.' 15 August (available at: https://www.gov.uk/government/publications/future-customs-arrangements-a-future-partnership-paper).

HM Government. 2017d. 'Northern Ireland and Ireland – A Position Paper.' 16 August (available at: https://www.gov.uk/government/publications/northern-ireland-and-ireland-a-position-paper).

HM Government. 2017e. 'The United Kingdom's Exit from the European Union – Safeguarding the Position of EU Citizens Living in the UK and UK Nationals Living in the EU.' Cm 9464.

Hobolt, Sarah B. 2016. 'The Brexit Vote: A Divided Nation, A Divided Continent.' *Journal of European Public Policy* 23(9): 1259–77.

Home Office. 2016. 'Explanatory Memorandum on Intention to Exercise Right to Opt into Revised Europol Framework Published.' Crown Copyright, Her Majesty's Stationery Office, July, London (available at: https://www.gov.uk/government/news/parliament-notified-of-europol-opt-in-intention).

Hooghe, Liesbet & Marks, Gary. 2008. 'A Postfunctionalist Theory of European Integration: From Permissive Consensus to Constraining Dissensus.' *British Journal of Political Science* 39(1): 1–23.

House of Commons Justice Committee. 2017. 'Implications of Brexit for the Justice System.' 9th Report of Session 2016–17 (available at: https://www.publications.parliament.uk/pa/cm201617/cmselect/cmjust/750/750.pdf).

House of Lords European Union Committee. 2016. 'Brexit: UK – Irish Relations.' 6th Report of Session 2016–17, HL Paper 76.

House of Lords, Delegated Powers and Regulatory Reform Select Committee. 2017. 'Special Report: Second Submission to the House of Commons Procedure Committee on the Delegated Powers in the "Great Repeal Bill".' 30th Report of Session 2016–17, HL Paper 164 (available at: https://www.publications.parliament.uk/pa/ld201617/ldselect/lddelreg/164/164.pdf.

Huber, John D. 1996. 'The Vote of Confidence in Parliamentary Democracies.' *American Political Science Review* 90(2): 269–82.

Hufnagel, Saskia. 2016. "Third Party' Status in EU Policing and Security: Comparing the Position of Norway with the UK Before and After the "Brexit".' *Nordisk politiforskning* 3(2): 165–80 (available at: https://www.idunn.no/nordisk_politiforskning/2016/02/third_party_status_in_eupolicing_and_security_-_comparin).

Hume, David. 1741. [1987]. 'Superstition and Enthusiasm.' In *Essays: Moral, Political and Literary*. Indianapolis, IN: Liberty Fund.

Ignazi, Pierre. 2003. *Extreme Right Parties in Western Europe*. Oxford: Oxford University Press.

Informal meeting of the EU 27. 2016. 'Informal Meeting of the Heads of State or Government of 27 Member States and the Presidents of the European Council and the European Commission.' 15 December. Brussels: European Council.

Inglehart, Ronald. 1970. 'Public Opinion and Regional Integration.' *International Organization* 24(4): 764–95.

Inglehart, Ronald & Norris, Pippa. 2016. 'Trump, Brexit, and the Rise of Populism: Economic Have-Nots and Cultural Backlash.". HKS Faculty Research Working Paper Series, No. 26, August.

Innerarity, Daniel. 2014. 'What Kind of Deficit? Problems of Legitimacy in the European Union.' *European Journal of Social Theory* 17(3): 307–25.

Irish Government. 2017. 'Ireland and the Negotiations on the UK's Withdrawal from the European Union under Article 50 of the Treaty on European Union: The Irish Government's Approach.' May.

Isiksel, Turkuler. 2016. *Europe's Functional Constitution: A Theory of Constitutionalism Beyond the State*. Oxford: Oxford University Press.

Islam, Faisal. 2017. 'Long Read: Why the Car Industry is Getting Worried.' Sky News (available at: http://news.sky.com/story/brexit-forensics-why-car-industry-is-getting-worried-11041671).

Johnson, Alan. 2017. 'Why Brexit is Best for Britain: The Left-Wing Case.' *The New York Times*, March 28.

Jopson, Barney & Sevastopulo, Demetri. 2016. 'Farage's Brexit Message Woos Trump Fans.' *Financial Times*, 25 August (available at: https://www.ft.com/content/ 21279dc4-6a44-11e6-a0b1-d87a9fea034f).

Juncker, Jean-Claude. 2016. 'Towards a Better Europe – a Europe that Protects, Empowers and Defends.' State of the Union Address 2016, Strasbourg, 14 September.

Kant, Immanuel. 1789. [1996]. *Anthropology from a Pragmatic Point of View*. Edited by H. Rudnick. Carbondale: Southern Illinois University Press.

Khan, Shehab. 2017. 'British Passengers Spend Six Times More on Train Fares than European Counterparts.' *Independent*, 4 January (available at: https://www.msn.com/en-gb/ travel/news/british-rail-passengers-spend-six-times-more-on-train-fares-than-european-counterparts/ar-BBxPTVj?li=BBoPU0T).

King, Anthony. 2007. *The British Constitution*. Oxford: Oxford University Press.

King, Jeff, Hickman, Tom & Barber, Nick. 2016. 'Pulling the Article 50 'Trigger': Parliament's Indispensable Role.' *UK Constitutional Law Blog*, 27 June (available at: https://ukconstitu-tionallaw.org/2016/06/27/nick-barber-tom-hickman-and-jeff-king-pulling-the-article-50-trigger-parliaments-indispensable-role/).

Kissinger, Henry. 1994. *Diplomacy*. New York: Simon & Schuster.

Kitschelt, Herbert. 1995. *The Radical Right in Western Europe: A Comparative Analysis*. Ann Arbor, MI: University of Michigan Press.

Krause, Sharon R. 2008. *Civil Passions: Moral Sentiment and Democratic Deliberation*. Princeton, NJ: Princeton University Press.

Kriesi, Hanspeter, Grande, Edgar, Dolenzal, Martin, Helbling, Marc, Hoglinger, Dominic, Hutter, Swen & Wüest, Bruno. 2012. *Political Conflict in Western Europe*. Cambridge: Cambridge University Press.

Kröger Sandra & Bellamy, Richard. 2016. 'Beyond a Constraining Dissensus: The Role of National Parliaments in Domesticating and Normalising the Politicization of European Integration.' *Comparative European Politics* 14(2): 131–53.

Kundnani, Hans. 2014. *The Paradox of German Power*. London: Hurst.

Kuper, Simon. 2017. 'Brexit Reveals Britain's Enduring Flaws.' *Financial Times*, 5 August (available at: https://www.ft.com/content/b3d62bcc-7713-11e7-90c0-90a9d1bc9691).

Kymlicka, Will. 1996. *Multicultural Citizenship: A Liberal Theory of Minority Rights*. Oxford: Oxford University Press.

Ladrech, Robert. 1994. 'Europeanization of Domestic Politics and Institutions: The Case of France.' *Journal of Common Market Studies* 32(1): 69–88.

Laffan, Brigid. 2014. 'Framing the Crisis, Defining the Problems: Decoding the Euro Area Crisis.' *Perspectives on European Politics and Society* 15(3): 266–80.

Le Galès, Patrick. 2016. 'UK as an Exception or the Banal Avant-garde of the Disintegration of the EU.' *Socio-Economic Review*, 15: 42–8.

Le Monde. 2017. 'Paris et Berlin envoient un signal fort pour l'Europe de la défense.' 14 July.

Le Pen, Marine. 2017. 'Engagements présidentiels Marine 2017' (available at: https://www.mar-ine2017.fr/programme/).

Leibfried, Stephan. 2015. 'Social Policy: Left to the Judges and the Markets?' In *Policy-Making in the European Union*, edited by Helen Wallace, Mark A. Pollack and Alasdair R. Young. 7th edition. Oxford: Oxford University Press.

Leuffen, Dirk, Rittberger, Berthold & Schimmelfennig, Frank. 2012. *Differentiated Integration: Explaining Variation in the European Union*. Basingstoke: Palgrave Macmillan.

Levy, Jacob T. 2000. *Multiculturalism of Fear*. New York: Oxford University Press.

Lijphart, Arend. 1999. *Patterns of Democracy: Government Forms and Performance in Thirty-Six Countries*. London: Yale University Press.

Lindseth, Peter L. 2014. 'Equilibrium, Demoi-cracy, and Delegation in the Crisis of European Integration.' *German Law Journal* 15: 529–68.

Maas, Willem. 2005. 'The Genesis of European Rights.' *Journal of Common Market Studies* 43(5): 1009–25.Macron, Emmanuel. 2017. 'Discours du Président de la République devant le Parlement réuni en congrès.' Paris: L'Elysée (available at: http://www.elysee.fr/declarations/article/discours-du-president-de-la-republique-devant-le-parlement-reuni-en-congres/).

MacShane, Denis. 2015. *Brexit: How Britain will Leave Europe*. London: I.B. Tauris.

MacShane, Denis. 2017. 'Time For An EU Fair Movement Directive.' *Social Europe*, 10 July (available at: https://www.socialeurope.eu/time-eu-fair-movement-directive).

Madelin, Robert & Ringrose, David. eds. 2016. *Opportunity Now: Europe's Mission to Innovate*, The Publications Office of the European Union, July.

Maidment, Jack. 2017. 'Germany Hints at Soft Brexit amid Fears Theresa May could be Ousted during Talks.' *Daily Telegraph*, 19 June.

Majone, Giandomenico. 1994. 'The Rise of the Regulatory State in Europe.' *West European Politics* 17(3): 77–101.

Marcus, George E. 2002. *The Sentimental Citizen: Emotion in Democratic Politics*. Philadelphia: Penn State University Press.

Marsh, David. 2017. 'Bumpy Post-Brexit Ride: German, UK Central Bankers on Euro Clearing.' *OMFIF Blog*, 27 February (available at: https://www.omfif.org/analysis/commentary/2017/february/bumpy-post-brexit-ride/).

Martinico, Giuseppe. 2017. 'The Asymmetric Bet of Europe.' *Verfassungsblog*, 3 December (available at: http://verfassungsblog.de/the-asymmetric-bet-of-europe/).

Martinsen, Dorte Sindbjerg & Vollaard, Hans. 2014. 'Implementing Social Europe in Times of Crises: Re-established Boundaries of Welfare?' *West European Politics* 37(4): 677–92.

May, Theresa. 2017a. 'Brexit Speech in Full.' *Daily Telegraph*, 17 January.

May, Theresa. 2017b. 'Florence Speech in Full.' *Independent*, 22 September.

McCall, Cathal. 2015. 'How "Brexit" Could Destabilise the Irish Peace Process.' In *Cross-Border Review Yearbook 2016 – European Crisis and its Consequences for Borders and Cooperation*, edited by James W. Scott, 157–9. Budapest: European Institute of Cross Border Studies.

McCall, Cathal. 2017. 'Borders of the Future: Brexit and Bordering Ireland.' *QPol*, 13 June (available at: http://qpol.qub.ac.uk/brexit-bordering-ireland/)

McCourt, David M. 2009. 'What was Britain's "East of Suez Role"? Reassessing the Withdrawal, 1964–1968.' *Diplomacy and Statecraft* 20(3): 453–72.

McDonald, Henry. 2017. 'DUP's Opponents Say Tory Deal is not Blank Cheque for Hard Brexit.' *Guardian*, 26 June (available at: https://www.theguardian.com/politics/2017/jun/26/dup-to-seek-cuts-in-air-passenger-duty-and-corporation-tax-to-back-tories).

McKibbin, Ross. 2014. 'Labour Vanishes.' *London Review of Books*, 20 November.

McNamara, Kathleen. 2015. *The Politics of Everyday Europe: Constructing Authority in the European Union*. Oxford: Oxford University Press.

Meloni, Giulia & Swinnen, Johan. 2014. 'The Rise and Fall of the World's Largest Wine Exporter – and Its Institutional Legacy.' *Journal of Wine Economics* 9(1): 3–33.

Menéndez, Augustín José. 2009. 'European Citizenship after Martínez Sala and Baumbast: Has European Law Become More Human but Less Social?' ARENA Online Working Paper No .11 (available at: http://www.sv.uio.no/arena/english/research/publications/arena-working-papers/2001-2010/2009/WP11_09_Online.pdf).

Miller, David. 2000. *Citizenship and National Identity*. Cambridge: Polity.

Milward, Alan. 2000. *The European Rescue of the Nation-State*. 2nd edition. London: Routledge.

Mindus, Patricia. 2017. *European Citizenship after Brexit: Freedom of Movement and Rights of Residence*. Basingstoke: Palgrave Macmillan

Moloney, Niamh. 2010. 'EU Financial Market Regulation after the Global Financial Crisis: "More Europe" or More Risks?' *Common Market Law Review* 47(5): 1317–83.

Moloney, Niamh. 2017. 'EU Financial Governance and Brexit: Institutional Change or Business as Usual?' *European Law Review* 42(1): 112–28.

Monnet, Jean. 1955. 'Speech to the Common Assembly of the ECSC, Strasbourg, 12 January 1953.' In *The United States of Europe Has Begun: The European Coal and Steel Community Speeches and Addresses 1952–1954*. University of Pittsburgh Archive of European Integration, microfiche, Paris.

Moravcsik, Andrew. 1993. 'Preferences and Power in the European Community: A Liberal Intergovernmentalist Approach.' *Journal of Common Market Studies* 31(4): 473–524.

Moravscik, Andrew. 2008. 'The Myth of Europe's "Democratic Deficit".' *Intereconomics* November/December: 331–40.

Morgan, Glenn. 2012. 'Supporting the City: Economic Patriotism in Financial Markets." *Journal of European Public Policy* 19(3): 373–87.

Morgan, Glyn. 2005. *The Idea of a European Superstate*. Princeton: Princeton University Press.

Morgan, Glyn. 2016. 'Union Citizenship for UK Citizens.' *EUDO Citizenship Forum* (available at: http://eudo-citizenship.eu/commentaries/citizenship-forum/citizenship-forum-cat/1586-freedom-of-movement-under-attack-is-it-worth-defending-as-the-core-of-eu-citizenship?showall=&start=11).

Mortimore, Roger. 2016. 'Polling History: 40 years of British Views on "in or out" of Europe.' *The Conversation* (available at: https://theconversation.com/polling-history-40-years-of-british-views-on-in-or-out-of-europe-61250).

Mudde, Cas. 2012. 'The Comparative Study of Party-based Euroscepticism: The Sussex vs the North Carolina School.' *East European Politics* 28(2): 193–202.

Mudde, Cas & Kaltwasser, Cristóbal Rovira. 2013. 'Exclusionary vs. Inclusionary Populism.' *Government and Opposition* 48(2): 147–74.

Müller, Jan-Werner. 2011. *Contesting Democracy: Political Ideas in Twentieth-Century Europe*. New Haven: Yale University Press.

Müller, Jan-Werner. 2016a. 'Europe's Sullen Child.' *London Review of Books*, 2 June, 38(11): 3–6.

Müller, Jan-Werner. 2016b. 'Capitalism in One Family.' *London Review of Books*, 1 December, 38(23): 10–14.

Murphy, Mary C. 2017. 'Northern Ireland: A Casualty of Brexit?' *Alliance Europa Blog*, 21 March (available at: http://allianceeuropa.ideasoneurope.eu/2017/03/21/northern-ireland-casualty-brexit/).

Nash, Kate. 2003. 'Cosmopolitan Political Community: Why Does It Feel So Right?' *Constellations* 10: 506–18.

National Audit Office. 2017. 'Comptroller and Auditor General's Report on the Department for Education's financial statements 2014–15' (available at: https://www.nao.org.uk/report/comptroller-and-auditor-generals-report-on-the-department-for-educations-financial-statements-2014-15/).

Neely, Allen. 1991. 'British Resistance to European Integration: An Historical and Legal Analysis with an Examination of the UK's Recent Entry into the European Monetary System.' *Penn State International Law Review* 10(1): 113–36..

Nicolaïdis, Kalypso. 2004. 'We, the Peoples of Europe ...' *Foreign Affairs*, November/December: 97–110.

Nicolaïdis, Kalypso. 2010a. 'EU 2.0? Towards Sustainable Integration.' *Open Democracy* (available at: https://www.opendemocracy.net/kalypso-nicola%C3%AFdis/project-europe-2030-towards-sustainable-integration).

Nicolaïdis, Kalypso. 2010b. 'Sustainable Integration: Towards EU 2.0? – The JCMS Annual Review Lecture.' *Journal of Common Market Studies* 48 (Annual Review): 21–54.

Nicolaïdis, Kalypso. 2010c. 'Project Europe 2030: Reflection and Revival.' *Open Democracy*, May (available at: https://www.opendemocracy.net/kalypso-nicola%C3%AFdis/project-europe-2030-reflection-and-revival-part-one).

Nicolaïdis, Kalypso. 2013. 'European Demoicracy and its Crisis.' *Journal of Common Market Studies* 51(2): 351–69.

Nicolaïdis, Kalypso. 2016. 'The EU Global Strategy: 40 Expert Opinions' *European Institute for Strategic Studies* (available at: https://europa.eu/globalstrategy/en/eu-global-strategy-expert-opinion-no40-11-march-2016).

Nicolaïdis, Kalypso. 2017. 'Taking Back Control: Brexit and the Transformation of European Order.' In *The Law & Politics of Brexit*, edited by Federico Fabbrini. Oxford: Oxford University Press.

Nicolaïdis, Kalypso & Watson, Max. 2015. 'Sharing the Eurocrats' Dream: A Demoi-Cratic Approach to EMU Governance in the Post-Crisis Era.' In *The End of the EUrocrat's Dream*, edited by Markus Jachtenfuchs, Damian Chalmers and Christian Joerges. Cambridge: Cambridge University Press.

Nicoli, Francesco. 2017. 'Hard-line Euroscepticism and the Eurocrisis: Evidence from a Panel Study of 108 Elections Across Europe.' *Journal of Common Market Studies* 55(2): 312–31.

Niskanen, William A. 1973. *Bureaucracy: Servant or Master*. London: Institute of Economic Affairs.

Notre Europe. 2017. *Brexit and the EU Budget: Threat or Opportunity*. Bertelsmann Stiftung.

Nowotny, H. 2003. 'Science in Search of its Audience.' *Nova Acta Leopoldina*, 87(325): 211–15.

Nussbaum, Martha. 2001. *Upheavals of Thought: The Intelligence of Emotions*. Cambridge, Cambridge University Press.

O'Brien, Charlotte. 2017. 'There's Only One Woman on the UK Brexit Negotiating Team – Here's why that Matters.' *The Conversation*, 25 July (available at: https://theconversation.com/theres-only-one-woman-on-the-brexit-negotiating-team-heres-why-that-matters-81506).

OECD. 2014. 'Social Expenditure Update.' Directorate for Employment, Labour, and Social Affairs. November (available at http://www.oecd.org/els/soc/OECD2014-Social-Expenditure-Update-Nov2014-8pages.pdf).

Offe, Claus. 2000. 'The Democratic Welfare State. A European Regime Under the Strain of European Integration.' IHS Political Science Series, No 68. Institute for Advanced Studies.

Offe, Claus. 2015. *Europe Entrapped*. Cambridge: Polity.

Official Journal of the European Union. 2006. 'Agreement between the European Union and the Republic of Iceland and the Kingdom of Norway on the Surrender Procedure between the Member States of the European Union and Iceland and Norway.' *Official Journal of the European Union* L 292/2, 21 October, 2–19.

Official Journal of the European Union. 2009. 'Council Decision 2009/371/JHA of 6 April 2009 establishing the European Police Office (Europol).' *Official Journal of the European Union*, L 121/37, 15 May, 37–66.

Official Journal of the European Union. 2016. 'Regulation 2016/794 of the European Parliament and of the Council of 11 May 2016 on the European Union Agency for Law Enforcement Cooperation (Europol) and Replacing and Repealing Council Decision 2009/371/JHA, 2009/934/JHA, 2009/935/JHA, 2009/936/JHA and 2009/968/JHA.' *Official Journal of the European Union*, L 135/53, 24 May, 53–114.

O'Neill, Brendan. 2016. 'Brexit Voters are not Thick, not Racist, just Poor.' *Spectator*, 2 July (available at: https://www.spectator.co.uk/2016/07/brexit-voters-are-not-thick-not-racist-just-poor/)

Open Europe. 2017. 'Global Britain: Priorities for Trade Beyond the EU.' April.

O'Riordan, Tim & Voisey, Heather. 2013. 'The Politics of Agenda 21.' In *The Transition to Sustainability: The Politics of Agenda 21 in Europe*, edited by Tim O'Riordan and Heather Voisey, 31–56. London: Earthscan.

Orwell, George. 1941. *The Lion and the Unicorn: Socialism and the English Genius* (available at: https://www.orwellfoundation.com/the-orwell-prize/orwell/essays-and-other-works/the-lion-and-the-unicorn-socialism-and-the-english-genius/).

Parker, Owen. 2017. 'Critical Political Economy, Free Movement and Brexit: Beyond the Progressive's Dilemma.' *British Journal of Politics and International Relations* 19(3): 479–96.

Parsons, Craig. 2017. 'France and the Evolution of European Integration: The Exemplary and Pivotal Case for Broader Theories.' In *The Oxford Handbook of French Politics*, edited by Robert Elgie, Emiliano Grossman and Amy G. Mazur, 585–605. Oxford: Oxford University Press.

Patel, Kiran Klaus. 2017. '(BR)EXIT: Algerien, Grönland und die vergessene Vorgeschichte der gegenwärtigen Debatte.' *Studies in Contemporary History* 14: 112–27.

Paterson, William E. 2011. 'The Reluctant Hegemon? Germany Moves Centre Stage in the European Union.' *Journal of Common Market Studies* 49 (Annual Review): 57–75.

Peers, Steve. 2017. 'The Brexit Talks: Opening Positions on the Status of UK and EU citizens.' *EU Law Analysis Blog*, 30 June (available at: http://eulawanalysis.blogspot.co.uk/2017/06/the-brexit-talks-opening-positions-on.html).

Pettit, Phillip. 2010. 'A Republican Law of Peoples.' *European Journal of Political Theory* 9(1): 70–94.

Pew Survey. 2014. 'Faith and Skepticism about Trade' (available at: http://www.pewglobal.org/2014/09/16/faith-and-skepticism-about-trade-foreign-investment/trade-08/).

Philippe, Édouard. 2017. 'Déclaration de politique générale d'Édouard Philippe.' Paris, Gouvernement (available at: http://www.gouvernement.fr/declaration-de-politique-generale-d-edouard-philippe).

Phinnemore, David. 2013. *The Treaty of Lisbon: Origins and Negotiation*. Basingstoke: Palgrave.

Phinnemore, David & Warleigh-Lack, Alex. 2009. *Reflections on European Integration*. London: Palgrave.

Pisani-Ferry, Jean, Röttgen, Norbert, Sapir, André, Tucker, Paul & Wolff, Guntram B. 2016. 'Europe after Brexit: A Proposal for a Continental Partnership.' Centre for European Studies Working Paper, Harvard University, September (available at: http://bruegel.org/2016/08/europe-after-brexit-a-proposal-for-a-continental-partnership/).

Polanyi, Karl. 1944. [2001] *The Great Transformation: The Political and Economic Origins of Our Time*. Boston, MA: Beacon Press.

Politico. 2017. 'Merkel's Thunderbolt is Starting Gun for European Defense Drive.' 30 May.

Portes, Jonathan. 2017a. 'Reduction in Net Migration is not "Good News".' *The UK in a Changing Europe*, 30 May (available at: http://ukandeu.ac.uk/reduction-in-net-migration-is-not-good-news/).

Portes, Jonathan. 2017b. 'Why you're Wrong if you Think Clamping down on Immigration from Europe will Help Low-paid British Workers.' *Independent*, 18 July (available at: http://www.independent.co.uk/news/business/comment/uk-europe-immigration-brexit-freedom-movement-eu-citizens-low-paid-british-workers-theresa-may-a7846686.html).

Putnam, Robert D. 1988. 'Diplomacy and Domestic Politics: The Logic of Two Level Games.' *International Organization* 42(3): 427–60.

Quatremer, Jean. 2016. 'Brexit: amis anglais, merci pour votre sacrifice.' *Libération*, 24 June (available at: http://bruxelles.blogs.liberation.fr/2016/06/24/brexit-amis-anglais-merci-pour-votre-sacrifice/).

Rachman, Gideon. 2016. 'Rival Historians Trade Blows over Brexit.' *Financial Times*, 13 May.

Rahman, Arshadur. 2015. 'Over-the-counter (OTC) Derivatives, Central Clearing and Financial Stability.' In *Quarterly Bulletin* Q3: 283–95. London: Bank of England.

Rawls, John. 1971. *A Theory of Justice*. Cambridge/MA: Harvard University Press.

Rawls, John. 1999. *The Law of Peoples*. Cambridge, MA: Harvard University Press.

Reynolds, David. 2016. *Britannia Overruled: British Policy and World Power in the Twentieth Century*. 2nd edition. London: Pearson Educational.

Reynolds, Stephanie. 2017. 'Explainer: UK's Offer to EU Citizens Living in the UK.' Liverpool University Expert Opinion, 6 July (available at: https://news.liverpool.ac.uk/2017/07/06/explainer-uks-offer-to-eu-citizens-living-in-the-uk/).

Rhodes, Martin. 2013. 'Labour Markets, Welfare States and the Dilemmas of European Social Democracy.' In *The Crisis of Social Democracy in Europe*, edited by Michael Keating and David McCrone. Edinburgh: Edinburgh University Press.

Rittel, Horst W. J. & Webber, Melvin M. 1973. 'Dilemmas in a General Theory of Planning.' *Policy Sciences* 4(2): 155–69.

Robin, Corey. 2004. *Fear: The History of a Political Idea*. Oxford, Oxford University Press.

Rodrik, Dani. 2011. *The Globalization Paradox*. Oxford: Oxford University Press.

Rosamond, Ben. 2000. *Theories of European Integration*. Basingstoke: Palgrave Macmillan.

Ross, Wilbur. 2017a. 'IMF Warnings of Protectionism "Rubbish" says Ross.' *Financial Times*, 16 April (available at: https://www.ft.com/content/ef20b50a-2252-11e7-8691-d5f7e0cd0a16).

Ross, Wilbur. 2017b. 'US Reopens Door to Reviving EU Trade Talks.' *Financial Times*, 21 April (available at: https://www.ft.com/content/7996f226-282a-11e7-9ec8-168383da43b7).

Ross, Wilbur. 2017c. 'Donald Trump will Make Trade Fair Again.' *Financial Times*, 5 April.

Rousseau, Jean-Jacques. 1782. [1985]. *Considerations on the Government of Poland*. Indiannapolis: Hackett.

Rozenberg, Olivier. 2016. 'France in Quest of a European Narrative.' Paris: Les Cahiers européens de Sciences Po, No. 4/2016.

Ruggie, John Gerard. 1982. 'International Regimes, Transactions, and Change: Embedded Liberalism in the Postwar Economic Order.' *International Organization* 36(2): 379–415.

Salamońska, Justyna & Recchi, Ettore. 2016. 'Europe between Mobility and Sedentarism: Patterns of Cross-border Practices and their Consequences for European Identification.' Migration Policy Centre, RSCAS Working Paper 2016/50 (available at: http://cadmus.eui.eu/handle/1814/43545).

Salomone, Anthony. 2017. 'Free Movement is Not a Problem to be Solved.' Scottish Centre for European Relations, Comment, 21 July (available at: https://www.scer.scot/database/ident-3011).

Sanders, David & Houghton, David Patrick. 2017. *Losing an Empire, Finding a Role: British Foreign Policy since 1945*. 2nd edition. London: Palgrave Macmillan.

Sapir, André, Schoenmaker, Dirk & Véron, Nicolas. 2017. 'Making the Best of Brexit for the EU-27 Financial System.' Peterson Institute for International Economics, Policy Brief 17-8, February. Washington D.C.: Bruegel.

Savage, Deborah & Weale, Albert. 2009. 'Political Representation and the Normative Logic of Two-Level Games.' *European Political Science Review* 1(1): 63–81.

Savage, Michael. 2017. 'German Industry in Stark Warning to UK over Brexit.' *Observer*, 9 July.

Schain, Martin. 1988. 'Immigration and Changes in the French Party System.' *European Journal of Political Research* 16(6): 597–621.

Scharpf, Fritz. 1997. 'Economic Integration, Democracy, and the Welfare State.' *Journal of European Public Policy* 4(1): 18–36.

Scharpf, Fritz W. 2002. 'The European Social Model: Coping with the Challenges of Diversity.' *Journal of Common Market Studies* 40(4): 645–70.

Schedler, Andreas. 2007. 'Mapping Contingency.' In *Political Contingency: Studying the Unexpected, the Accidental, and the Unforeseen*, edited by Ian Shapiro and Sonu Bedi, 54–78. New York: NYU Press.

Schelkle, Waltraud. 2017. *The Political Economy of Monetary Solidarity: Understanding the Euro Experiment*. Oxford: Oxford University Press.

Schelkle, Waltraud & Lokdam, Hjalte. 2016. *Financial Regulation and the Protection of Eurozone Out: Report of the Hearing on Brexit, 27th November, 2015*. London: LSE.

Schoenmaker, Dirk & Véron, Nicolas. eds. 2016. 'European Banking Supervision: The First Eighteen Months.' Blueprint Series, No. 25. Brussels: Bruegel.

Schrauwen, Annette. 2017. '(Not) Losing out from Brexit.' *Europe and the World: A Law Review* 1(1): 1–18.

Schuman, Robert. 1950. 'Declaration of May 9th 1950' (available at: http://www.cvce.eu/).

Schwartz, Herman. 2017. 'Size, Scope and why the American Welfare Model Remains Exceptional.' In *Growth Strategies and Welfare States*, edited by Anke Hassel and Bruno Palier. Oxford: Oxford University Press.

Scientific American. 2012. 'Best Countries in Science' (available at: https://www.scientificameri-can.com/article/global-science-best-countries-science-scorecard/).

Shackleton, Michael. 2017. 'Transforming Representative Democracy in the EU? The Role of the European Parliament.' *Journal of European Integration* 39(2): 191–205.

Shaw, Jo. 2016a. 'Where Does the UK belong?' In *Residence, Employment and Social Rights of Mobile Persons: On how EU Law Defines where they Belong*, edited by Herwig Verschueren, 301–16. Cambridge: Intersentia.

Shaw, Jo. 2016b. 'Citizenship, Migration and Free Movement in Brexit Britain.' *German Law Journal* 17 (Brexit Supplement): 99–104.

Shaw, Jo. 2017. 'The Quintessentially Democratic Act? Democracy, Political Community and Citizenship in and after the UK's EU Referendum of June 2016.' *Journal of European Integration* 39(5): 559–74.

Shaw, Jo & Štiks, Igor. 2012. 'Citizenship in the New States of South Eastern Europe.' *Citizenship Studies*, 16(3–4): 309–21.

Shaxson, Nicolas & Christensen, John. 2016. 'Tax Competitiveness – A Dangerous Obsession.' In *Global Tax Fairness*, edited by Thomas Pogge and Krishen Mehta. Oxford: Oxford University Press.

Shipman, Tim. 2016. *All Out War: The Full Story of How Brexit Sank Britain's Political Class*, London: William Collins.

Simson Caird, Jack. 2017. 'Legislating for Brexit: The Great Repeal Bill.' House of Commons Library Briefing Paper, Number 7793, 2 May (available at: http://researchbriefings.files.parliament. uk/documents/CBP-7793/CBP-7793.pdf).

Sinn, Hans-Werner. 1997. 'The Selection Principle and Market Failures in Systems Competition.' *Journal of Public Economics* 66(2): 247–74.

Slaughter, Anne Marie. 2017. *The Chessboard and the Web: Strategies of Connection in a Networked World*. New Haven: Yale University Press.

Slawson, Nicola. 2017. 'French Presidential Favourite Macron May Drive Hard Bargain in Brexit Matters.' *Guardian*, 24 April (available at: https://www.theguardian.com/world/2017/apr/24/french-presidential-favourite-emmanuel-macron-hard-bargain-brexit-talks).

Smith, Adam. 1759. [1976] *The Theory of Moral Sentiments*. Edited by D.D. Raphael and A.L. Macfie. Oxford, Oxford University Press.

Smith, Michael E. 2004. *Europe's Foreign and Security Policy: The Institutionalization of Cooperation*, Cambridge: Cambridge University Press.

Somek, Alexander. 2008. *Individualism: An Essay on the Authority of the European Union*. Oxford University Press.

Special EU Programmes Body. 2017. 'PEACE IV Programme Overview: What is the PEACE IV Programme?' 1 August (available at: http://www.seupb.eu/piv-overview#).

Springsteen, Bruce. 1980. 'The Ties That Bind.' New York: Columbia Records.

Statistical Database of Estonia. 2011. 'Population and Housing Census 2011 – Native and Immigrant Population (Data of Several Generations).' 31 December 2011. Updated 21 June 2013 (available at: http://www.stat.ee/sdb-update?db_update_id=13687).

Streeck, Wolfgang. 2000. 'Competitive Solidarity: Rethinking the 'European Social Model.' In *Kontingenz und Krise: Institutionenpolitik in Kapitalistischen und Postsozialistischen Gesellschaften*, edited by Karl Hinrichs, Herbert Kitschelt and Helmut Wiesenthal. Frankfurt: Campus.

Streeck, Wolfgang. 2014. *Buying Time: The Delayed Crisis of Democratic Capitalism*, London: Verso.

Streeck, Wolfgang. 2016a. *How will Capitalism End: Essays on a Failing System*, London: Verso.

Streeck, Wolfgang. 2016b. 'Where are We Now? Responses to the Referendum.' *London Review of Books*, 14 July, 38(14).

Sus, Monika. 2017. 'Towards the European Union's Foreign Policy 2025 – Taking Stock of the Dahrendorf Foresight Project.' *Global Policy* 8(4): 115–25.

Swales, Kirby. 2016. 'Understanding the Leave Vote.' NatCen Social Research (available at: http://natcen.ac.uk/media/1319222/natcen_brexplanations-report-final-web2.pdf).

Swank, Duane & Betz, Hans-Georg. 2003. 'Globalization, the Welfare State and Right-wing Populism in Western Europe.' *Socio-Economic Review* 1(2): 215–45.

Syal, Rajeev. & Walker, Peter. 2017. 'John Major: Tory-DUP Deal Risks Jeopardising Northern Ireland Peace.' *Guardian*, 13 June (available at: https://www.theguardian.com/politics/2017/jun/13/john-major-tory-dup-deal-could-jeopardise-northern-ireland-peace).

Tannam, Etain. 2017. 'Cracks are Beginning to Appear in British-Irish relations.' *LSE Brexit Blog*, 26 July (available at: http://blogs.lse.ac.uk/brexit/2017/07/26/cracks-are-beginning-to-appear-in-british-irish-relations/).

Tardy, Thierry. 2014. 'CSDP: Getting Third States on Board.' Issue/Brief, European Union Institute for Security Studies, March. Brussels: EUISS (available at: http://www.iss.europa.eu/uploads/media/Brief_6_CSDP_and_third_states.pdf).

Taylor, Charles. 1994. *Multiculturalism: Examining the Politics of Recognition*. Princeton, NJ: Princeton University Press.

Taylor, Zachary. 2016. *The Politics of Innovation: Why some Countries are Better than others at Science and Technology*. Oxford: Oxford University Press.

Tetlock, Philip & Gardner, Dan. 2015. *Superforecasting: The Art and Science of Prediction*. New York: Crown.

Thatcher, Margaret. 1988. 'Bruges Speech.' Delivered at the College of Europe.

Thatcher, Margaret. 1993. *The Downing Street Years*. London: Harper Collins.

Thatcher, Margaret. 2002. *Statecraft: Strategies for a Changing World*. London: Harper Collins.

Thomas, Landon. 2017. 'IMF Raises Outlook for Global Economic Growth.' *New York Times*, 8 April (available at: https://www.nytimes.com/2017/04/18/business/dealbook/imf-raises-forecast-for-global-economic-growth.html).

Tombs, Robert. 2015. *The English and Their History*. London: Penguin.

Towers, Brian. 1992. 'Two Speed Ahead: Social Europe and the UK after Maastricht.' *Industrial Relations Journal* 23(2): 83–89.

Tsebelis, George. 2002. *Veto Players: How Political Institutions Work*. Princeton, NJ: Princeton University Press.

Tuck, Richard. 2016. 'The Left Case for Brexit.' *Dissent*, 6 June (available at: https://www.dissentmagazine.org/online_articles/left-case-brexit).

Tullock, Gordon. 1965. *The Politics of Bureaucracy*. Washington DC: Public Affairs Press.

Turner, Adair. 2015. *Between Debt and the Devil: Money, Credit, and Fixing Global Finance*. Princeton: Princeton University Press.

Turner, Ed & Green, Simon. 2017. *Priorities, Sensitivities, Anxieties: German and Central European Perceptions of Brexit*. Birmingham: Aston Centre for Europe.

Usherwood, Simon & Startin, Nick. 2013. 'Euroscepticism as a Persistent Phenomenon.' *Journal of Common Market Studies* 51(2): 1–16.

Valentino, Nicholas A., Hutchings, Vincent L., Banks, Antoine J. & Davis, Anne K. 2008. 'Is a Worried Citizen a Good Citizen? Emotions, Political Information Seeking, and Learning via the Internet.' *Political Psychology* 29(2): 247–73.

van Ham, Peter. 2017. 'Brexit: Strategic Consequences for Europe.' The Hague: Clingendael Institute (available at: https://www.clingendael.org/sites/default/files/2016-02/Brexit%20Report%20February%202016.pdf).

van Middelaar, Luuk. 2013. *The Passage to Europe*. New Haven and London: Yale University Press.

van Middelaar, Luuk. 2016. 'Sept theses sur le *Brexit.' Revue trimestrielle de droit europeen*, October–December, 705–10.

Van Parijs, Philippe. 2013. 'The Euro-dividend.' In *The Eurozone Crisis and the Democratic Deficit*, edited by Richard Bellamy and Uta Staiger, 16–17. London: UCL European Institute.

Van Parijs, Philippe. 2015. 'An Unconditional Basic Income in Europe will Help End the Crisis.' *EurActiv*, 11 April (available at: http://eurac.tv/hiI).

Van Parijs, Philippe & Vanderborght, Yannick. 2017. *Basic Income: A Radical Proposal for a Free Society and a Sane Economy*. Cambridge, MA: Harvard University Press.

Vasilopoulou, Sofia & Wagner, Markus. 2017. 'Fear, Anger and Enthusiasm about the EU: Effects of Emotional Reactions on Public Preferences towards European Integration.' *European Union Politics* 17(3): 1–24.

Verdun, Amy. 2000. *European Responses to Globalization and Financial Market Integration: Perceptions of Economic and Monetary Union in Britain, France and Germany*. Houndmills: Palgrave Macmillan.

Verdun, Amy. 2015. 'A Historical Institutionalist Explanation of the EU's Responses to the Euro Area Financial Crisis.' *Journal of European Public Policy* 22(2): 219–37.

Verdun, Amy & Wood, Donna. 2013. 'Governing the Social Dimension in Canadian Federalism and European Integration.' *Canadian Public Administration* 56(2): 173–84.

Verhofstadt, Guy. 2017. *Europe's Last Chance: Why the European States Must Form a More Perfect Union*. New York: Perseus Books.

Vidmar, Jure. 2014. 'The Scottish Independence Referendum in an International Context.' *Canadian Yearbook of International Law* 51: 259–88.

Wadsworth, Jonathan. 2015. 'Immigration and the UK Labour Market.' LSE Centre for Economic Performance, Election Analysis.

Wall Street Journal. 2017a. 'European Central Bank Gets Political.' *Wall Street Journal*, 10 February.

Wall Street Journal. 2017b. 'The Calculated Rise of Macron.' *Wall Street Journal,* 29–30 April.

Wall Street Journal. 2017c. 'France in Troubling but Beware of Italy.' *Wall Street Journal*, 13 April.

Wall Street Journal. 2017d. 'Italy in a Bind over Bank Bailout.' *Wall Street Journal*, 16 December.

Wallace, Helen. 2000. 'Possible Futures for the European Union: A British Reaction.' Jean Monnet Working Paper (available at: http://www.jeanmonnetprogram.org/archive/papers/00/00f0701.html).

Walzer, Michael. 2004. *Politics and Passion: Towards a More Egalitarian Liberalism*. New Haven, Yale University Press.

Webber, Douglas. 2017. 'Can the EU Survive?' In *The European Union in Crisis*, edited by Deesmond Dinan, Neill Nugent and William E. Paterson. London: Palgrave Macmillan.

Weber, Max. 1968. *Economy and Society: An Outline of Interpretative Sociology*, edited by Guenther Roth and Claus Wittich. Berkeley: University of California Press.

Whitman, Richard G. 2016. 'The UK and EU Foreign and Security Policy: An Optional Extra.' *Political Quarterly* 87(2): 254–61.

Williams, Zoe. 2017. 'Think the North and the Poor caused Brexit? Think Again.' *Guardian*, 7 August (available at: https://www.theguardian.com/commentisfree/2016/aug/07/north-poor-brexit-myths).

Williamson, Oliver E. 2002. 'The Theory of the Firm as a Governance Structure: From Choice to Contract.' *Journal of Economic Perspectives* 16(3): 171–95.

Wintour, Patrick. 2017. 'Austria Threatens EU Funding Cuts over Hungary's Hard Line on Refugees.' *Guardian*, 8 March (available at: https://www.theguardian.com/world/2017/mar/08/austria-calls-for-less-funding-for-eu-countries-refusing-refugees).

Withnall, Adam. 2017. 'UK could Become 'Tax Haven' of Europe if it is Shut out of Single Market after Brexit, Chancellor Suggests.' *Independent*, 15 January (available at: http://www.independent.co.uk/news/uk/politics/brexit-eu-chancellor-philip-hammond-welt-am-sonntag-uk-tax-haven-europe-a7527961.html).

Yeo, Colin. 2017. 'Analysis: What is the UK Proposing for EU Citizens in the UK and EU Citizens in the EU?' *Free Movement Blog*, 27 June (available at: https://www.freemovement.org.uk/analysis-what-is-the-uk-proposing-for-eu-citizens-in-the-uk-and-eu-citizens-in-the-eu/).

Young, Iris Marion. 1990. *Justice and the Politics of Difference*. Princeton, NJ: Princeton University Press.

Index